THE INSTITUTIONALIZED PRESIDENCY

Special Editors

Norman C. Thomas and Hans W. Baade

Series Editor

John C. Weistart

OCEANA PUBLICATIONS, INC.

Dobbs Ferry, New York

1972

Library of Congress Cataloging in Publication Data
Main entry under title:

The Institutionalized Presidency.
    (Library of law and contemporary problems)
    Originally published as the summer 1970 issue (v. 35, no. 3) of
Law and contemporary problems, Duke University School of Law.
    Includes bibliographical references.
    1. Presidents—U. S.—Addresses, essays, lectures.
I. Thomas, Norman C., ed.   II. Baade, Hans Wolfgang, ed.
III. Series: Law and contemporary problems, v. 35, no. 3.
JK516.I55   1972   353.032   75—37118
ISBN 0-379-11514-X

74-4983
Manufactured in the United States of America

Titles Published in

The Library of Law and Contemporary Problems

CONTENTS

FOREWORD

It has been fifteen years since *Law and Contemporary Problems* published its initial symposium on the presidential office.[1] During that interval, President Eisenhower completed his term of office, two Democratic Presidents have come and gone, and now Eisenhower's former Vice President is over half through his first term. Although the office still basically resembles the institution that existed at midcentury, each of the four most recent Presidents has left his mark on it in several important respects. Changes have also occurred in the office that are the product of exogenous events and conditions. Since the Eisenhower years the nation has passed through a series of profound social, economic, and political crises and transformations that have sharply altered presidential roles and the expectations held for the presidency. The office itself has expanded in both structure and functions. Yet, with the exception of the Twenty-fifth Amendment relating to presidential succession and disability, there have been few alterations in the legal or constitutional position of the presidency. An objective foreign observer might be prompted to remark, *"plus la difference, plus la meme chose,"* and he would not be wholly in error. Nevertheless, the changes have been substantial, and they are reflected in the issues that excite the interest of students and other observers of the presidency and presidents.

With these considerations in mind, the editors agreed with the suggestion advanced by Hans Baade and myself that it was time to reappraise the presidential office with a view toward developing a new set of perspectives for the 1970's. The papers fall into three categories: those that focus on the office itself, those that examine efforts to improve and rationalize the office through reorganization, and those that examine the operational dynamics of the office. From the papers should come a broad, although not necessarily comprehensive, set of perspectives on the presidency and the issues that surround it. Only one observation can be made with any degree of certainty: the presidency is in a constant state of flux. The extent to which the people of the United States manage to adapt the presidency to the solution of their needs and to meeting the challenges that confront them will be a major determinant of the nation's ultimate fate. Although the presidency has definite limitations, and many of the papers explicitly recognize them, it remains the focal

---

[1] See 21 LAW & CONTEMP. PROB. 607 (1956).

point of American political life and is still the most effective means available for mobilizing energy and resource; for the achievement of national goals.

Two papers in the symposium warrant special mention. Thomas E. Cronin's contribution is based on extensive field research conducted during the past two years. It represents the first original empirical scholarship in the area since the seminal writings of Richard E. Neustadt fifteen years ago.[2] Hopefully it will set the stage for additional innovative analyses of the presidency. Hans Baade, a foreign-trained scholar permanently resident in an American university, served in 1969 as a consultant to the West German equivalent of the Hoover Commission. His participant-observer's account of the work of that body includes a highly interesting analysis of the relevance, and irrelevance, of American experiences with governmental reorganization in the West German context. It furnishes a comparative perspective that should serve as an antidote to any imbalance resulting from a reading of the American-oriented pieces.

This symposium is in no way intended to provide definitive answers to the questions and problems surrounding the presidency. Its purpose is to stimulate interest and continued concern in the expectations held for the presidency and the uses made of it as its development unfolds.

Norman C. Thomas

June, 1971

---

[2] Neustadt's contribution to the 1956 symposium, *The Presidency at Mid-Century*, 21 Law & Contemp. Prob. 609 (1956) became the core of his classic Presidential Power (1960).

PERSPECTIVES ON THE PRESIDENCY*

David L. Paletz†

I

Introduction

With the inevitable procrustean effects, this paper attempts to summarize familiar and arcane writing on the presidency and its incumbents. I divide the literature into six categories, each of which, I suggest, represents a relatively distinctive perspective on the presidency. I portray these approaches by comparing and contrasting the beliefs and assertions of representative writers along four dimensions: first, presidential responsibilities; second, the powers of the office; third, the importance of the occupant's behavior; and fourth, prescriptions for institutional changes—which often but not invariably stem from the first three dimensions. These beliefs and assertions may be refurbished, revised, or modified in some way by the actions of Presidents, and by the horde of words which scholars, politicians, journalists, and other scribes compose and, with the encouragement and sometimes at the behest of publishers, purvey. I therefore attempt not only to distinguish the six different perspectives, but also to suggest why and how some of them have undergone change.[1]

This paper is not an attempt to canvass the entire range of literature about the presidency or about particular Presidents. I concentrate on selected and representative works. Writings which treat particular facets of the office and its incumbent—subjects such as elections, advisory systems, presidential personality, and so on—are excluded from my purview.[2] Nor do I include epiphenomena from the *Saturday Review* and *New York Times Sunday Magazine*. Moreover, by concentrating on the written word, I totally ignore television which, primarily because of its pervasiveness and its personalization of the presidency, has a far more important impact on the mass public's knowledge and myths than any of the works

* This is a revised version of a paper delivered at the 41st Annual Meeting of the Southern Political Science Association, Miami Beach, November 1969. I am indebted to my friend Thomas F. Cronin for our illuminating conversations which helped me formulate some of the categories contained herein. I am further indebted to Leonard Rubin and to my colleague Norman C. Thomas for penetrating comments on the previous draft.

† Assistant Professor of Political Science, Duke University.

[1] According to Norman Mailer in a review of *The Group*, 1 N.Y. Rev. Books 3 (1963): "lists and categories are always the predictable refuge of the passionless, the mediocre, the timid, and the bowelbound who will not make another move until they have exhausted the last." He exaggerates.

[2] Works in these areas are so well-known as to require no footnote. I would, however, draw the reader's attention to three publications deserving particular attention. They are: Barber, The President and His Friends, paper presented at the 65th Annual Meeting of the American Political Science Association, New York, 1969; E. Flash, Economic Advice and Presidential Leadership: The Council of Economic Advisers (1965); The Presidential Advisory System (T. Cronin & S. Greenberg, eds. 1969).

I discuss.[3] My focus is on the authors whose books deal in a general way with the presidency and its incumbents.

One final introductory comment is necessary. This paper is exploring uncharted territory. The classificatory scheme, therefore, is intended to be both suggestive and tenative rather than logically and analytically distinct.

II

THE PERSPECTIVES

A. Roles

The most prevalent and academically respectable way of viewing the presidency is in terms of the President's roles. Indeed, it may be dubbed the received view of the office. Presidential roles are arrayed, and range from those provided for in the Constitution (Chief Executive, Commander-in-Chief), to those which assertedly now devolve upon the office. The latter include Chief Legislator and World Leader. Clinton Rossiter's widely used text[4] is a typical example of this genre and has the roles all specified—from Chief Executive to World Leader—in the first chapter.[5]

Obviously each role is a presidential responsibility. But the authors of this view also often contend that no other American governmental institution can adequately compensate for presidential dereliction. And, without necessarily adducing specific evidence, they emphasize that the public expects an incumbent President to perform his roles. Thus, an almost inevitable concomitant of a role perspective is the contention that the President is possessed of "far more responsibility than he has power."[6] Nonetheless, the occupant of the office does make an enormous difference; for the presidency is malleable and some Presidents are far more able than others. Rossiter, for example, compares Franklin D. Roosevelt, Harry S. Truman, and Dwight D. Eisenhower in terms of their ability to meet their abundant responsibilities. Perhaps inevitably, Rossiter depicts Roosevelt's conception and conduct of the presidency most favorably, while Eisenhower receives fewest plaudits.[7]

Thomas A. Bailey exemplifies the zenith (some might say the nadir) of the "roles" approach in his book on presidential greatness.[8] The forty-three roles he provides[9] are not only measuring criteria of presidential greatness as he conceives it, but also a compendium of presidential responsibility (also as he conceives it). The President is proclaimed Administrator-in-Chief, Bureaucrat-in-Chief, Legislator-in-

---

[3] For an example of a discussion of public images of the presidency, see Sigel, *Image of the American Presidency—Part II of an Exploration into Popular Views of Presidential Power*, 10 MIDWEST J. POL. SCI. 123-41 (1966).

[4] C. ROSSITER, THE AMERICAN PRESIDENCY (rev. ed. 1960).

[5] *Id.* at 5-43.

[6] F. HELLER, THE PRESIDENCY: A MODERN PERSPECTIVE 87 (1960).

[7] ROSSITER, *supra* note 4, at 142-81.

[8] T. BAILEY, PRESIDENTIAL GREATNESS (1966).

[9] *Id.* at 262-66.

Chief, Chief of State, Spokesman-in-Chief, Financier-in-Chief, Diplomat-in-Chief, Appropriator-in-Chief, General-in-Chief ("of so-called free-nations,"),[10] and so on. By adding other criteria such as a President's skill at handling his press conferences, his ability to bypass the Senate with executive agreements, the quality of his leadership, and his management of public opinion, Bailey makes it clear that he views the powers of the office as elastic. By evaluating Presidents against his criteria (although with becoming modesty he does admit to the difficulty of the task), Bailey demonstrates his belief in the importance of the occupant of the office and his conviction that a President who extends his powers for the benefit of the nation merits the appellation "great."

Interestingly, Bailey alludes to the war in Vietnam. "Great Presidents generally have had big wars, and with the escalation of bombing and shooting in South Vietnam, Johnson may enjoy this added advantage as he eagerly seeks an honored place beside Lincoln, Wilson, and Franklin Roosevelt."[11] Although it is problematic whether he would revise it as one of his criteria, I doubt that Bailey would be so sanguine now about the relationship between this war and presidential greatness.

Given his inclination to endorse activist Presidents, we might expect Bailey to prescribe structural changes in the Presidency and also propose additional powers for the office. That he does not do so is probably a result of the consciously evaluative rather than prescriptive purpose of his book. Other authors of the "roles" approach are not so reticent. And, on the grounds that a President's responsibilities are so overwhelming, while the powers of the office are inadequate to meet them, these writers often suggest ways of increasing the presidency's formal powers. Such proposals include according the President greater autonomy in making appointments, further curtailing the ability of Congress to impede executive reorganization, and endowing the President with an item veto.[12]

These proposals to enlarge the power of the presidency are rarely accompanied by any disquiet among proponents of the "roles" approach. Their emphasis is on the difficulty a President encounters in handling his job and fulfilling the manifold expectations pressed upon him. As Tugwell puts it:

> [i]f the President cannot, by using the cleverist administrative devices and by devoting to his duties the utmost industry, stretch his personal directions over the enormous machine he commands; and if he often cannot find the time, to say nothing of the capability, to make all the vital decisions he is supposed to make —then we do have to ask ourselves in what other way the institution can be enlarged to meet the looming responsibilities of an even more demanding future.[13]

The possible solution for Tugwell is some form of plural executive. But what is important is the formulation of the problem, not the solution. There is no

---

[10] *Id.* at 266.

[11] *Id.* at 334. This was probably written in 1965.

[12] F. HELLER, *supra* note 6, at 88-89.

[13] R. TUGWELL, THE ENLARGEMENT OF THE PREIDENCY 492 (1960).

concern about the possibility (however remote) of tyranny in any form; nor is there much discussion about possible repercussions resulting from the aggrandizement of the presidency. It may be, for example, that more powers not only beget more responsibilities but that they make a President more vulnerable by imposing upon him requirements for the kinds of explicit and detailed involvements in the political process which he may need to avoid. Thus, an item veto might demonstrate for the public the political dimension of the presidency and exacerbate conflict with Congress. A dissatisfied Congress (especially if controlled by the party without the presidency) could reduce authorized expenditures, conduct even nastier and more frequent inquiries into Administration department management and policies than it does at present, and even withhold some appropriations altogether. And more explicit and clear power for the President is likely to make the party holding the office more accountable to the electorate, which is not necessarily desirable either for the President, or his party, or those who see blurred distinctions between America's political parties as essentially beneficial for social cohesion. Despite this, for most of those authors who emphasize presidential roles, the question is how the office can be strengthened to enable its occupant better to run the country. It is assumed that additional responsibilities and increases of power will work in both the President's and the public's interest.

B. Obligations

As discussed under the "roles" category, much of the literature identifies the President as the repository of his country's hopes and characterizes him as Chief Executive, Chief Legislator, Voice of the People, Protector of Peace, etc. Implicit in this characterization is the expectation that he will carry out these responsibilities. There is, however, a more extreme version of this perspective which merits its own category. This is the writing which identifies an area, defines it as falling clearly within presidential responsibility, proceeds to complain about presidential dereliction, and exhorts the present and future occupants of the office to action. Such work is replete with illustrations of the reasons for action and includes constitutional justification. Often the presidency is chosen as the necessary source of action because the other institutions of government at the national, state, and local levels are assertedly unwilling or incapable of adequate response.

In *The Presidency and Individual Liberties*,[14] Richard P. Longaker, although he denies any intention "to suggest that the burden on the President to protect constitutional rights is ultimately any greater than it is for the other institutions of American government or for the least of us,"[15] belies his disavowal by the following kind of statement:

---

[14] R. Longaker, The Presidency and Individual Liberties (1961).
[15] *Id.* at vii-ix.

Wise and persistent use of the instruments of the presidency—the appointing power, the selective and vigorous use of law enforcement, and the cumulative advances by means of the imaginative application of administrative discretion, to name only a few—can nourish freedom even in the face of Cold War pressures. Executive neglect, on the other hand, may lead to the undermining of the very substance of American constitutionalism. What must be recognized today is that sustained leadership in the field must originate in White House direction, coordination, and sensitivity . . . . Because the major problems will find their way to the White House, to be dealt with or neglected, here in particular there should be individuals who speak of liberty rather than security and who feel committed to a positive role for the Federal executive in civil rights.[16]

The responsibility is depicted as pressing, and its neglect is supposedly dangerous to the health of the body politic.

The "obligations" and "roles" perspectives both place considerable importance on the actions of the President. Indeed, Presidents can be differentiated on the basis of their responses to their responsibilities. Yet, whereas the "roles" approach often explicitly and invariably implicitly stresses the necessity of increasing presidential powers, this is not to the same extent a theme of the "obligations" writers.

Thus, Longaker makes clear that so far as protecting constitutional rights is concerned, the President possessed adequate powers—he merely needed to use them. Both perspectives, however, generally share an absence of the fear that presidential activity can be anything other than beneficial and humane.

Probably the most flamboyant example of the "obligations" category, and it is consciously hortatory, appeared in 1966. In it Bertram Gross argues that "the new role of the White House is to provide a center of creative stability in the midst of turbulent change."[17] The President is charged with some of his conventional responsibilities, such as Peacemaker and Champion of Justice, but to these Gross adds Truth Teller, Humanist, and Learner. This article was probably written during the period of the Johnson administration's greatest legislative success when, for a few euphoric months, Congress no longer seemed an obstacle to presidential legislative leadership. And Gross certainly sees the presidency and its occupant as pivotal in the American political system. Yet responsibilities like Truth Teller and Learner may well represent reactions by Gross to President Johnson's conduct of his office. There is an awareness of presidential fallibility here relatively absent from other works.

Yet the "obligations" writers are politically disingenuous in the sense that they rarely encourage the President to follow their prescriptions by adumbrating the gains in power, prestige, and popularity that might accrue. Conversely, they neglect to discuss the negative repercussions that might result if he undertakes the proposed activity. Their books, then, remain academic in their effects on the President. The

---

[16] *Id.* at 232.

[17] Gross, *Some Questions for Presidents*, in A GREAT SOCIETY 305-50 (B. Gross ed. 1966). The quote is at 309.

effect of these books on the public, however, is probably to convey an impression of presidential dereliction while simultaneously raising expectations about the ability of Presidents to act and the beneficial results to be expected from such action were it to be undertaken.

It has been observed that generals develop strategy to win the last war rather than the next. Similarly, writers on the presidency address themselves to the model and experiences provided by the President in power or the one who has recently left office. The "roles" and "obligations" perspectives became particularly prevalent during the late fifties and early sixties. They may well have been a response to the problems that seemed to accumulate in the United States during the complacency and apparent stagnation of the Eisenhower presidency. Those wishing to see an attempt made to solve these problems identified the presidency as the most, if not the only, appropriate institution. Since Eisenhower had essentially a passive conception of his office, he became something of a symbol and focal point for dissatisfaction—especially among liberal academics. Rossiter's book, for example, seems to reflect this irritation with Eisenhower.

Clearly Eisenhower did not fully accept many of the responsibilities thrust upon him by either the "roles" or the "obligations" schools. And although it is often a tenet of the "roles" approach that the presidency needs additional power, Eisenhower was criticized by both "roles" and "obligations" authors for not using the power he did possess. Accordingly, with their emphasis on the importance of the occupant, both views placed great expectations on the next incumbent. Indeed, Longaker's book, published in 1961, appears to be a clear rebuke to Eisenhower and an appeal to his successor.

The next President was John F. Kennedy and his experience graphically demonstrated the gap between presidential responsibility, as conceived by scholars in the first two categories, and the President's powers. Koenig put the restraints-and-constraints point of view colorfully when he described the source of President Kennedy's discouragement as the "far-stretching chasm between the ideal of a vigorous, creative Presidency he envisaged in his gallant 1960 campaign and the reality of the complicated, restraint-bound, frustrating office he discovered after his inauguration."[18] And Sidney Warren in 1964 similarly sounded the motif of ever greater obligations on the President combined with the limitations and constraints on the Chief Executive's course of action:

> The nation has come to look to the White House for an immediate answer to any and all significant problems. Yet, ironically, in a period when the presidency is at the very peak of its influence, probably nowhere in the world is executive leadership more hemmed in, more limited by political considerations, more vulnerable to pressures from within and without than in the United States.[19]

---

[18] L. KOENIG, THE CHIEF EXECUTIVE 3 (1964). When Koenig published a revised version of his book in 1968 his views were essentially unchanged.

[19] S. WARREN, THE PRESIDENT AS WORLD LEADER 431 (1964).

Hence, the views of the presidency held by the scholars who dominated the first two categories began to change as the experiences of the Kennedy administration provided fresh empirical data. The limitations and frustrations of the office began to be accentuated. These difficulties were most immediate to the men in the Kennedy administration and their perspectives provide our next category.

C. Constraints

For the men who serve in an administration and subsequently strive to depict their experiences, the story is a combination of achievement and frustration. The Kennedy presidency exemplifies this category because it generated such an outburst of prose from the assassinated Chief Executive's cohorts (many of whom justified their efforts by claiming they were merely inadequately trying to write the book he would have written had he lived).

John F. Kennedy was an activist President whose rhetoric proclaimed vast responsibilities for his office. There is, therefore, inevitably an inclination for those who served in his administration to blame his frustrations, disappointments, and failures on the constraints surrounding the presidency and the President's lack of power to overcome them. Such a tendency was reinforced when the President was killed before he really had a sufficient opportunity fully to pursue his policies, let alone implement them. Conversely, the late President's accomplishments are lauded and cited as examples of his ability to overcome his office's lack of power. This is the tenor of the "histories" emanating from participants in the Kennedy administration. The President had enormous responsibilities (getting America moving again, for example); his powers were inadequate to the task; but by dint of his ability, skill, effort, and concern, he was able to make a start. Implicit in this approach is a general prescription that the presidency be strengthened. But more important, is the explicit assumption that an activist conception of the presidency is appropriate and necessary and that men like John F. Kennedy are the kind to occupy the office. It is not surprising that many members of the Kennedy administration joined Robert F. Kennedy's 1968 campaign.

Nonetheless, men who have actually participated in the conduct of government at the presidential level tend to emphasize the burdens and difficulties of the office. They suggest (although not necessarily expressly) that a President, even when he wants to face and deal with his manifold responsibilities (as the writers conceive and identify them), is constrained in at least four ways. First, the problems are often intractable or difficult to solve. Second, the President is limited in his options and constrained in his choices of which problems to tackle, let alone try to resolve. Third, the decision-making process is a complex and inordinately difficult one, particularly if the decision-maker takes into account the manifold sources of information and views and the sensibilities (personal and political) on which his decisions impinge. Two and three are obviously interrelated. Finally, even when a decision is reached, the obstacles to its implementation and then execution are so extensive as often to render it nugatory.

The views I have outlined can be found, in between the paeans, in the books by Schlesinger,[20] Sorensen,[21] and Hilsman[22] as they chronicle the experiences of the Kennedy administration.

A distinction should be made, however, between domestic and foreign policy. Here, the participants' books confirm the impression conveyed by some scholars that a President is somewhat more confined in his domestic policy where he must often deal with the mastodons of Congress.

Yet even Hilsman, who specifically concentrates on foreign policy-making even more than Schlesinger, and who asserts that President Kennedy was successful in surmounting many of the administrative, political, and legislative obstacles to decision-making and implementation, quotes President Truman's famous comment which the latter made as he contemplated turning over the presidency to Eisenhower: "He'll sit here and he'll say, 'Do this! Do that!' And nothing will happen. Poor Ike—it won't be a bit like the Army."[23] And, at the end of his book, Hilsman elaborates:

> In the field of foreign affairs, the President's power is immense. His is the monopoly in dealing with other states. But he, too, must build a consensus for his policy if it is to succeed. He must bring along enough of the different factions in Congress to forestall revolt, and he must contend for the support of wider constituencies, the press, interest groups, and "attentive publics." Even within the Executive Branch itself, his policy will not succeed merely at his command, and he must build cooperation and support, obtain approval from some, acquiescence from others, and enthusiasm from enough to carry it to completion.[24]

So, although a President is sometimes less frustrated and confined in his conduct of foreign policy than in domestic affairs, he is still constrained. This is the essential view conveyed by the participant-observers.

Most of the participants cited do not propose to place more responsibilities on the President, perhaps because they construe such responsibilities primarily as burdens. And although they may believe that the presidency needs stregthening, this does not necessarily lead them into specific proposals for increasing the powers of the office. One reason may be that most of the writers in this category began their Washington sojourns when the White House was occupied by John F. Kennedy and ended them during the tenure of Lyndon B. Johnson. Under the onslaught of Johnson's aggressive conduct of the office, not to mention the expanded war in Vietnam, they are conscious that presidential activity may not always be beneficial.

---

[20] A. SCHLESINGER, JR., A THOUSAND DAYS (1965).

[21] T. SORENSEN, KENNEDY (1965).

[22] R. HILSMAN, TO MOVE A NATION (1967).

[23] *Id*. at 6.

[24] *Id*. at 561-62. Presidents may have objectives, I'm not sure they have policies.

The one apparent exception is McGeorge Bundy who, in his Godkin lectures delivered at Harvard in March 1968, argued forcefully that American government, including the presidency, must be strengthened.[25] His position is clear, even simple. There is what he characterizes as "explosive need,"[26] in such areas as race, poverty, communication, and nuclear energy. These needs are the responsibility of government. But government's capacity to respond is limited by "alarming weakness."[27] The solution is to strengthen government, which means strengthening the presidency, first to meet "present responsibilities," and second, to meet the "new ones that are coming."[28]

Yet, returning to Cambridge from his Washington duties, Bundy encountered pervasive distaste for the war in Vietnam. Hence he is constrained to admit that "rhetorically, at least, there is difficulty in presenting an argument for greater strength in our government in a year when many of our most concerned and conscientious citizens are inclined to believe that it is precisely the strength of a government they disagree with that has brought us to great trouble in Vietnam."[29] Subsequently, he scarcely treats Vietnam and his argument is independent of it. Nonetheless, he does ask those "who have strong feelings about Vietnam to consider how much they would give to a President they approved."[30] This seems to beg the issue. It may be that Lyndon Johnson's conduct of the Vietnam war manifested a lack of presidential power rather than the reverse; this is too complex an issue to argue here. The point is that to some observers the war reveals two things: first, that Presidents can make mistakes; and secondly, that the effects of such errors can be devastating. Accordingly, there has been a diminution in the enthusiasm for loading responsibilities onto the President and in the proposals for increasing his power.

In any event, Bundy's suggestions for change are of an order different from those made by writers who adopt the "roles" perspective. It is true that he proposes to increase the President's power by empowering him to change basic tax rates within certain limits. But among his more significant suggestions is one designed to increase the prestige and authority of Cabinet-level executives. The job of these men, as Bundy explains it somewhat unclearly, would be to help the President and be more responsive to him than the present Cabinet officers. At the same time, however, they would tend to diminish "excessive personalism,"[31] if the President had such a tendency.

Here, Bundy is in a muted way responding to the presidency of Lyndon B. Johnson because his proposal, if adopted, would probably have the effect of in-

[25] M. BUNDY, THE STRENGTH OF GOVERNMENT (1968).
[26] Id. at 1. It is the title of the first chapter.
[27] Id. at 27. It is the title of the second chapter.
[28] Id. at 29.
[29] Id. at x.
[30] Id.
[31] Id. at 55.

creasing the power of the presidency but not necessarily the power of the President. In the same refrain, Bundy has a sober paragraph on presidential fallibility.[32]

One conclusion possibly to be derived from Bundy's discreet comments and proposals is that, despite the ambiguities of meaning inherent in America's sorry relations with Vietnam, the episode generally serves as a warning, chastening experience; and that we are unlikely to see an abundance of works in the near future proposing to increase the President's power—at least with respect to foreign relations. In fact, we may expect the reverse.

Perhaps representing the start of a trend, towards the end of 1966 Arthur Schlesinger, Jr. engaged in a partial debate with Alfred de Grazia (a propounder of the "anti-aggrandizement" approach to be discussed as category five) under the auspices of the American Enterprise Institute.[33] He advocated giving Congress "a more authoritative and continuing voice in fundamental decisions in foreign policy,"[34] and argued that the citizen's obligation is to support Congress or the presidency depending on the results desired. This view, Schlesinger hastened to add, was not "simply a consequence of the Vietnam war."[35] Still, the Johnson presidency then in full swing, and the Vietnam war increasingly conspicuous and bothersome, do appear to have raised questions about presidential power and its employment which Schlesinger had previously slighted.

Yet, despite Bundy's proposals for strengthening the presidency and Schlesinger's caveats about presidential power, this category is one of the least susceptible to change. The view from the White House and the Executive Office is one of good intentions and difficult decisions impeded by bureaucratic inertia, incompatible demands, and rampageous pluralism. Experience in governing leads to the realization that additional power to the President may not resolve problems but increase them; that administrative re-organizations have been tried in the past without noticeable success; and that clear-cut triumphs for a President are few and often overshadowed by frustrations and mistakes. The constraints gradually take on a rather immutable cast.

D. Statecraft

Looming over the three previous categories, and apparently required reading for members of the Kennedy administration both during and after their sojourns in Washington, is Richard Neustadt's *Presidential Power*.[36] Hilsman's book in particular reflects the Neustadt approach to and conception of leadership.

---

[32] *Id.* at 57.

[33] A. SCHLESINGER, JR., & A. DE GRAZIA, CONGRESS AND THE PRESIDENCY (1967). It was a partial debate because the two participants never appear to have confronted and argued with each other orally.

[34] *Id.* at 28.

[35] *Id.* at 101.

[36] R. NEUSTADT, PRESIDENTIAL POWER (1968). For an intelligent explication of some of the merits and defects in the book see Sperlich, *Bargaining and Overload*, in THE PRESIDENCY (A. Wildavsky ed. 1969). For a work which considers leadership in a comparative and less instrumental fashion, see POLITICAL LEADERSHIP IN INDUSTRIALIZED SOCIETIES (L. Edinger ed. 1967), and the bibliography therein.

Neustadt, of course, is in the tradition of Machiavelli, a tradition which for its apparent hard-headed devotion to the realities of power has only appeared in American politics in the form of such blatantly cynical and droll books as Riordon's *Plunkitt of Tammany Hall* and the acidulous comments of *Mr. Dooley.*

Neustadt's positions on my four criteria can be briefly summarized. The President has overwhelming responsibilities; his powers are conspicuously limited; the views and actions of the occupant are vital; and such Presidents as Franklin D. Roosevelt with an activist conception of the office are infinitely preferable to passive occupants like Dwight D. Eisenhower. Neustadt is not, however, particularly interested in prescribing structural change. Rather, his book is a manual (although not always a clear one) advising the President how best to employ those powers he already possesses.

Since Neustadt is the primary contemporary American exponent of the "statecraft" category, we must look to him for changes in this perspective. The main source is the afterword on JFK contained in the latest paperback edition of *Presidential Power.* Neustadt's closing paragraphs in this new section are instructive:

> The President remains our system's Great Initiator. When what we once called "war" impends, he now becomes our system's Final Arbiter. He is no less a clerk in one capacity than in the other. But in the second instance those he serves are utterly dependent on his judgement—and judgement then becomes the mark of "leadership." Command may have a narrow reach but it encompasses irreparable consequences. Yet persuasion is required to exercise command, to get one's hands upon subordinate decisions. With this so-nearly absolute dependence upon presidential judgment backed by presidential skill, we and our system have no previous experience. Now in the 1960's we begin to explore it.
>
> Hopefully, both citizens and Presidents will do so without fear, or histrionics, or withdrawals from reality, or lurches toward aggression. Regardless of the dangers, presidential power, even in this new dimension, still has to be sought and used; it cannot be escaped. We now are even more dependent than before on the mind and temperament of the man in the White House.[37]

The approach remains the same. The objective—to guide the President in gaining, preserving, and employing his power is unchanged. Yet the lines quoted above are suffused with awareness of the dangers that inhere in the presidency and the damage which may result from presidential errors or abuses of power. It may be that Neustadt is unhappy over the conduct of the presidency of Lyndon B. Johnson. More likely, he is concerned over what that conduct revealed about the damage which could result from a misapplication of presidential powers (or a President's ability to extend them through such dubious instrumentalities as the Tonkin Gulf resolution). In any event this "afterword: JFK" contains a note of caution and concern generally absent from the remainder of the book.

---

[37] NEUSTADT, *supra* note 36, at 213-14.

E. Anti-aggrandizement

"Anti-aggrandizement" is a perennial thread in the literature on the presidency. Constitutionalists who put their faith in the balance and separation of powers look with dismay at the increased powers and importance of the presidency. They might agree that the United States faces many difficult problems, but they scarcely consider this sufficient reason sanguinely to increase the number and nature of presidential roles, or to enhance presidential power—particularly at the expense of Congress. Consequently, in his magisterial *The President: Office and Powers,*[38] Edward S. Corwin describes "a long-term trend at work in the world that consolidates power in the executive departments of all governments."[39] The result is an institutionalized presidency which may jeopardize[40] private and personal rights. Individual Presidents may differ, and their impacts on the office vary considerably, yet the impetus to institutionalization of the office is apparently irresistible unless specific changes are implemented in order to control presidential power. Accordingly, Corwin proposes that the President's Cabinet be constructed from a joint Legislative Council containing the leading members of Congress.[41]

Just as some of the men included in the "obligations" category were responding to the somewhat lacadaisical conduct of the office by President Eisenhower, Corwin's book may have been influenced by a distaste for the increase in presidential power occurring under Franklin D. Roosevelt. Similarly, shortly after Roosevelt's death, C. Perry Patterson's book on the presidency appeared in which he advocated cabinet government. His purpose, however, was not to strengthen the presidency but to weaken it. As Patterson put it, "responsible cabinet government is the best possible means in the absence of constitutional restraint to prevent the permanent establishment of irresponsible executive government in this country in the hands of one man."[42]

In recent years the "anti-aggrandizement" approach has been a reaction to and a direct rejection of the "obligations" and, to a somewhat lesser extent, the "roles" views. "Anti-aggrandizement" is now propounded most eloquently by Alfred de Grazia. De Grazia spells out his views in *Republic in Crisis* where he attacks the conventional views of the presidency with radical scepticism.[43] He is not convinced that we are now more inundated by crises than ever and he observes that the cry of emergency (which may be created by the President) results in an increase in the already too great presidential power. "Congressmen, being only human, are themselves subject to the man-on-horseback hallucinations. The releasing of power

---

[38] E. Corwin, The President: Office and Powers (1957). This book first appeared in 1940. Were it not for Corwin's pronounced "anti-aggrandizement" view, his book could be included under the "roles" category.

[39] *Id.* at 304.

[40] Although Corwin refrains from using so strong a word, his concern is evident.

[41] *Id.* at 297.

[42] C. Patterson, Presidential Government in the United States, at vi (1947).

[43] A. de Grazia, Republic in Crisis 69-144 (1965).

in generous and vague terms to President Johnson in 1965 to deal as he saw fit with the Vietnam conflict was typical."[44]

Even if this is an age of crisis (which de Grazia is not really willing to admit), it is, in his opinion, a mistake to turn to the presidency and its occupant for solutions. For the President is part of an executive force. Americans do not realize this because of their penchant (reinforced by the media and historians) to personalize this executive force in the President. By the executive force, de Grazia is apparently referring to the bureaucracy or more precisely the civil service. The presidency is merely its spearhead. This means that although there are differences in the attitudes, temperaments, and inclinations of Presidents, the policies they support are similar:

> Because of how he is chosen and because of his role in the system, the President will emphasize certain policies and propound certain ideas. It appears, for example, that it is very difficult for a federalist, "voluntarist" decentralizing, "isolationist" politician to be elected President, or if elected President to espouse such policies.[45]

De Grazia's prescriptions for change are quite explicit. "The President should be seen as a person furnished with a license to capture as much as he can, and as Congress will let him, of the flora and fauna of a gigantic reservation."[46] Such imperialism must be resisted. The solution is to strengthen Congress against the executive force.[47] This should be done not only because in terms of coordination, integration, and efficiency, Congress is a more responsible institution, but because the executive force is already too powerful. Conversely, all the proposals for increasing the power of the President, such as an item veto and unfettered authority to reform agencies, should be strenuously opposed. Otherwise we may experience rule by the bureaucratic state with the President supplying the face just "as the frozen pond needs a skater to make a winter scene perfectly human."[48]

It may not be entirely accurate to attribute to the presidency the qualities of an increased bureaucracy in the overall administration; for the presidency is in many of its essentials separate and different from the administrative branch. Nor is it entirely clear how presidential irresponsibility necessarily follows from possessing many powers or even from their misuse. I suspect that presidential irresponsibility is more likely to be a function of the relationship between the office and the "legitimate" demands placed upon it, with "legitimate" being, as often as not, redefined from one problem to another. Nonetheless, given the Johnson presidency and America's external entanglements, we can probably anticipate a spate of books in the "anti-aggrandizement" category.

---

[44] *Id.* at 95.

[45] *Id.* at 79.

[46] *Id.*

[47] For his specific proposals, see *id.* at 215-43, 298.

[48] *Id.* at 105.

F. Power Elite

C. W. Mills provides a deliberate attempt to refute those he calls "the image makers." "The images they now offer us are not those of an elite in irresponsible command of unprecedented means of power and manipulation, but of a scatter of reasonable men overwhelmed by events and doing their best in a difficult situation."[49] This view, which smacks of the embattled and constrained President discussed under category C, is replaced in Mills' analysis by a "power elite," and the presidency is only one among a nexus of institutions controlled by this elite.

Since the power elite approach is ostensibly concerned with the presidency only as a small component of a much broader phenomenon, it might seem inappropriate to treat it as a distinctive category. I do so because I regard it as an important emerging perspective on the presidency which can be usefully compared and contrasted with the five perspectives previously outlined.

According to Mills, it is the power elite who are

in command of the major hierarchies and organizations of society. They rule the big corporations. They run the machinery of state and claim its prerogatives. They direct the military establishment.[50]

Obviously, then, there is not much point discussing the distribution of responsibilities and powers because, on issues of pith and moment, it is the power elite which decides. One would assume, further, that this view downgrades the importance of the President's behavior. Yet, when Mills adduces evidence to confirm his analysis he refers to pivotal moments in which small circles (meaning the power elite) "do decide or fail to decide."[51] Mills cites as such moments "the dropping of the A-bombs over Japan ... the decision on Korea ... the confusion about Quemoy and Matsu, as well as before Dienbienphu ... the sequence of maneuvers which involved the United States in World War II."[52] These instances refer to decisions ultimately made by three different Presidents. All are foreign policy decisions. Consequently, implicit in Mills' analysis is the idea that in the membership of the power elite the President is *primus inter pares* in his decision-making ability, although in making his decisions the President acts in consonance with other members of the elite and follows what Mills refers to in a different context as its "community of interests."[53]

Mills' portrayal of the power elite is directed by a populist anger and moral fervor. This leads him, therefore, into a discussion of the "higher immorality," as if the combined weight of his exposé and indignation will lead to beneficial results. Otherwise, he seems pessimistic about the prospects for change. "At the top there has emerged an elite of power. The middle levels are a drifting set of stalemated,

---

[49] C. MILLS, THE POWER ELITE 325 (1956).

[50] *Id.* at 4.

[51] *Id.* at 22.

[52] *Id.*

[53] *Id.* at 283.

balancing forces . . . . The bottom of this society is politically fragmented, and even as a passive fact, increasingly powerless."[54] Of course, proposals for structural changes in the presidency are not important in Mills' analysis.

In 1967 G. William Domhoff wrote a book in an attempt, among other things, empirically to demonstrate or at least to bolster Mills' thesis.[55] As Domhoff put it: "We will not assume, as Mills did, that the Executive branch of the federal government is part of a power elite, but will instead show that its leaders are either members of the upper classes or former employees of institutions controlled by members of the upper class."[56] Domhoff then tries to document that the power elite controls the executive branch through prior control of the presidential nominations which, in turn, it controls through the financing of political campaigns.[57]

Like Mills, Domhoff too has received considerable criticism of his thesis and methodology. I cite him merely to indicate the persistence of the power elite theme.

Whereas Domhoff tends to repeat Mills' theme, Noam Chomsky develops it. For Chomsky,[58] although he may never use Mills' term, America is ruled by a power elite and this elite, as demonstrated by the Vietnam war, can be both evil and dangerous in its effects on America and other countries which bear the brunt of its policies. And, more explicitly than Mills, Chomsky denigrates the importance of the presidency. "There is a growing realization that it is an illusion to believe that all will be well if only today's liberal hero can be placed in the White House."[59]

Chomsky differs from Mills in tone and prescription. Mills is sarcastic and biting; Chomsky is angry and bitter. Ironically, while Mills appeared pessimistic about prospects for change, Chomsky sees in the course of the Vietnam war an opportunity, for it has provoked opposition not only to those in political power who were involved in its conception, execution, and defense, it has also engendered questioning and threatens to undercut the legitimacy of those who occupy positions of importance in the American political system and many of the institutions themselves—including the presidency. Finally, whereas Mills did not appear to proffer a solution, Chomsky advocates draft resistance, and endorses the "revival of anarchist thinking [which] . . . offers some real hope that the present American crisis will not become an American and world catastrophe."[60]

III

CONCLUSIONS

I have briefly canvassed the component parts of six perspectives on the presidency, tried to explain their sources, and suggested a few of the reasons why they

---

[54] *Id.* at 324.

[55] G. DOMHOFF, WHO RULES AMERICA? (1967).

[56] *Id.* at 9.

[57] *Id.* at 85. *See generally id.* at 84-105.

[58] N. CHOMSKY, AMERICAN POWER AND THE NEW MANDARINS (1967).

[59] *Id.* at 18.

[60] *Id.* at 19.

might have been modified in recent years. Certainly my list is not complete. Furthermore, given the varieties of conduct available to Presidents; the different viewpoints and concerns of authors; and the fact that the presidency is, if not protean, at least an office both of extraordinary power and extraordinary limitations, we can expect diverse perspectives to persist.

As for the six perspectives discussed in this paper, I would speculate that they may correspond to particular segments of the political spectrum.[61] To oversimplify grossly, conservatives would be inclined to be "anti-aggrandizement"; moderates would tend to have a "constraints" perspective;[62] liberals would be partial to the "roles" approach; more extreme liberals might be found in the "obligations" school; and the "power elite" perspective is probably peculiar to radicals or, more precisely, nascent revolutionaries.[63] If my formulations have any semblance of accuracy, some intriguing areas of research emerge. I shall mention only one. Presidential perspectives may provide useful indices of changing attitudes among the public, especially among the political activists. For example, the differences in tone and prescriptions between C. Wright Mills and Noam Chomsky may well reflect changes in the revolutionary temper if the Chomsky version of the "power elite" perspective is accepted. Even more important than changes within a category would be changes in acceptance between categories. A decline in "obligations" and corresponding increase in the "constraints" perspective might reflect a reduction in the more extreme liberalism with its optimism and belief in government action (especially presidential action) to solve social ills.

In conclusion, I suggest that we need to examine and test some of the assumptions and assertions about the extent of presidential responsibilities, the adequacy of the President's powers, the importance of individual Presidents' behavior, and the impact of proposed changes in the presidency, inherent in each of the six perspectives. Perhaps because of the difficulty of achieving adequate access (in comparison to Congress), scholars have failed to generate sufficient data about the actual workings of the presidency. Without such empirical data, however, it is difficult to compare or evaluate the various perspectives; and we are often confined to exposition.

---

[61] The words liberal, extreme, etc. are used here without conscious pejorative intent.

[62] Irrespective of their initial ideological inclinations, many participant-observers, chastened by their experiences in office, probably leave the White House or Executive Office as confirmed moderates—at least in their perspectives on the presidency.

[63] I have excluded the statecraft category. Although statecraft is putatively the province of political scientists, it requires a bolder man than this writer to identify his professional brethren with any particular political positions. Besides, Machiavelli's unfortunate experiences, and Professor Neustadt's lonely eminence in this category, suggest that a statecraft perspective may require qualities denied most political scientists.

THE PRESIDENCY AND THE CONSTITUTION: A LOOK AHEAD

Joseph E. Kallenbach*

Current fashion in scholarly discussions of the presidency is to focus upon its internal organizational arrangements and operational methods, the "style" and the "public image" of the occupant of the moment. This emphasis is by no means misplaced. The dimensions of the presidency are determined in large measure by the occupant's capacity and skill in converting his post into a center for policy-initiation and leadership in the political process. Without question, it has become a highly *personalized* office. Yet it is well to remind ourselves from time to time that with reference to this great office, the Constitution still "does matter."[1] Underlying all that it has come to be is the constitutional framework which gives it form and substance.

I

THE CONSTITUTIONAL FOUNDATION

In formulating the constitutional phraseology creating this office the framers of the Constitution wrote on a clean slate. They were in the rather enviable position of being able to give concrete form to what was in their collective judgment a "model" plan of executive organization. Blending theory with practical wisdom derived from the British model and from American experience with various types of "republican" executive organization, they set down as their contribution on this subject the language of article II of the Constitution.

Viewing these original constitutional provisions in the perspective afforded by time, one is impressed first of all by the extraordinary viability and durability of the terminology hit upon in defining the President's powers, functions, and relations with the other elements making up the governmental scheme. It remains to this date without alteration. One notes further, however, that the formal amending procedure has been resorted to with unusual frequency to tinker with certain structural features of the original plan—chiefly those concerned with the mode of selection.

Since 1791, when the perfecting Bill of Rights amendments were incorporated into the Constitution, there have been fifteen amendments engrafted upon the handiwork of the framers. No less than five of these—the twelfth (1804), twentieth (1933), twenty-second (1951), twenty-third (1961), and the twenty-fifth (1967)— have dealt with what may very properly be described as structural aspects of the

---

* Professor of Political Science, University of Michigan.
[1] *Cf.* Fairlie, *Thoughts on the Presidency*, THE PUBLIC INTEREST, Autumn, 1967, at 48.

office of President. To these might well be added three others—the fifteenth (1870), nineteenth (1920), and twenty-fourth (1963) amendments. These revisions of the original document, to be sure, were directed generally toward broadening the popular electoral base upon which government in the United States rests. But these amendments were adopted after developments through state legislation and party usage had already occurred that had converted the original plan of presidential selection into a system of indirect popular choice. These franchise-extending amendments therefore contributed very materially toward democratizing in greater measure the office of President.

Formal amendments adopted to date have been essentially responses to change in conception of the functions assigned to this office. As has been noted, the original phraseology detailing its formal powers and defining its relationships to the other organs of government remains unchanged. But it is precisely *because* new conceptions of the President's role in the governmental process have become institutionalized that it has been deemed necessary to introduce structural modifications by resort to the amendment procedure.

Constitutional revisions effected to date have been, essentially, accommodations dictated by the President's having assumed a more open, active leadership role in government affairs. This has resulted from the new interpretations read into his original grants of constitutional authority. Supplemented further by congressional enactments, these grants have become a vast reservoir of power and influence. The President's "headship" of the government has become far more than symbolic. The primacy of the *presidency*, if not of the *President*, as an element in the governing process, has become apparent to all. Simultaneously developments have occurred that have placed in his hands also a national party leadership role, supplementing his official governmental "headship" powers at almost every point.

II

THE ROLES OF THE PRESIDENT

Implicit in these developments there is discernible a certain ambivalence, even a contradiction, of purpose and result. This ambivalence arises from a duality in the roles that have come to be associated with this office. On the one hand, providing a direct popular base on which the office rests, coupled with a broadened conception of his official powers and authority, has given the President a new source of support for vigorous assertion and use of his constitutional powers vis-à-vis Congress, the courts, and the states. He speaks and acts as the *people's* agent. He lays claim to a mandate from them for his acts. Authority *descends* upon him from the nation, not from the other organs of government. *Vox populi legati suprema lex est* becomes his credo.

Thus when Franklin D. Roosevelt addressed Congress in 1942 in his role as President, requesting that it pass a more effective price and wage control bill, he underscored his request with a threat to act on his own authority if Congress failed to respond promptly. He concluded his remarkable statement with these significant words:

> When the war is won, the powers under which I act (will) automatically revert *to the people—to whom they belong*.[2]

Essentially what FDR was enunciating was a kind of fuhrership principle of executive authority. As National Leader and Head of Government he was laying claim to a right to act in the name of the people for the public good, independent of congressional sanctioning of his action. Granted, he may well have been bluffing, knowing that the Congress would respond to his request, given the state of public opinion at the time;[3] but this statement is a clear illustration of the ultimate reach of executive prerogative in an "emergency."

Added to this latitudinarian conception of the powers of the office is the idea that the President should exercise a "moral leadership" role in the affairs of the American people generally. Again it was FDR, echoing views earlier expressed by Theodore Roosevelt and Woodrow Wilson, who can be cited as voicing most emphatically this view. Shortly before his assumption of office, he characterized it as "pre-eminently a place of moral leadership." This responsibility, he went on to say, far outweighs the purely administrative functions of the office.[4] The range of this responsibility extends to every matter of vital concern to the people and their welfare. The presidency thus becomes an office of spiritual as well as political leadership. It combines the functions of a Caesar and a Pope.[5]

But when the "people" invest the President with his powers of office, they do so through a partisan electoral contest. He speaks through and for the political party whose acknowledged champion and spokesman he has become by virtue of his emerging as its nominee. Of course, his objective as a leader of a partisan faction is only to prevail over a Loyal Opposition party (or parties) with regard to certain policies he believes the government should pursue. His objective is not to utterly destroy them.[6] His mandate as party leader is limited by the democratic dogma of toleration for opposing views—a concept that supplies the key to successful operation of democratic systems of government generally. In view of the non-ideological, quite decentralized character of the two major parties in the United States, moreover, this partisanship of toleration extends in great degree into the area of intra-party politics as well. Over neither his "congressional party" wing

---

[2] 88 CONG. REC. 7044, 77th Cong., 2d Sess. (1942) (emphasis added).

[3] *Cf.* Roche, *Executive Power and Domestic Emergency: The Quest for Prerogative*, 5 W. POL. Q. 610 (1952).

[4] Warn, *Roosevelt's Approach to the Great Task*, N.Y. Times, Nov. 13, 1932, § 8, at 1, col. 1.

[5] Fairlie, *supra* note 1, has coined the term "Caesaropapism" to express this concept.

[6] The development of a sophisticated partisan politics of toleration and accommodation in the United States, with the President playing a leading role therein, is explored in illuminating fashion in R. HOFSTADTER, THE IDEA OF A PARTY SYSTEM: THE RISE OF A LEGITIMATE OPPOSITION IN THE UNITED STATES, 1780-1840 (1969).

nor the state and local party cadres upon whose shoulders he has ridden into power can the President realistically expect to exercise a discipline and control that unites them into a solid phalanx under his leadership.

Joining in his hands these two kinds of leadership roles places the President in a somewhat awkward position. He becomes at once the surrogate of a united people and at the same time, the leader and spokesman of a faction of the people. In his first capacity he wields broad "moral leadership" and none-too-closely defined official powers as Head of State. In his latter capacity, by contrast, he speaks and acts for a segment of the people aligned in opposition to other important elements in American political society. As such, he must expect to encounter, and be obliged to tolerate, a great amount of sniping, criticism, and mulish obstructionism, if not downright sabotage, of his undertakings. Those in and out of government who speak and act for an organized, constantly evolving partisan opposition will see to that. Intent upon scoring points that will enhance their chances of taking over control of this power center at the next election, his partisan opponents are naturally loath to act in ways that might make the President and the partisan element he represents "look good" in the eyes of the national electorate; for his partisan opposition is committed to an attempt to oust him and his party when the contest for preferment is staged anew.

Because of this duality of roles, the presidency necessarily presents to the nation and the world a kind of schizophrenic aspect. As influences and pressure play upon the President from the two poles of his sometimes inconsistent roles, he performs his functions in a state of continual tension. Let him address the Congress—and his national constituency as well—in discharge of his constitutional responsibility to "give to the Congress information on the state of the Union, and recommend to their consideration such measures as he shall deem necessary and expedient," and the cry arises immediately for "equal time" on the communications media for his Loyal Opposition to reply. His engagement in active congressional campaigning to further election of partisan colleagues pledged to support of his policies immediately sparks charges of "slicksterism" and misuse of the prestige of his office for partisan ends. Searching and sometimes embarrassing questions are raised on exactly how and by whom the expenses entailed by his campaign tours and speeches are being met. On the other hand, his failure to include an active, effective party leadership role in his conception of his official responsibilities exposes him to criticism from other directions for ineptness and unwillingness to exploit to the fullest extent the potential of his office for advancing the public welfare.

The "moral leadership" aspect of the President's modern role in governmental affairs serves further to magnify the tensions arising from his having assumed a party leadership function in addition to a greatly broadened conception of an official authority derived from the constitutional sources. One commentator recently began a short discussion of this problem in its current context in this fashion:

Around the White House they worry quite sincerely that a lot of Americans are confusing the President with God. Their concern, of course, stems from the fear that if the populace approaches the Oval Office with spiritual expectations and then finds only a human in there, the result will be general despair and a tendency to blame everything from riots and race hatred to dope and divorce on Richard Nixon.[7]

In the eyes of the populace—with some assistance from Presidents themselves as well as from none-too-discerning learned commentators—the President is elevated to the status of the Great Wizard, the Healer of All the Nation's Woes. Let him fail to express his views and concern about one of the great problems of the day, and he is assailed for failure to exert appropriate "moral leadership." All would be well, it is said, if he would only sound the tocsin to battle against this or that evil in American life. It is his function to inspire the people and point the way to realization of every man's conception of the American Dream. Yet if he announces a position and issues a call for action on some burning social or economic issue—with the inevitable result of offending some elements in society who do not agree with his point of view—his critics will be quick to charge him with "creating divisiveness," "alienating" important elements of society, or "polarizing" the American Public.

III

THE PROSPECTS FOR CHANGE

It is within the context of these built-in conflicts between the roles the modern presidency has assumed that one must approach the question of the possibility and desirability of change in the Constitution as it relates to this office. Given the history of failure of past efforts, both from within Congress and from outside it, to effect fundamental changes of this kind (except as to the mode of filling the office and keeping it filled), the prospects appear to be practically nil. The method by which the popular choice of the nation is determined in the selection of the President and Vice President will probably soon be brought into closer focus with political realities by formal amendment of the Constitution. Beyond that, however, the prospects for change appear slim indeed. Change in a fundamental sense is likely to occur only if some great catastrophe in the nation's life—such as, God forbid! an all-out nuclear war, or an internal upheaval of the sort apparently sought by some of our young revolutionary nihilists—should befall us.

It should never be forgotten that the modern Presidency is the product of a continual struggle for power and influence deliberately invited by the nature of the original constitutional plan. So far as concerns the constitutional ground rules setting up the arena and allocating weapons of political warfare as among the three branches of the national government, they have to date resisted all efforts to alter

[7] Sidey, *The Presidency: Demand for "Moral Leadership,"* LIFE, Oct. 23, 1970, at 2.

them by the formal amendment route. There is no good reason to believe they will not continue to do so.

Note, for example, the controversies that have arisen over the question of alteration of the original veto arrangements in the Constitution. An unusually vigorous use of this authority by Andrew Jackson produced in reaction a series of serious but unsuccessful attempts by the Whigs to cut back the veto power by constitutional amendment during the 1840's. Enactment by a run-away Congress of 15 of 21 measures vetoed by President Andrew Johnson in the 1860's ultimately demonstrated that the veto was not an absolute weapon in the hands of the President. It could be blunted by a determined congressional majority.

Later the pendulum swung the other way again. Every President from Grant to Eisenhower has expressed dissatisfaction with the original veto arrangements and pleaded for a constitutional amendment granting them the item veto over appropriation bills. Numerous pundits have endorsed the idea as a sound one. When no favorable response came from Congress, the Presidents eventually turned increasingly to the device of "impoundment" of appropriated funds which in their judgment were improvidently authorized by Congress.[8] Still more recently, enactment by Congress of a major appropriation bill over President Nixon's veto has demonstrated anew that the "pull and haul" system set up by the framers as between Congress and the President in the enactment of money bills is by no means outmoded. It still works both ways.

All this is not to say, of course, that changes in the constitutionally ordained equilibrium of power as between the President, the Congress, and the courts, and as between him and state authorities has not occurred, or will not continue to occur. The role of the President in the constitutional scheme will doubtless be altered as the future unfolds; but alteration will come about through the more subtle, informal methods of constitutional change rather than by constitutional amendment. Changes in the balance of powers between Congress and the Executive that will be effected cannot be expected to eliminate the state of tension that exists between them. They may well cause it to become even more acute from time to time as the President appears in his various roles before the Congress and the American public.

For the moment it would appear that the mood in Congress and in the nation is one of seeking and exploiting new, and refurbishing old, ways of redressing the balance more explicitly on the side of congressional power and influence. This would appear to have been a more or less inevitable result, given the fact that in four of the last eight Congresses (five out of nine if the new 92nd Congress chosen

---

[8] For a discussion of this development, see Goostree, *The Power of the President to Impound Appropriated Funds: With Special Reference to Grants-in-Aid to Segregated Activities,* and Kranz, *A Twentieth Century Emancipation Proclamation: Presidential Power Permits Withholding of Federal Funds from Segregated Institutions,* in THE PRESIDENCY 727 (A. Wildavsky ed. 1969); Church, *Impoundment of Appropriated Funds; The Decline of Congressional Control Over Executive Discretion,* 22 STAN. L. REV. 1240 (1970).

in November, 1970 is included) both Houses have been under the control of the President's political opposition.

It can be predicted that among the strategies Congress may be expected to pursue in the future in its never-ending tug-of-war with the President will be the following:

1. Further efforts to exploit more effectively its inquisitorial and other types of authority to command production of information relevant to public policy in the hands of the President or his agents.

2. More frequent use of a built-in concurrent resolution "cut-off" device, whereby grants of authority to the President by legislative act may be cancelled without running the risk of a veto.[9]

3. Wider employment of the committee-clearance-in-advance procedure for supervising administration of particular statutes.[10]

4. Increased resort to House and/or Senate resolutions declarative of attitudes, intent, and understandings of the respective bodies on questions of public policy, as illustrated by the Senate's passage of the National Commitments Resolution in 1969.[11]

5. Freer use by the Senate of its power to reject nominations to major posts by the President. Illustrative of the point was the Senate's breaking a precedent of some forty years standing by refusing to confirm two presidential nominations to the Supreme Court within the past two years. This followed soon after a resignation of an incumbent Justice was induced by a Senate inquiry into his qualifications while he was being considered as the President's nominee for the post of Chief Justice.

6. Fuller exploitation by Congress of its "power of the purse" to limit presidential discretion in various policy-initiating and policy-executing areas. The ultimate reach of this potent weapon remains unexplored, at least in the minds of some members of Congress. As indicated in the Senate debates on the Cooper-Church Amendment to the Military Procurement Act of 1970, it might conceivably be used in such a way

---

[9] Cf. Buchwalter, *The Congressional Concurrent Resolution: A Search for Foreign Policy Influence*, 14 MIDWEST J. POL. SCI. 434 (1970).

[10] Cf. J. HARRIS, CONGRESSIONAL CONTROL OF ADMINISTRATION 237 *et seq.* (1965). As a result of repeated clashes between President L.B. Johnson and Congress on inclusion of various types of "committee veto" provisions in statutes, a subcommittee of the Senate Judiciary Committee chaired by Senator Ervin, of North Carolina, conducted extensive hearings on this problem in 1967. *See Hearings on the Separation of Powers Before the Subcomm. on Separation of Powers of the Senate Comm. on the Judiciary*, 90th Cong., 1st Sess. (1967).

[11] S. RES. 85, 91st Cong., 1st Sess. (1969). The resolution, which was passed by a 70-16 vote, reads as follows:

Resolved, That (1) a national commitment for the purpose of this resolution means the use of armed forces of the United States on Foreign territory, or a promise to assist a foreign country, government, or people by the use of armed forces or financial resources of the United States, either immediately or upon the happening of certain events, and (2) it is the sense of the Senate that a national commitment by the United States results only from affirmative action taken by the executive and legislative branches of the United States by means of a treaty, statute, or concurrent resolution of both Houses of Congress specifically providing for such commitment.

as to substitute Congressional judgment for that of the President in the exercise of his commander-in-chief functions with respect to matters of military strategy and tactics in an area of actual combat. It might be observed, in passing, that when Congress in 1942 sought to use the "power of the purse" to usurp the President's constitutionally based power of removal over subordinate executive officials, it was rebuked by the Supreme Court.[12] But the Court's ruling in that instance turned on a point of constitutional construction that carefully evaded the basic question of implied limits on the power of the purse growing out of the Constitution's allocation of executive powers to the President.

The long-range impact of these and other devices Congress may be expected to experiment with in the next decade on the constitutional balance of power between the two branches cannot be fully appraised at this point. They may well prove to be futile and ineffective. The pressures that exist both in the foreign and domestic policy-making areas appear to make aggrandizement of the executive side of government an imperative. Efforts in Congress to retrieve for itself a wider decision-making authority may simply prove to be impractical.

IV

CONSTITUTIONAL AMENDMENTS

Meanwhile, the impact of both recent and anticipated constitutional revisions pertaining to the office of President can be evaluated. These changes by amendment, it has been pointed out above, have reference to the mode of election and perfecting the arrangements for succession, rather than to the powers of the office per se. Nevertheless they have a significance with respect to the extra-constitutional role of the President as party leader in ways that have not been widely appreciated.

The twenty-second amendment, which became a part of the constitutional plan in 1951, has usually been conceived of as an instrument for enforcing a rule of rotation with respect to the holding of the *official* powers of the office. And so it is. But it may be suggested that the amendment was understood by its more perceptive advocates as significant primarily as an instrument for regulating *party* government. Its immediate impact was to enforce a rule of limited tenure on a national party head by arbitrarily displacing him after an interval as the dominant force in his party nationally.

After all, as had been demonstrated by the Taft and Hoover candidacies in 1912 and 1932, respectively, an incumbent President seeking re-election could be turned out of office after one term if the people were so inclined. But no incumbent President since 1900 who had sought renomination by his party had been rejected as its *nominee*. It was the domination of the national party convention by an incumbent President so as to compel his own renomination that was the primary target of the amendment. Rather than tinker with the constitutional arrangements relating to the official

---

[12] United States v. Lovett, 328 U.S. 303 (1946).

powers and duties of his office (on the terms of which probably no agreement could have been achieved in Congress), this indirect bi-partisan approach to the end desired —a freeing of the *party* from one-man rule—was adopted.

Again, one may discern a connection between the twentieth amendment and the twenty-fifth amendment in their bearing on the question of succession in the party leadership aspect of the presidency. The main object of the twentieth amendment, of course, was to effect a closer coordination between the beginning of an in-coming President's term of office and the functioning of the newly-chosen Congress under his leadership. An infrequently noted provision of the amendment, however, was the language of its third section. This section makes clear that in the contingency of an inconclusive presidential election and an ensuing deadlock in the House of Representatives, the new Vice President-elect must temporarily assume the post of *Acting* President until the deadlock is resolved. His doing so, it is made clear, does not permanently displace the President-to-be.

This language went part way, at least, toward resolving the question whether a Vice President might legitimately *act* as President without *becoming* President—an unresolved issue that had been a serious barrier to implementation of the original constitutional arrangements regarding succession in the event of the President's disability. Beyond that, however, it implied that the President and the Vice President, rather than being regarded as candidates for two separate offices, should be looked upon as a "team." The Vice President, as the potential deputy party leader, should therefore be politically compatible with and enjoy the confidence of the President in that capacity.

In addition to legitimizing either a temporary or permanent Head of State role for the Vice-President—an important criterion for any arrangement relative to the presidential succession[13]—this provision led almost immediately to introduction of the usage of the national party convention's deferring to the presidential nominee's wishes in the selection of a vice presidential running mate. In other words, the national party leader was accorded the privilege of naming the deputy leader. This practice manifested itself in the Democratic Party's convention in 1940 when F.D.R. imposed upon a rather reluctant body of delegates his choice of running mate. The precedent of consulting the presidential nominee and deferring to his wishes in the matter of the vice presidential nomination has been followed in every national major party convention, with one exception, since then.[14]

This usage, in its turn, led directly to inclusion of the language of section 2 in the twenty-fifth amendment. That section, which follows immediately upon language

---

[13] *Cf.* Wildavsky, *Presidential Succession and Disability: Policy Analysis for Unique Cases*, in THE PRESIDENCY 777 (A. Wildavsky ed. 1969).

[14] Adlai Stevenson, the Democratic Party's nominee in 1956, permitted the party convention to exercise a free choice in the matter of the vice presidential nomination. His endorsement of Senator Sparkman, of Alabama, as his running mate in the 1952 election had given rise to considerable criticism in certain "liberal" circles of the party, who maintained that it had weakened the ticket.

in the amendment declaring that the Vice President shall "become" President in case of the removal of the President, or his death or resignation, reads as follows:

> Whenever there is a vacancy in the office of the Vice President, the President shall nominate a Vice President who shall take office upon confirmation by a majority vote of both Houses of Congress.

Potentially this provision of the amendment is of far greater significance than the other sections concerning succession to the powers and duties of the office of President by the Vice President in the event of the President's disability. It has as its objective keeping the line of succession filled by a President-in-waiting, thus obviating the necessity, for all practical purposes, of going beyond the vice presidency in providing a successor. In view of the increasing importance that has come to attach to the vice presidential post so far as the party leadership aspect of the office of President is concerned, it is remarkable that this provision in the amendment received comparatively little attention in the Congressional debates. It deserved far more attention than it was given. Of all the provisions in the amendment, it is the one that may well prove to be either unworkable in practice or, if it works, of profound significance in its impact upon the office of President in its party leadership aspect.

Since World War II, the vice presidency has become the most frequently used stepping stone to the presidency, or at least to preferment as the nominee for that post by the President's party. Two presidentially designated deputy party leaders, Harry S. Truman and L. B. Johnson, have succeeded to the office of President upon the death of incumbents and have gone on to win election in their own right for full terms. Two other incumbent Vice Presidents, Richard Nixon in 1960 and Hubert Humphrey in 1968, were nominated with the blessing of the incumbent President of their respective parties, but were defeated in their runs for the big prize. Nixon, of course, was successful in a second try after an intervening election. Increasing reliance of Presidents from F.D.R. to Nixon on their Vice Presidents to carry a major share of the party campaigning burden in off-year congressional elections demonstrates the point that the Vice President's *ex officio* role as deputy party leader is something more than an empty title.

It is this dimension of the President's position in relation to his party that raises doubts about the feasibility of this provision of the amendment. Placing the responsibility in his hands to nominate a person to fill a vice presidential vacancy, insofar as that officer becomes an *ex officio* deputy party leader, is of course, in line with the practice that has come to prevail at the national party convention in selecting the vice presidential nominee. Presumably a President will consult other party leaders in and out of Congress in settling on his choice, in case the post becomes vacant, as he does at a national party convention. But his filling a vacancy in the *office* is not merely that of selecting a candidate for election, subject to the suffrage of the people. It is to fill an office with prescribed constitutional and statutory powers and duties plus other important partisan political functions.

The twenty-fifth amendment proposes to give legitimacy to a new incumbent in the vice presidency as an *officer* by requiring that his appointment be confirmed by a majority vote in both Houses of Congress. This is likely to be forthcoming if the President's party has a majority in both Houses. But what if the President's party does not have majority control in Congress?

This is no idle speculation. In no less than six of the last thirteen Congresses, the President's party has been in the minority in both Houses of Congress. May it be readily assumed in this kind of situation that as a matter of partisan "courtesy" the majority party in the two Houses will readily go along with the President's selection of a person who will become his "heir apparent" as party leader? Would the temptation not be too strong for the President's loyal opposition to simply "sit" on the nomination, keep the vice presidency vacant, and thereby, under arrangements regarding the presidential succession presently set forth in the Presidential Succession Act of 1947, retain the opposition party's House Speaker in the position of being only "one heartbeat away" from the presidency itself?[15]

Other features of the twenty-fifth amendment are less open to criticism on the ground that they fail to take into account the fact that the presidency has become a party leadership post as well as a powerful Headship of State office. The arrangements of section 3 of the amendment providing for temporary assumption of the powers and duties of the office of President by the Vice President upon due notice and request by a temporarily disabled President are in line with understandings reached on an informal basis by President Eisenhower and his Vice President, as well as by Presidents Kennedy and Johnson and their "Deputy Presidents." These "understandings," it should be noted, had followed upon resolution of the point in the twentieth amendment that a Vice President might "act" as President without "becoming" President.

The rather complex procedure provided for effecting a temporary succession by a Vice President when the President is unable to declare his disability commendably takes into account the partisan political aspects of the succession problem as well as the official duty aspects. On the partisan side, associating the heads of the principal departments (or of "such other body as Congress may by law provide") with the

---

[15] Senator Birch Bayh's *One Heartbeat Away* (1958) is an illuminating, detailed account of the struggle in Congress to get the Presidential Disability Amendment drafted and passed. Senator Bayh played a leading role in this effort on the Senate side. The suggestion to incorporate a provision in the amendment to cover the matter of filling a vice presidential vacancy in the manner eventually adopted came from a number of sources. *See Id.* at 32. In earlier drafting endeavors it was planned to incorporate provisions abolishing the provisions in the Presidential Succession Act of 1947 which placed the House Speaker and President *pro tem* of the Senate in the line of succession; but for reasons of legislative strategy this feature was omitted from the amendment. Had this provision been included and the Secretary of State been named as the next officer in the succession line beyond the Vice President, the provision for filling the vice presidency incorporated in the amendment would be much less vulnerable to criticism.

decision of the Vice President to assume the powers of the presidency in this kind of contingency affords protection against a rash challenge of the party head by an ambitious Vice President, or perchance, may spur him to take necessary action.

A similar procedure must be invoked by a Vice President to resist a President he deems still disabled who seeks to resume the powers of office. But the support of a two-thirds majority in both branches of Congress must be secured by a Vice President within a specified time limit if he is to be permitted to retain the official powers of the presidency in the face of a claim by the incumbent President that his disability has been eliminated.

In simpler terms, the amendment provides a rational procedure by which a President regarded as unable to exercise his official powers as head of state, and his unofficial functions as party chief as well, may be *suspended* though not permanently *removed*. The procedure adopted seeks to provide a check upon the Vice President's action in such a case both as to its impact on the party leadership role as well as upon the head of state role of the President. A contingency of the sort that might involve Congress as the ultimate judge of the merits of the claims of rival contenders for the office is very unlikely to occur; but if it does, requiring a substantial bi-partisan majority in each House of Congress to suspend the regularly elected President from office is appropriate insurance that this step will be taken only in the event a crisis of major proportions has arisen—one transcending ordinary considerations of partisan advantage.

A final point of consideration concerns the impact of what will probably become the twenty-sixth amendment on the dual roles of head of state and party head the President has come to occupy. The likelihood appears strong that a constitutional amendment will soon be adopted abolishing the electoral college procedure for registering the will of voters of the nation in the selection of the President and Vice President, and making a direct vote of the people from the nation at large determinative of the outcome. But a nagging problem has appeared with regard to such an amendment. What procedure should be provided to deal with the contingency of there not being a conclusive enough plurality in the popular voting for any pair of candidates for these offices to be deemed elected?

In the version of the direct election amendment proposal passed by the House in September, 1969, by approximately a five-to-one majority, this contingency is dealt with by a provision that if no ticket receives a plurality of forty per cent or more of the total vote, a run-off popular election will be held within a matter of weeks between the two leading pairs of candidates. In Senate debate on the amendment proposal during the months of September and October of 1970, opponents of the direct election plan centered their fire heavily on these provisions of the House-passed plan. Alternatives advanced by opponents to the direct election system looked toward preserving the present electoral vote system, with possibly an "automatic" electoral vote based on the present electoral vote distribution formula. These alternative plans also embraced the idea of resolving an inconclusive electoral vote result by referring the presidential and vice presidential contests, as now provided, to the House and Senate respectively; or possibly by reference of these contests to a joint session of the two Houses, with each Senator or Representative casting an individual vote in each contest.

Whatever the new elective system adopted may prove to be, if the present method of resolving an inconclusive first step result is retained or a system of joint voting by the two Houses is substituted as the method for achieving a final result in this contingency, extremely serious repercussions may well be felt. The "near miss" scored by Governor Wallace in his proclaimed intention to capture enough electoral votes to produce an inconclusive electoral vote result in the 1968 election, following upon the four-party contest in 1948 and the "unpledged elector" ploy used by dissident States Rights Democrats in 1960, has brought home the point to many of the leading members of the two major parties that to continue to rely on the present electoral vote method may well lead to disaster so far as the two-party system is concerned. A presidential election resolved by the "bartering" of a bloc of third or fourth party electoral votes, or by political horse-trading in the House and/or Senate, would shake the structure of the two major parties to their foundations.

While this thought has proved to be the catalyst that has finally produced some movement in Congress to substitute a more realistic, politically logical mode of electing the President for the electoral college system, there has been inadequate attention given to the question in Congress of what would be in store for its members if ever they should be called upon to resolve an inconclusive first stage in the election of the President. A realistic appraisal of the situation confronting them should be made.

In the 1968 election, if less than one-half of one per cent of the major party vote in Ohio and Missouri had shifted from Nixon to Humphrey, the electoral votes of those states, totaling 38, would have gone to the latter rather than the former. An electoral vote deadlock would have resulted, with no pair of candidates for President and Vice President receiving a majority. Assume further that neither of the major party candidates, in line with their pledges during the course of the campaign, would have struck a political bargain with Wallace for enough of his electoral votes to surmount the majority vote hurdle. If the election had been referred to the House, the following situation would have resulted in the 91st Congress:[16]

Thus eleven House delegations in states carried by Nixon would have been under a heavy political "cross-pressure." That is to say, the Democrats who were in the majority in each of those states would have been confronted by the difficult choice of sticking with their party's candidate and giving their states' votes in the House voting to the rejected popular choice therein, or going along with the will of a

---

[16] The electoral results used in deriving this and the following tables are those found in the CONGRESSIONAL QUARTERLY 1968 ELECTIONS SUPPLEMENT (1969).

TABLE 1
DISTRIBUTION OF HOUSE UNIT VOTES FOR PRESIDENT, 1968

States carried in popular vote:	Total	House delegation Rep.	House delegation Dem.	House delegation AIP	Evenly divided
By Nixon	32	17	11	0	4
By Humphrey	13	2	10	0	1
By Wallace	5	0	5	0	0
Totals	50	19	26	0	5

plurality of the voters in their states and casting their states' votes for the opposition party's candidate. In like fashion two delegations in states carried by Humphrey would have been under "cross-pressure"; and five state delegations in states carried by Wallace would have been similarly pressured. Five state votes would presumably have been nullified by an even split in the partisan make-up of the delegation.

If the election had been referred to a joint session of the two Houses, with each member having an individual vote, the "cross-pressure" factor would simply become more wide-spread and acute, as the following analysis shows:

TABLE 2
SENATE SEATS COMPARED WITH PRESIDENTIAL ELECTION RESULTS, 1968

	Rep. Senators (Elected & Holdovers)	Dem. Senators (Elected)	Dem. Senators (Holdovers)	Total
State for Nixon:	33	11	20	64
	Dem. Senators (Elected & Holdovers)	Rep. Senators (Elected)	Rep. Senators (Holdovers)	
State for Humphrey:	16	3	7	26
		Dem. Senators (Elected)	Dem. Senators (Holdovers)	
State for Wallace:	0	4	6	10

So far as the Senate is concerned 51 newly-elected or holdover Senators would have been "out-of-line" in a partisan sense with the recently expressed popular results in their respective states. Of these, 31 would have been Democratic Senators in states carried by Nixon; 10 would have been Republican Senators in states carried by Humphrey; and 10 would have been Democratic Senators in states carried by Wallace.

The House picture would have been equally muddled on the matter of the popular vote in the district as compared with the partisan character of the representative chosen as shown by. table 3:

TABLE 3

HOUSE SEATS COMPARED WITH PRESIDENTIAL ELECTION RESULTS, 1968

	Rep. elected	Dem. elected	AIP elected	Total
District for Nixon	160	66	0	226
District for Humphrey	28	133	0	161
District for Wallace	4	44	0	48
Total	192	243	0	435

A total of 142 House seats would have been held by partisans "out-of-line" with the presidential election results in their districts. Nixon carried 66 districts in which Democrats were elected; Humphrey 28 districts in which Republicans were elected; and 44 Democrats and 4 Republicans were elected in districts that voted for Wallace.

Thus on a joint voting basis in Congress a total of 193 members would have had to make the difficult choice between supporting their party's candidate or registering the revealed wishes of their constituencies for another party's candidate. Caught in this kind of "bind" would have been 110 Democratic and 32 Republican House members, and 41 Democratic and 10 Republican Senators. This amounts to approximately 44 per cent of the entire membership. How they would actually have resolved this dilemma one can only guess.

V

CONCLUSION

Viewed in its long range aspect, retention of language in a presidential election reform amendment reserving to Congress power to resolve in one way or another an inconclusive first step result in the election of the President might well prove to have most far-reaching consequences. Depending on the nature of the provisions for resolving the election on the basis of the first stage results, candidates for Congress might well become *de facto* presidential electoral candidates. The national party organization could be expected in that case, as they have done with the problem of the "disloyal" elector candidates on their party tickets, to exert pressure on the local party organization to put up under the party label only candidates for Congress whose loyalty to the national party leadership can be depended on. A "fence-straddling" congressional candidate on the matter of his choice for President would be opposed by a party "regular" whose loyalty is secure. Candidates for Congress would necessarily have to tie themselves more closely to the national party leadership, and rise or fall with the fortunes of the national party in their respective constituencies. The relationship of the President to his congressional party element would become closer, and party discipline in Congress would doubtless approach more closely to that found in a parliamentary democracy.

Use of some other method than referral to Congress of an inconclusive popular election for President, such as a run-off election device, on the other hand, would tend to keep the constituency bases of members of Congress and of the President more distinct and separate. While it might strengthen him in his role as head of government by giving him a political base different from that of the local and state party hierarchy, his party's members in Congress would by the same token remain in a stronger position to challenge his leadership, if so inclined. In fashioning a presidential election reform amendment, it would be well, therefore, for the members of Congress to recognize that the mechanics of the system they devise can have profound implications with respect to their relationship to their presidential candidate and the national party organizational leadership generally. It may further continuance of a viable system of checks and balances, or it may promote movement toward subordinating the congressional party of the President to a much greater degree of executive leadership than is now the case.

REORGANIZING THE FEDERAL EXECUTIVE BRANCH: THE LIMITS OF INSTITUTIONALIZATION*

Harvey C. Mansfield†

Introduction

Reorganization, in the broad sense, is one of the instruments for managing social change. Managing change in the structure of government is a political operation. Reorganization in the federal executive branch, on a scale or at a level that attracts external notice, is accordingly a process caught up in the stresses of rivalry between the President and his entourage, the bureaucracy, the Congress and its committees, and organized outside forces, for the control of governmental offices and operations —for whatever uses that control may be put to. It is a process that has been undertaken on a comprehensive scale at least spasmodically ever since 1887, and more systematically during the past twenty or thirty years. Numerous approaches have been tried, sometimes with positive results but often ending in stalemates, at least for the time being.

It is commonly supposed that the Reorganization Act of 1939, with its subsequent modifications and extensions, finally succeeded in resolving the earlier impasse by institutionalizing the process—by stating acceptable criteria, by focusing responsibility for the initiative in the form of a Reorganization Plan proposed by the President, and by providing an orderly and assured disposition of it through the expression of congressional acquiescence, implicitly or explicitly, or by the imposition of a congressional veto. There is an element of truth in this but also a considerable exaggeration. The Reorganization Act has indeed introduced an important problem-solving innovation in a sensitive area, but it is far from becoming the standard institutionalized method for accomplishing reorganizations in the executive branch.

I take institutionalizing here to mean the emergence of a patterned response to the need for handling a growing volume of cases involving recurrent issues through specialized agencies that develop an expertise in the subject and, by methods that establish routines, generalize acceptable rules and goals and minimize procedural and personal controversies.[1] In this sense legislation is an institutionalized process, with limits upon its applicability for various purposes in various circumstances. So is the reorganization plan procedure.

I have dealt in another article with this procedure and with the congressional

---

* I am indebted to the Brookings Institution for support in studies of which this is a partial product.
† Professor of Government, Columbia University.
[1] *Cf.* Polsby, *The Institutionalization of the U.S. House of Representatives*, 62 Am. Pol. Sci. Rev. 144 (1968).

reception accorded reorganization plans.[2] My aim here is to examine how and to what extent the initiative in reorganizations has come to devolve upon the chief executive, and how, among possible alternatives, he has chosen to equip himself with assistance in the formulation of concrete proposals. The first topic calls for a review of leading historical instances of the exercise of the initiative, in the context of shifting objectives from "economy" to program controls by the Congress as well as by the President. The second involves tracing the shift from reliance on public and mixed commissions to unpublicized presidential task forces. From these bodies of evidence some tentative conclusions about the limits of institutionalization may seem warranted. This article is confined to the civilian establishment in the executive branch. Reorganization in the military establishment would, I believe, show analogies; but it would be a separate enterprise to deal with them.[3]

Before coming to the evidence it is appropriate to start briefly with the constitutional sources of difficulty, for the seeds of later contests were planted there. I take it that what the Constitution says, and fails to say, about organization applies also to reorganization.

I

CONSTITUTIONAL ISSUES

The framers of the Constitution took the existence of departments for granted, in two phrases of article II, section 2: "The President . . . may require the opinion, in writing, of the principal officer in each of the executive departments upon any subject relating to the duties of their respective offices" and "the Congress may by law vest the appointment of such inferior officers as they think proper . . . in the heads of departments." An intervening phrase in the same section speaks, in connection with Senate confirmation, of "all other officers of the United States whose appointments are not herein otherwise provided for, and which shall be established by law . . . ." The opening sentence of article II vests "the Executive power" in the President and section 2 makes him "Commander-in-Chief of the Army and Navy," but beyond what has already been quoted, and the injunction upon him to "take care that the laws be faithfully executed," no correspondingly explicit language defines his relationships with the civilian establishment. The silences and ambiguities are crucial, for they allowed two contradictory doctrines respecting the unity of the executive branch to take root in 1789. The issues were exhaustively canvassed in the great debate over the President's removal power in the first Congress; again in connection with the Tenure of Office Act after the Civil War; and still

---

²Mansfield, *Federal Executive Reorganization: Thirty Years of Experience*, 39 PUB. AD. REV. 332 (1969).

³For a start, see W. MILLIS, H. MANSFIELD, & H. STEIN, ARMS AND THE STATE 139-85 (1958); S. HUNTINGTON, THE SOLDIER AND THE STATE (1957); P. HAMMOND, ORGANIZING FOR DEFENSE (1961); D. CARALEY, THE POLITICS OF MILITARY UNIFICATION (1966).

later in the Supreme Court's decisions in the *Myers* and *Humphrey* cases.[4] They are relevant also to reorganization.

It can be plausibly argued that the purpose in assuring the President the written opinions of department heads on request was not only to provide him with informed advice and to make them answerable to him for past actions. It would also enable him to establish clear responsibility before he acted on a pending matter himself or directed the department chief how to act on it—a protection of the principle of hierarchy. George Washington, coming to the Presidency from the Convention, took it so and acted in that fashion.[5] A President who can direct the exercise of any powers committed to a subordinate can afford to take a relaxed view of the formal structure of the establishment of which he is the pinnacle. In Washington's case the statutes commonly delegated final authority directly to him.

Simultaneously, however, when the Congress established the Treasury Department it fixed the main features of the department's organization by specifying five distinct offices—Secretary, Comptroller, Auditor, Treasurer and Register—and their duties, so arranged as to provide internal safeguards for the integrity of the fiscal transactions of the government, and to bring direct reports from the Secretary to Congress.[6] This produced no difficulties between Washington and Hamilton, but it set a precedent for what presently became the prevailing practice, in the 19th Century and after, of statutory powers and instructions running to specified officials of or below Cabinet rank, rather than to the President.[7] Not quite half a century later, Andrew Jackson in 1833 asserted a constitutional prerogative as direct representative of the people to order his Secretary of the Treasury to remove the government's deposits from the Bank of the United States. But he found it necessary to that end first to remove the Secretary, in favor of another more amenable to instruction. And when in the aftermath of that episode the same claim was again made in defense of an action on the part of Jackson's Postmaster General, the Supreme Court rejected this "alarming doctrine."[8] Congress could confer such powers as it saw fit directly on such administrative offices as it chose to create—powers to be exercised on the responsibility of each incumbent, with whatever degree of independence he found it

---

[4] Myers v. United States, 272 U.S. 52 (1926); Humphrey's Executor (Rathbun) v. United States, 295 U.S. 602 (1935); *see* E. CORWIN, THE PRESIDENT: OFFICE AND POWERS ch. 3 (1940).

[5] L. WHITE, THE FEDERALISTS: A STUDY IN ADMINISTRATIVE HISTORY, 1789-1801, chs. 2-4 (1948).

[6] Act of Sept. 2, 1789, 1 Stat. 65. White surmises that Hamilton drafted the statute. WHITE, *supra* note 5, at 118n.

[7] Congressional preference for this arrangement is reinforced today by a consideration not yet apparent in 1789: lesser officials can be summoned before congressional committees and made to testify about their statutory responsibilities, as the President cannot. This was the point that Congressman Chet Holifield (D., Calif.) made in opposing (unsuccessfully) Reorganization Plan 2 of 1970 which created a cabinet-level Domestic Council to be presided over by a confidential assistant to the President. 126 CONG. REC. H43118 (daily ed. May 13, 1970), H.R. REP. No. 91-1066, 91st Cong., 2d Sess. (1970); *Hearings on Reorganization Plan No. 2 Before the Subcom. on Executive Reorganization of the Senate Comm. on Government Operations*, 91st Cong., 2d Sess. (1970); *Hearings on Reorganization Plan No. 2 Before the Subcomm. of the House Comm. on Government Operations*, 91st Cong., 2d Sess. (1970).

[8] Kendall v. U.S. ex rel. Stokes, 12 Pet. 524 (1838); *see* E. CORWIN, THE CONSTITUTION OF THE UNITED STATES: ANALYSIS AND INTERPRETATION 478-80 (1953); L. WHITE, THE JACKSONIANS (1954).

possible to maintain. Unity and hierarchy in the executive branch have seldom ranked high in the congressional scheme of order.

Down at least through the 19th Century it would have been generally agreed in principle that an office, or unit of government—apart from such a harmless hybrid anomaly as the Smithsonian Institution—which did not belong to the legislative or judicial branch must of necessity be a part of the executive; these three exhausted the logical possibilities. On that premise inferences of constitutional powers were often drawn from the attachment of one or another of these labels, as utility lawyers did in arguing against the finality of administrative decisions, by calling them "judicial," and as Chief Justice Taft did on behalf of the President's removal power in the *Myers* case, by calling it inherently "executive." But the establishment of the regulatory commissions, constituting a "headless 'fourth branch,'" as the Brownlow Committee characterized them,[9] was not to be undone by name-calling. And when the Reorganization Act of 1949 called the General Accounting Office and the Comptroller General—the lineal descendant of the Comptroller of the Treasury and inheritor of his statutory powers—"a part of the legislative branch of the Government,"[10] the change was purely semantic. The Budget and Accounting Act of 1921 had described the GAO only as "independent of the executive *departments*"[11]—a description equally applicable to, for example, the Securities and Exchange Commission or the Veterans Administration—and the substantive change took place at that time, not by altering the statutory powers of the Office but by the reorganization that gave the Comptroller General a 15-year term and made him virtually irremovable. Today, we may conclude, the labels have symbolic and propaganda uses, and little more. They do not make a "branch" of government cohesive. They are compatibles with hunting licenses for Presidents and congresses, each as they can, to augment their control over the organization of the executive branch.

The constitutionality of the Reorganization Plan method—of a presidential action that acquires the force of law after a stipulated lapse of time unless sooner vetoed in Congress—is another issue as to which a pound of practice weighs more than an ounce of doctrine. When the Congress in the Economy Act of 1932 included an authorization to President Hoover to promulgate reorganization by executive orders subject to veto in either legislative chamber, his Attorney General expressed the opinion that the proviso was unconstitutional.[12] But he also recognized that it was inseparable, that without it there would have been no delegation. There the question has rested, "no tickee, no washee." Presidents have taken the power on the terms they could get.

---

[9] PRESIDENT'S COMMITTEE ON ADMINISTRATIVE MANAGEMENT, REPORT WITH SPECIAL STUDIES 32 (1937).

[10] Reorganization Act of 1949, § 7, 63 Stat. 203. Comptrollers General had repeatedly been calling themselves "agents of Congress" and the draftsman here went them one better.

[11] 31 U.S.C. § 41 (1964) (italics supplied).

[12] 37 OP. ATT'Y GEN. 56, 63 (1933). The subject is reviewed in E. NOBLEMAN, STAFF MEMORANDUM 89-1-6 (Feb. 9, 1965), prepared for the Senate Committee on Government Operations on the Constitutional and legal aspects of the Reorganization Act procedures.

A collateral attack on a 1933 reorganization order, by shipping concerns challenging the validity of regulations issued by the Department of Commerce, to which the old Shipping Board and its powers had been transferred, was lost in the courts.[13] So far as I am aware no reorganization plan under the 1939 or later statutes has been challenged in litigation. And issues that might arise if the veto power were claimed for a congressional committee or its chairman, instead of the full chamber (as has happened in connection with military construction authorizations and other subjects),[14] have so far remained moot.

II

INITIATIVES AND OBJECTIVES

The source of a reorganization initiative is closely related to the motives that inspire it and to the objectives in view, obviously. This section reviews experience with the major alternatives that have emerged. Its general argument is that while piecemeal reorganization proposals directly connected with material policy shifts may arise from any quarter, the initiative for government-wide reorganization studies and programs, once thought to be the province of Congress, has passed decisively to the Executive Office of the President. At least two sorts of reasons contributed to this result, one having to do with the difficulties of sustaining the degree of cohesion of interests in Congress necessary for securing legislation, and the other with congressional incapacity to translate the objectives proclaimed into self-executing standards. As reorganization became a politically attractive course, the Congress proved unable to institutionalize the process except by a delegation of authority that transferred discretion, and with it the initiative, and that recognized new and less congenial objectives.

The dissatisfactions that set major policy changes in motion commonly, if not always, include objections to the way previous policy has been administered. Often, indeed, expedient political tactics have dictated stress on complaints about administration rather than on the underlying grievances against policy. It is natural, therefore, that a reform package should contain some reorganization proposals. The initiative for these is then to be found somewhere in the coalition that proves successful in pushing the policy change through. In the case of the consolidation of agencies that became the Veterans Administration in 1930, for example, the impetus came largely from outside, from the clientele veterans' organizations. The overhaul of the Office of Education, on the other hand, in connection with the breakthrough in federal policy in that field in the mid-1960's, was largely an inside job spurred by the top command in HEW. Jurisdictional rivalry furnishes another motivating impetus.

---

[13] Isbrandtsen-Moller Co. v. United States, 300 U.S. 139 (1937); Swayne & Hoyt, Ltd. v. United States, 300 U.S. 297 (1937); 37 Op. Att'y. Gen. 238 (1933). The Economy Act of 1933 provided for a waiting period but no legislative veto. The lower court found the argument of implied congressional ratification conclusive. Isbrandtsen-Moller Co. v. United States, 14 F. Supp. 407 (1936).

[14] *See* J. Harris, Congressional Control of Administration (1964).

Innovations in water resource policy authorized through the Interior or Public Works committees for the Reclamation Service or the Corps of Engineers, for example, will spark legislation from the Agriculture committees to give counterpart authority and programs to the Soil Conservation Service. The source of the initiative is more problematical when reorganization is approached in a government-wide context. Historically it was first asserted in Congress.

A. Congressional Initiatives

Instances of congressional investigations and committee reports on particular features of organization and especially on the financial operations of the executive branch can be found at least as early as 1795[15] when Albert Gallatin took up the cudgels against the Secretary of the Treasury, Oliver Wolcott, over the issue of observing the limits of specific appropriations. House select committees and the House Committee on Public Expenditures from time to time, for example, in 1822, 1828, and 1842, responded helplessly to resolutions seeking "reorganization" and "retrenchment in public expenditure." In an era when amateur members met for short sessions and worked without professional staff assistance, and when financial records were dispersed and uninformative, the committees were unable to cope with the mass of detail that a sustained study of the departments would have involved. After 1842 the committees on expenditures (by then, one for each department) virtually ceased to function.

A generation later the problem revived on a larger scale. The federal establishment expanded rapidly in the post-Civil War decades. Federal civilian employment more than tripled, from 51,000 to 157,000 between 1871 and 1891, although Treasury receipts rose only from $383 million to $393 million while expenditures went from $292 million to $366 million in the same period.[16] Massive arrearages nevertheless accumulated in the major government offices: the Land Office and the Pension Bureau in the Interior Department, the claims and auditors' offices of the War and Treasury Departments. Hundreds of thousands of letters were unanswered, claims and applications remained undisposed, vouchers went unexamined, and so on. Apparently, complaints and frustrations arising from these delays and their attendant abuses, rather than the financial condition of the Treasury (which was in surplus for every year from 1866 to 1894), supplied the impetus for the first comprehensive congressional investigation of organization and procedures in the executive branch. It was set in motion by Senator Marion Cockrell (Dem., Mo.) who in 1887 secured

---

[15] A list of these is included in PRESIDENT'S COMMISSION ON ECONOMY AND EFFICIENCY, THE NEED FOR A NATIONAL BUDGET, H.R. DOC. 851, 62d Cong., 2d Sess. (1912); the list was reprinted in G. WEBER, ORGANIZED EFFORTS FOR THE IMPROVEMENT OF METHODS OF ADMINISTRATION IN THE UNITED STATES (1919), a publication of the Institute for Government Research. For an entertaining as well as instructive historical account of the futility of congressional efforts to control executive application of appropriations see L. WILMERDING, JR., THE SPENDING POWER (1943).

[16] BUREAU OF THE CENSUS, HISTORICAL STATISTICS OF THE UNITED STATES, COLONIAL TIMES TO 1957, at 710-11 (1960).

the appointment of a select committee of three Democrats and two Republicans, at a time when Republicans controlled the Senate, midway in Cleveland's first administration.

1. *The Cockrell Committee and the Dockery-Cockrell Commission*

With the aid of a clerk, subpoena power, and questionnaires to department heads, followed up by time-and-motion studies of its own, the Cockrell Committee in two years compiled enough detailed descriptive material on bureaucratic procedures to fill a report and appendices that ran to over 2,000 printed pages. It found plenty of grist for its mill, in a pre-typewriter era when clerks at $1,000 or $1,200 a year copied letters and accounts longhand into registers and journals, and when it was neither unlawful nor uncommon for appointed clerks to hire proxies, by private arrangement at lower rates, to come in and perform their daily stints.[17]

The results of the committee's labors were soon lost to sight. It did not touch any large organizational questions but confined itself to office methods in Washington. Field offices, where then as now nine-tenths of federal employees were located, were beyond its purview. Its principal statutory relic was the establishment of a Joint Committee on the Disposition of Useless Papers in the Executive Departments (itself later the butt of ridicule) and a law authorizing department heads, after submitting lists and getting the joint committee's approval, to dispose of old records as waste paper.[18] Its main substantive accomplishment was to prod the Secretary of the Treasury, and less effectively the Secretary of War, to set up departmental committees to review and simplify procedures and record-keeping in their bureaus. In consequence, its chronicler concludes,

> Workloads were increased, the workday was lengthened, proxy employment was prohibited, employees were shifted and many incompetents were dismissed. . . . Removal of the Chief of the Record and Pension Division of the Surgeon General's Office was forced by the Committee, because he had reported that no improvements were possible in his bureau.[19]

Six years later, at the opening of the second Cleveland Administration in 1893, a more ambitious effort of the same general character was mounted, this time by a joint committee of six members, the so-called Dockery-Cockrell Commission. For the first time it employed outside experts as staff—three accountants, two of them, Charles W. Haskins and Elijah W. Sells, later the founders of a famous firm. Over the next two years the Commission filed some 29 reports, dealing mostly, as might be expected, with financial procedures and office methods, in the Land Office, the Treasury, and the Post Office. The Pension Bureau, the Office of Indian Affairs, and field offices generally—notorious patronage preserves—were excluded from its jurisdiction. It held no public hearings but accepted statements and made its own

[17] For an account of the Committee's work, and of the later Dockery-Cockrell Commission, see O. KRAINES, CONGRESS AND THE CHALLENGE OF BIG GOVERNMENT (1958).

[18] Act of Feb. 16, 1889, ch. 171, 25 Stat. 672 (1889).

[19] KRAINES, *supra* note 17, at 45.

surveys. It compiled the first exhaustive list of laws relating to the organization of all departments and agencies. It offered numerous legislative and administrative recommendations, with varying degrees of success, and succeeded only later in introducing the typewriter. It got nowhere with a proposal to abolish the office of Solicitor of the Treasury as obsolete after the establishment of the Department of Justice in 1870.[20]

The Commission's major accomplishment by far was the passage of the Dockery Act,[21] which effected a general overhauling of procedures and consolidation of offices in the accounting operations of the Treasury and the Post Office. A half dozen lesser legislative changes were adopted, while others fell by the wayside. In the end the Commission put a price tag on the reforms it secured: a continuing annual saving in expenditures of $607,591, and another, of $449,928 annually, on the recommendations that failed of adoption, in addition to its claims of intangible benefits. In the fiscal year 1895, federal expenditures amounted to $356 million.

Several incidental features of these episodes deserve notice. First, those who seek change run up against the jurisdictional sensitivities of those who are content with the *status quo*. The Commission, being authorized by its enabling resolution to report bills, encountered the jealousy of a standing committee as soon as it tried to do so. Its very first bill, altering the routing of postal certificates of deposit, though endorsed by the Postmaster General and the Secretary of the Treasury, was denounced in the Senate by members from both parties on the Committee on Post Offices, who argued that the Commission itself was unconstitutional and, besides, that its bill should be referred to their committee. To keep the peace, it entailed a month's delay in passage. Similarly, executive officials whose jurisdictions were endangered—the Postmaster General, the Commissioner of the General Land Office, the First Comptroller and the Sixth Auditor—came out in opposition; and a union of clerical employees was formed to lobby against the Commission's work.

Second, the reform of one generation, embodied in a statute, may become the reorganizer's target in the next. The Committee on the Disposition of Useless Papers, which mainly functioned to provide its chairman with a little patronage, was abolished by the Legislative Reorganization Act of 1946.[22] The Dockery Act's consolidation of postal accounting in the Sixth Auditor's office, though the Postmaster General objected, did little harm in 1894, considering conditions in the Post Office then and the nominal nature of the Sixth Auditor's connection with the Treasury. In operation his office was a part of the postal establishment, as it had been for sixty years. But when the Budget and Accounting Act of 1921 lumped together the offices of the Comptroller of the Treasury and the six Auditors to form the new and aggressively independent General Accounting Office, the effect, barely noticed at the last minute, was to deprive the Post Office, alone among all the depart-

---

[20] *Cf.* H. CUMMINGS & C. McFARLAND, FEDERAL JUSTICE, chs. 8, 11 (1937).

[21] Act of July 31, 1894, ch. 174, 28 Stat. 162.

[22] Act of Aug. 2, 1946, ch. 753, 60 Stat. 812.

ments, not only of the fundamental elements of an administrative accounting system of its own but also of legal authority to remedy its internal needs. When Postmaster General Farley in 1933 imported an energetic and capable business executive to be Comptroller of the Post Office and to modernize postal accounting, he found most of his tools in the possession of an uncooperative Comptroller General who was as little disposed to yield them as the Postmaster General had been forty years earlier.[23]

Third, reorganization studies helped launch a profession. When the Second Hoover Commission in 1953 farmed out its study topics to task forces, one of its contractors was Haskins and Sells, by then a management consultant as well as an accounting firm.

Finally, a more general lesson was learned regarding the underlying rationale of these two congressional initiatives. Functionally, they were an exercise in shifting the monkey of political responsibility from congressional to bureaucratic backs. The unforgivable official was the one who said no improvements were possible. The federal departments were indeed performing unsatisfactorily. Frustrated constituents, it is fair to suppose, took their complaints to their congressmen. When these complaints in turn were referred to the department heads and bureau chiefs the nearly uniform reply was a form of confession and avoidance. Yes, they said, there are delays because we are understaffed, for want of adequate appropriations to cope with the growing volume of business; the fault lies with the Congress; give us more money and we will improve the service. Senator Cockrell and his colleagues struck a popular note in rejecting this line. Let the departments, he said in effect, stop doing the time-honored but useless things they are now engaged in, and let them also install modern methods in place of their antiquated ways of doing what still needs doing; then they will find they can make out very well with their present allowances; the fault lies with them, and if they will not mend their ways we will show them how to.

Thus were the twin, interlocked goals of economy and efficiency invoked. They have ever since remained potent symbols. But they rest on the assumption that all right-minded observers can see, and agree upon, what are the useless and dispensable activities—in this case, almost exclusively, routine clerical functions in headquarters offices. The ratio of $600,000 in savings to $356 million in expenditures might have served as a caution against great expectations from reorganizations undertaken for these goals.

2. Joint Committee on Reorganization, 1921-23

Only once has the congressional leadership been sufficiently moved to launch a broad congressional initiative toward reorganization. The occasion was the aftermath of World War I and Republican recapture of the government. The business

---

[23] H. MANSFIELD, THE COMPTROLLER GENERAL 171-75 (1939).

community, and conservatives generally, were appalled at the size of the national debt
and the scale of federal activities; the 1920 platform promised improved organization
and methods. The agenda consisted mainly of the unfinished business worked up
by the Taft Commission of 1912 (of which, more presently) and its successors, public
and private. The Retirement Act of 1920, the Budget and Accounting Act of 1921,
and the Classification Act of 1923, all milestones in the renovation of the executive
branch, were carried through to the statute books. The topic with which the Taft
Commission had made least headway, however, and to which the Wilson Administration had meanwhile added complexities, was the rationalization of departmental
jurisdictions. To this the congressional reorganizers addressed themselves.

In the lame-duck session after the 1920 elections a joint resolution on the Dockery
Commission model was adopted on December 17; President Wilson let it become
law unsigned. It created a Joint Committee on Reorganization, composed of three
senators and three representatives. Reed Smoot (R., Utah), soon to become chairman
of the Senate Finance Committee, was its chairman. It was directed

> to make a survey of the administrative services for the purpose of securing all
> pertinent facts . . . also to determine what redistribution of activities should be
> made . . . with a view to the proper correlation of the same . . . so that each
> executive department shall embrace only services having close relation with each
> other and ministering directly to the primary purpose for which the same are
> maintained.[24]

The committee was authorized to report bills to this end. Shortly after his inauguration in March 1921, Harding suggested that he be authorized to name a personal
representative to cooperate with the joint committee and to be paid from its funds.
This was agreed to. Harding named Walter F. Brown, a Toledo lawyer later to be
Hoover's Postmaster General, who now became chairman of the reconstituted body.
The President, after a cabinet session on the subject, blessed the undertaking in a
letter to the committee:

> The executive and cabinet are of one mind that a bill reallocating the government
> services upon the principle above outlined [related services grouped according to
> major purpose] should be prepared and strongly recommended to Congress for as
> speedy passage as possible. . . . To this end we pledge your committee our hearty
> consideration.[25]

Chairman Brown replied that the "members of the committee are entirely in
accord with your suggestion." If Congress were capable of such a thing, it seemed
no enterprise was launched under fairer skies. W. F. Willoughby's Institute for
Government Research was ready to help with a detailed blueprint based upon "the
principles that should be followed by the National Government, or, for that matter,

---

[24] Act of Dec. 17, 1920, ch. 7, 41 Stat. 1083.
[25] Quoted in L. SHORT, DEVELOPMENT OF NATIONAL ADMINISTRATIVE ORGANIZATION IN THE UNITED
STATES 461-62 (1923).

by any government, in providing for the organization of the administrative branch . . . ."[26] The National Budget Committee, a civic group based in New York City, offered a less drastic proposal along similar lines. The Budget Bureau, though empowered by its recent statute to cover the same ground, prudently kept out of the way. The Joint Committee shrewdly avoided one major source of potential controversy: it was not authorized to propose either the contraction or the enlargement of any existing government service, but only its organizational location. It also escaped partisan controversy.

The whole effort nevertheless came to naught. In January, 1922, the committee presented a plan informally to the President; it was discussed with his cabinet members collectively and individually. A year later the President returned a modified and less ambitious plan to the committee, whose life was extended in March, 1923, to July 1, 1924. Before that date arrived the President was dead, and his administration clouded in scandal. The plan was moribund and President Coolidge did nothing sufficient to revive it. The committee, though it held hearings in January, 1924, expired with its report, which Coolidge transmitted to Congress.[27] It recommended an elaborate plan, at once comprehensive and specific. Bills were introduced and debated the next year but nothing was enacted.

This experience has been taken, probably correctly, to show that Congress is incapable of effecting, primarily on its own initiative, a comprehensive reorganization of the executive branch by direct statutory reassignment of jurisdictions across the board. If so, it would follow that if such a thing is to be done by Congress it must be done piecemeal; and conversely, that if it is to be done comprehensively it must be by way of a delegation that puts on the President a large measure of responsibility for initiating action, for its timing, and for its particular form.

It may be questioned whether one episode warrants so broad a conclusion. Some factors in the Joint Committee's failure—notably the collapse of public confidence in the integrity of several cabinet officers and the death of President Harding—were certainly specific to the time and circumstances. It is also pertinent that several main features of the Harding cabinet's proposal—consolidation of the army and navy in a department of defense, the transfer of non-fiscal agencies out of the Treasury, and the creation of a department of education and welfare—have subsequently been adopted by piecemeal action. The fact remains that only once since 1923 has a congressional committee mounted a comparably comprehensive study of executive branch organization, and this exception—the Byrd Committee in 1937—tends to prove the rule. Moreover, the Joint Committee encountered some generic difficulties that go far to explain the outcome.

---

[26] INSTITUTE FOR GOVERNMENT RESEARCH, REORGANIZATION OF THE ADMINISTRATIVE BRANCH OF THE NATIONAL GOVERNMENT at vii (1923); SHORT, *supra* note 25, at 462-70. Note the confident generalization of applicable principles.

[27] Message of June 3, 1924, S. Doc. No. 128, 68th Cong., 1st Sess. (1924). The recommendations included the transfer of the General Accounting Office bodily to the Treasury.

First, though Harding's cabinet could agree in principle at the outset on the generalities he stated, these yielded no single and unambiguous result in application; choices remained open to argument. Second, most department heads, if not all, were, in matters of jurisdiction, servants of the bureaucracies they headed—readier to take than to give up. The difficulty of reconciling views within the executive branch entailed a delay and loss of momentum over two years. The Joint Committee was in no position to knock heads together. Other factors influenced the Congress more directly. Clearing unrelated bureaus out of Treasury and Interior, unless it left them orphans, meant setting up a new department or departments for education, welfare, and health. The organized professions in these fields, then and for the next quarter century, opposed the elevation of these functions to cabinet status as a threat of increased federal control. Consolidating public works in one agency meant dislodging the Army Engineers from their historic connection with rivers and harbors. Finally, a sort of negative log-rolling—I will oppose what you don't want if you will oppose what I don't want—set in. It seems fair to conclude that the first lesson of the Joint Committee's experience was the abandonment of the Dockery Commission's first premise.

Nothing in this episode, however, disturbed the long-standing tradition that the Congress, when sufficiently moved, could and would reorganize a particular function. The transformation of a segment of the Corps of Engineers into the Inland Waterways Corporation, and the major changes in the handling of prohibition enforcement during the same period were proof enough of this.

3. *The Byrd Committee, 1936-1938 and Later*

What the congressional leadership never tried again was attempted in a very different context by a dissident Democrat in the Senate, Harry F. Byrd of Virginia. In February, 1936, he secured the adoption of a resolution setting up a select committee, of which he became chairman, "to investigate the executive agencies of the Government."[28] This move probably influenced the manner and timing of President Roosevelt's announcement, if not his actual decision (which had been under discussion for some months), to proceed with the appointment of his own Committee on Administrative Management.

Byrd had earlier made something of a reputation as Governor for reorganizing Virginia's state government and had employed the services of Luther Gulick and the Institute of Public Administration in New York City in doing so. By 1936 he was in right-wing opposition to the President and to the New Deal in virtually all its aspects—a true believer in retrenchment. With staff help from the Brookings Institution his committee conducted a series of voluminous and detailed studies of federal agencies. Despite advance efforts on both sides to prevent conflict by an agreed division of labor, the Byrd Committee reports stood in sharp contrast, in method,

---

[28] S. RES. No. 217, 74th Cong., 2d Sess. (1936).

plan, and conclusions, to the work of the President's Committee on Administrative Management proceeding simultaneously; the reports furnished ammunition that Byrd used in helping to defeat Roosevelt's reorganization bill in 1938.[29]

Whatever his capacity as a spoiler, however, Byrd's committee proved quite unable—and this is the important point here—to make headway with its own proposals. Four bills that the Senator introduced in 1937 failed to reach the floor after hearings by his committee. Fundamentally, this outcome may be thought to illustrate the inherent handicap of an anti-administration member of the dominant party, although the Republican-Southern Democratic coalition, formed the next year, was successful on some other issues. Byrd's difficulties here were compounded by the fact that another of his targets was Jesse Jones' Reconstruction Finance Corporation, with its immense resources and broad authority to lend and spend. Later on, after World War II and after Jones' political demise, Byrd was in on the killing of the RFC. But at this juncture the solid congressional support that Jones enjoyed embraced many of the conservative senators who were otherwise Byrd's natural allies. They would not follow him down that path to "economy." A reorganization initiative in Congress that aims at effects across the board needs more than a factional base.

One later congressional initiative needs notice, the work of the Jackson Subcommittee on National Security Policy during the latter part of the Eisenhower Administration, when the Democrats were in control on the Hill and Lyndon Johnson was the Senate Majority Leader. Using the broad charter of the parent Committee on Government Operations, and so bypassing the jurisdictions of the Armed Services and Foreign Relations committees, Senator Henry M. Jackson (Dem., Wash.) secured staff studies and expert testimony that challenged a good deal of contemporary doctrine on cold war topics, and therewith the fairly elaborate organizational machinery and procedures the Administration had built up to develop policy and supervise its carrying out. The Subcommittee succeeded in pointing up issues that became prominent in the 1960 presidential campaign. But when the election restored the executive branch to Democratic control, and President Kennedy installed an energetic reorganizer, Robert McNamara, as Secretary of Defense, the Jackson Subcommittee became a fifth wheel.

Two generalizations emerge here. First, there is more room for congressional initiatives in reorganization when the White House is in the hands of the other party. And second, the broader the scope of the executive jurisdictions encompassed in a reorganization survey, the less susceptible it becomes to specific congressional solution, since additional committee jurisdictions also become involved. Even in Congress the sentiment is widespread, if not unanimous, that a general reorganization of the executive is like a general tariff revision; for Congress it is a tempting prospect that cannot be brought off.

---

[29] S. REP. No. 1275, 75th Cong., 1st Sess. (1937). *See* R. POLENBERG, REORGANIZING ROOSEVELT'S GOVERNMENT, 1936-1939, at 31-41 (1966).

B. Outright Statutory Delegation

At the opposite end of the spectrum from congressional initiatives is a statutory delegation to an executive official to effectuate changes in organization by his own fiat. At lower levels in the executive hierarchy this is a common method, the more so because an implied delegation may be ratified by recognition in subsequent appropriations. Statutes and committee attitudes vary widely in the latitude they allow on this, from agency to agency and subject to subject. The reorganization in the executive office instituted by Plan 2 of 1970, renaming the Budget Bureau and setting up a Domestic Council, for example, could have been accomplished in substance by the President acting alone. The plan method was utilized instead for its greater psychological impact. But this opened up complicated questions of redelegation and of confidentiality and privilege, not pertinent here, that caused the House Government Operations Committee to recommend a veto of Plan 2, unsuccessfully as it turned out.[30]

An untrammeled delegation of reorganizing authority, by definition, vests the initiative, in law, entirely with the executive. But such a grant on a scale comprehending the executive branch has come to the President on only three emergency occasions, and then only for limited periods: in the Overman Act of 1918, in the Economy Acts of March 3 and March 20, 1933, and in the War Powers Act of December 1941, all of which carried expiration dates.[31] The pertinent point here about these instances is not only their temporary character, but also the fact that their rationale and objectives were altogether different from the congressional initiatives previously considered. These grants were made to enable the President to cope with needs, and in ways, not immediately foreseeable, and quickly, so as to absolve the Congress of responsibility for hindering remedial measures. These objectives were far from the goals of economy and efficiency that congressional reorganizers talked about, and the delegations tended away from the institutionalization of the process. Being addressed to temporary conditions they have left little lasting impression but the precedent[32] and the general lesson that although in a sufficient emergency more

---

[30] The Executive Office in 1970 was a large conglomerate of units formed, some by statute, some by reorganization plan, some by published executive order and some altogether informally. Congressman Holifield argued, in connection with the executive privilege point already noted above at note 7, *supra*, that if the Budget Bureau's statutory functions were all transferred to the President, for retention or redelegation at will, they could be redeployed without congressional review and placed in hands unresponsive to congressional inquiry. In the terms of this article, such a development would tend to de-institutionalize executive-congressional relationships. *See* H.R. REP. 91-1066, *supra* note 7, at 6-13.

[31] Act of May 20, 1917, ch. 77, 40 Stat. 556; Act of Mar. 3, 1933, ch. 212, § 401, 47 Stat. 1517; Act of Dec. 18, 1941, ch. 593, 55 Stat. 838. The Emergency Relief Appropriation Act of 1935 and the Defense Production Act of 1950 both authorized the President in sweeping terms to utilize existing agencies or to create new ones, and to delegate and redelegate his powers to them as he saw fit, in order to effectuate the statutory purposes. But these purposes, though broad, by no means encompassed the entire executive branch.

[32] Exec. Order No. 6166 of June 10, 1933, is an exception to this generalization: formulated by the Budget Bureau, it centralized civilian disbursing and strengthened centralized procurement in the Treasury and instituted the first Budget control over the flow of appropriated funds to departments, through quarterly apportionments.

people, even more members of Congress, look to the President for salvation than elsewhere, an emergency concentration of power in his hands will not outlast either his political downfall or the passing of the sense of urgency.

C. Public Commissions

A public commission, as a means of conducting studies and proposing a program of action, has at least two inherent attractions. It can be expected to transcend parochial interests and, by taking high ground, erect a standard that will be visible and command public support for its proposals. It confers legitimacy on the enterprise. And, with some attention to its composition, it can also hope to mediate, or at any rate to anticipate and mitigate partisan, interest group, and executive-legislative clashes in the formulation of its recommendations. So the device has come into frequent use in a variety of policy areas, both by public authorities and by private foundations.[33] For the purpose of furthering goals of general federal reorganization, as distinct from program revisions in specific policy fields, four official commissions have functioned in this century, each quite different from the others. Three are associated with the names of conservative Republican Presidents. Only two saw material changes brought about directly as a result of their labors. All but the last learned something from their predecessors. The obstacles they encountered tell something of the generic limitations of the method.

1. *The Taft Commission, 1910-1913*

President Taft created the first, the President's Commission on Economy and Efficiency, in the wake of the 1910 elections which ended a long period of Republican control of the House and, with the retirement of Nelson Aldrich, foreshadowed the break-up of the dominant Republican oligarchy he had headed in the Senate. Taft had started more informally a year earlier with a request to Congress that secured a rider on the sundry civil appropriation act for 1911:

> To enable the President, by the employment of accountants and experts from official and private life, to more effectively inquire into the methods of transacting the public business of the government in the several executive departments . . . with the view of inaugurating new or changing old methods . . . so as to attain greater efficiency and economy therein, and to ascertain and recommend to Congress what changes in law may be necessary to carry into effect such results of his inquiry as cannot be carried into effect by executive action alone . . . [there will be allocated] one hundred thousand dollars.[34]

The arrangements being thus left to him, Taft turned to his secretary, Charles D. Norton, who engaged Frederick A. Cleveland, then head of the New York Bureau of Municipal Research, to take charge of the inquiry; it got under way September, 1910.

---

[33] *See* F. POPPER, THE PRESIDENT'S COMMISSIONS (1970) for a discussion of some recent examples.

[34] Act of June 25, 1910, ch. 384, 36 Stat. 703. Successive supplements brought the total over a three-year period to $260,000.

But in the light of the election returns, as the partisan base for cooperation crumbled, the undertaking was reconstituted as a commission of six in the spring of 1911.[35] It comprised three experienced officials, including W. F. Willoughby from the Census, and three private citizens, including Cleveland, who became chairman, and Frank J. Goodnow, then professor of administrative law and municipal science at Columbia and author of well known treatises.

The Commission's contributions turned out to be almost purely educational, and promotional in a long-run sense. It addressed its studies to five major subjects: (1) a national budget system, (2) departmental and bureau organization and jurisdictions, (3) personnel practices, (4) financial procedures, and (5) business practices and methods. The last two of these were by this time familiar topics. A great deal of detailed information about them was collected and some changes were instituted as a result of administrative action, particularly through circulars from the Comptroller of the Treasury—Walter W. Warwick, a member of the Commission—looking toward standardization of departmental accounts. These accomplished the only actual changes in practice made as a result of the Commission's efforts. A published report on personnel problems—methods of appointment, efficiency ratings, mandatory retirement for age—dealt with matters that were the subject of legislation a decade later.

As to organization, the Commission compiled an exceedingly detailed inventory, running to over 1500 pages and purporting to catalog, though in a very formal and unrevealing way, the geographical and hierarchical location and duties of every extant unit of every federal department. From this overwhelming and unanalyzed factual mass, however, only a few specific recommendations emerged, mostly having to do with rationalizing and locating elsewhere some of the non-fiscal activities under Treasury jurisdiction—conclusions that scarcely needed the factual compilation. No action resulted from this first serious foray into a complex and sensitive subject, beyond grist for the mill of future talk about "overlapping and duplication."

From the beginning, however, the Commission gave its highest priority to the project for which it is chiefly remembered, the need for a national budget; and in pursuing that topic brought on a brief and symbolically characteristic showdown in presidential-congressional relations. Its report entitled *The Need for a National Budget* later furnished material for the campaign that eventuated in the passage of the Budget and Accounting Act of 1921. But the Commission, not content with a document, undertook to make a laboratory demonstration, at least, of "how to do it." In this endeavor it had Taft's earnest and active support. For its report it had worked out, using the current year's figures, a classification of expenditures, by appropriation headings, organization units, character (*i.e.*, capital, operating), function and object (*i.e.*, salaries, travel, etc.) Taft in June, 1912, directed his department heads to get

---

[35] For the facts in this section I have relied largely on WEBER, *supra* note 15. Weber had access to W. F. Willoughby's records and worked under his direction in the Institute for Government Research (later merged into the Brookings Institution), but his account eschews interpretations.

up their forthcoming estimates for fiscal 1914 both in the usual line-item form for the Secretary of the Treasury's annual *Book of Estimates,* and also in accord with the Commission's classifications.

This directive aroused the ire of the House Appropriations Committee chairman, now a Democrat, who told the House that "Congress knew best the character and extent of the information it desired . . . [and] that it would not be wise for Congress to abdicate, even by implication, its prerogative in this matter." He thereupon added a rider to a pending appropriation bill:

> Section 9. That until otherwise provided by law, the regular annual estimates
> . . . shall be prepared and submitted . . . only in the form and at the time now
> required by law, and in no other form and at no other time.[36]

Something of substance was ultimately at stake here, of course, in the difference between line-item and lump-sum or functional budgeting, although, with the information provided in both forms, the Committee was deprived of nothing tangible at the moment. But the prospect of a change in bargaining relationships, if the new form displaced the old, was enough to trigger the alarm.

The Committee's slap provoked the President in turn, who reiterated his instructions to department heads in September, 1912, invoking his constitutional right to recommend measures to Congress, and thereby to the people:

> If the President is to assume any responsibility . . . it is evident that he cannot
> be limited by Congress to such information as that branch may think sufficient for
> his purpose. . . . It is quite within his duty and power to submit to Congress and
> the country a statement of . . . estimates in the form he deems advisable. And
> this power I propose to exercise.[37]

Accordingly, in the last week of his term, February 26, 1913, the President transmitted to the expiring lame-duck session of the Sixty-second Congress the Commission's model demonstration, together with a number of supplementary statements. The election returns of the previous November, meanwhile, made that gesture that Commission's last official act.

The Commission raised the sights in its view of what reorganization was for, and earned a respected place in the intellectual history of professional public administration. It marked the first congressional acknowledgment that the President had a legitimate concern for reorganization, however fragile that acknowledgment was. It also gave an impetus to the reform movement that survived the indifference or preoccupation of the Wilson Administration. Willoughby, leaving government service, became head of the Institute for Government Research, founded with philanthropic support in 1916, and in that capacity championed reorganization causes for the next dozen years. Herbert D. Brown, the Commission's personnel expert, found official and congressional sponsorship, first in a niche in the Civil Service Commission,

---

[36] 58 CONG. REC. 13, 142 (1912).
[37] WEBER, *supra* note 15, at 90.

and, from 1916 on, as head of an independent agency, the Bureau of Efficiency, which lasted until 1933. The Taft Commission, nevertheless, as the President's creature, proved unequal to the task of mediating with a Democratic Congress. In fairness, probably no such commission could have surmounted the political tumult that overwhelmed the Taft administration in 1912. Institutionalization requires a greater stability in expectations.

2. *The Brownlow Committee, 1936-1939*

The President's Committee on Administrative Management, set up in 1936, is included here in the category of commissions because it made a public report, to the Congress as well as to the President. In other respects it resembled the presidential task forces considered below. More than the Taft Commission, it was a presidential enterprise, created by a letter to its chairman and announced in parallel letters from the President to the Speaker and Vice President. It had only the minimum congressional sanction of a line in a deficiency appropriation act, without a congressional mandate other than submission of its report.[38] Roosevelt appointed its three members. There would have been more if ex-Governor Lowden's health had permitted him to accept an offered place; a Republican, a pioneer state government reorganizer, and a onetime presidential aspirant, he would have given the outfit an overtly bipartisan cast. When he declined, other names were canvassed but Roosevelt decided to settle for a snug group, knowledgeable and congenial, with a minimum of uncertainties. He had talked with two of them a number of times earlier, in the preliminary planning, but when the work got under way he cut off further communication with the committee until after the November elections. When he saw the draft report he found little to alter and much to his liking.

The congressional leaders, on the other hand, although cordially invited at the beginning to set up select committees to cover the same ground, got no advance inkling of the contents of the Brownlow report until the very eve of its publication and transmittal. Nor, with one or two exceptions, did anyone in the executive branch outside the White House. Neither did Senator Byrd, who found in that fact evidence of bad faith and another ground for his opposition to the recommendations after he learned what these were. In the House the leadership was friendly in the beginning, by reason of personal ties between Brownlow and the speaker, but the Appropriations Committee chairman balked. In the Senate the leadership was indifferent until the report appeared.

The substance of the Brownlow report does not need recapitulation here.[39] For

---

[38] Act of June 22, 1936, ch. 689, 49 Stat. 1600. The Committee was released from the mandate stated there, to look for duplications that could be abolished, by an understanding with Chairman James P. Buchanan (D., Texas) of the House Appropriations Committee that involved turning over $10,000 of its appropriation to Brookings in support of the latter's studies for the Byrd Committee. L. BROWNLOW, A PASSION FOR ANONYMITY 355 (1958).

[39] PRESIDENT'S COMMITTEE ON ADMINISTRATIVE MANAGEMENT, REPORT WITH SPECIAL STUDIES

the first time, in an official study of this scope, it was short; it viewed the subject from the President's perspective; and it argued a simple theme, "the President needs help." The project was favored by three circumstances: the Committee was unanimous in presenting coherent views and proposals that coincided with ardent views of the President's; the President, at the time the report was made, had just won an overwhelming electoral victory and had majorities of over two-thirds of his party in both houses of Congress; and the Committee, by taking existing levels of substantive government activities as given and avoiding talk of transfers of jurisdictions among departments, minimized opposition by bureaucratic clienteles.[40] From the President's standpoint the report was an unqualified success.

These advantages were not enough to translate it into legislation, however, and in retrospect it seems plain that nothing the Committee could have done differently would have saved it. The defeat of the President's plan is attributable, rather, in the broad sense, to the convergence on Congress, at an unpropitious time, of highly emotional sentiments aroused by an incongruous combination of influences; and more narrowly, to the loss of two critical parliamentary moves, the first in the Senate and the second in the House. The general explanation is part of the larger history of Roosevelt's setbacks in the first half of his second term. The vote on the reorganizaton bill came in the ebb of the 1938 recession, in a mood of widespread frustration when Democrats were badly divided on many issues. But this by itself explains too much, for such major New Deal measures as the Fair Labor Standards Act and the revised AAA were enacted in that same session. The processes of coalition-building that passed these two and defeated the other were distinct.

Roosevelt, fresh and confident, sent the Brownlow Committee report to Congress with his endorsement on January 12, 1937. Early in February, and again without advance congressional consultation, he sent up another message, proposing to reorganize the Supreme Court. He read his reelection as an authorization to make over the basic relationships of his office with the rest of the government. Immediate success depended on securing these two legislative measures. The Court bill preempted the political stage, and the Senate's time, until the summer, when it was defeated.

By then the Byrd Committee was holding its hearings. But the political connection between the two reorganization bills, judicial and executive, did not emerge until the Senate took up the latter in the next session, at the end of February, 1938.

(1937). *See also* Brownlow, *supra* note 38; H. Emmerich, Essays on Federal Reorganization, ch. 3 (1950); R. Polenberg, Reorganizing Roosevelt's Government (1966); B. Karl, Executive Reorganization and Reform in the New Deal (1963).

[40] These actions minimized, but did not eliminate it. Friends of the Forest Service were alarmed that the well known covetousness of Secretary of the Interior Harold Ickes might be gratified; *see* Polenberg, *supra* note 39, chs. 3, 4. The report advocated taking the independent commissions apart, transferring important GAO functions to the Treasury, and remolding the Civil Service Commission. Friends of these agencies testified against the reorganization bill, as did the American Legion, the AFL, and many other organized interests.

After six weeks of mounting pressures in opposition, an omnibus bill passed, substantially intact, by a close margin. At this juncture an unfriendly ruling by the Vice-President sent it, not to conference but to floor consideration in the House, which had passed two bills embodying parts of the program the previous August. There, after ten days of a continuing build-up of opposition—by conservatives who had helped kill the Court bill and now saw a chance for another stroke; by the economy bloc led by Senators Byrd, Bailey and Burke; by friends of the Forest Service; by civil service reformers opposed to a one-man personnel administrator; by some Catholics opposed to a Department of Welfare; by Father Coughlin and his radio listeners—a stampede to beat the "dictatorship" bill moved enough members to carry a recommittal motion, 204 to 196, with 29 not voting. It was a near miss, but a miss nonetheless.

Defeated on both bills, Roosevelt turned in the summer and fall to a third course aimed at making good his conception of the presidency. Invoking party discipline, he campaigned to purge some leading Democrats who had opposed him. This failed too. The congressional elections returned reduced Democratic majorities, but these included, with one or two exceptions, the special objects of the President's attacks.

It was in this state of executive-congressional relations that the Reorganization Act of 1939 was put together and passed without serious controversy, except for one hurdle in the Senate, the following April. This time the President consulted the legislative leaders and they decided what could be salvaged. Congressman Lindsay Warren (D., N.C.) of the House Select Committee, perhaps drawing on the office of the legislative counsel, was responsible for the bill, and assured the House that he had not consulted the Brownlow Committee.

In short, the Brownlow Committee proved to be a device superior to its predecessors in the field as a means of formulating a program for the President, and it swung the main objective of a reorganization program away from "economy and efficiency" to the capacity of the President to wield the resources of the executive branch. But it was not an institution that, by repeated use, gave promise of containing or stabilizing the mercurial relationships between the President and Congress. The legislative veto which Congressman Warren introduced into the reorganization plan procedure of the 1939 Act, did hold out the prospect of becoming such an institution.

3. The First Hoover Commission, 1947-1949

The Commission on Organization of the Executive Branch was the first, and so far the only successful, essay in overt bipartisan collaboration in the formulation of a comprehensive reorganization program. Late in 1945, with his War Powers Act authority running out, President Truman had secured the revival of a reorganization statute on the 1939 model. But the Reorganization Act of 1945, though it required a concurrent resolution for the legislative veto, proved too frail a vessel for heavy cargo in the postwar storms over domestic issues, particularly public housing and labor relations. The House voted to reject all three of the reorganization plans that Truman submitted in the spring of 1946; two were rescued by narrow margins in the Senate. After the fall elections of that year he confronted a Republican majority in the House and two of his three 1947 reorganization plans again encountered adverse votes there; the Senate saved one and doomed the other. The single plan sent up in 1948, a second try for the transfer of the employment service to the Labor Department, defeated in 1947, was defeated again. Executive-legislative conflicts and, what was not quite the same thing, partisan conflicts were running high for the duration of the 80th Congress. Truman muted them in some ways and aggravated them in others.

The abortive mission of the 1945 law was superseded, in these circumstances, while it still had nearly a year to go, by an altogether different approach that opened up more far-reaching possibilities of action. The Hoover Commission served as an intermediary third party in the field of governmental reorganization; it enjoyed a higher degree of confidence from both sides than they had in each other and could communicate freely with both when direct communications were difficult. To that end it was a mixed body, carefully balanced in several ways. Of its twelve members, six held public office, two each from the Senate, the House and the executive branch; and six came from private life although all had had extensive experience in and with government. Six were Republicans and six Democrats; and four each were appointed by the President, the President *pro tem* of the Senate and the Speaker, respectively.

As an advisory body, the Commission's influence depended on the prestige of its members, the intrinsic merit of its proposals, the public backing it could arouse, and the degree to which its work turned out to suit the purposes of the President and of dominant elements in Congress. Unlike the Brownlow Committee, which did an inside job for the President, it was an autonomous body, committed to neither branch or party. Its terms of reference were sufficiently ambiguous to admit a good deal of latitude in the choice of objectives and emphases. In that ambiguity lay its opportunities and its risks.

The establishment of the Commission was a Republican and congressional idea. As in 1919, the federal debt and the current budget were alarmingly large, and an organizational shakedown, after the tumult of depression and war, had widespread appeal, at least in principle. But the change in party control in the House, for the first time since 1930, gave the congressional sponsors of the Lodge-Brown Act[41] more definite notions of the help they could expect from the commission they created. Republicans, again as in 1919, were confident of winning the forthcoming elections. Congress had preferred tax cuts to debt retirement in a period of inflation, and wanted budget cuts in the abstract but encountered opposition when specific pro-

---

[41] Act of July 7, 1947, ch. 207, 61 Stat. 246.

grams were threatened. Members like John Taber (R., N.Y.), chairman of the House Appropriations Committtee, saw in the Commission a means of exposing waste on a large scale and getting an authoritative blueprint for "painless economy" by dismantling some of the New Deal at the same time. Taber's axe swung on many targets, but he pledged and gave the Commission all the funds it asked for—ultimately, $2 million.

President Truman, from a quite different set of calculations, welcomed the proposal and supported the enabling legislation. He too saw opportunities in it, and for him it foreclosed few options that were otherwise open. He is reputed to have had a hand in the selection of the Commission's chairman and maintained cordial relations with ex-President Hoover throughout the study. He directed the Budget Director and all departments and agencies to cooperate fully; some of these officials saw opportunities also for changes they had vainly wanted for a long time.

A collegial body of twelve, so diversely composed and viewing such an array of problems, might have turned into a hung jury, hopelessly divided; or it might have confined itself to consensus on platitudes. That the Commission did neither is largely attributable to the prestige and labors of its chairman. He acted as his own staff director, engaged the numerous task forces assigned to investigate particular topics, supervised their work closely, and put the unmistakable stamp of his terse literary style on the Commission's own reports. For the task force studies he turned instinctively to business leaders, management consultant firms, and the like, chiefly, rather than to academic resources; the outlook of business administration pervaded the enterprise. The Commission members themselves, however, with two or three exceptions, were men in public affairs, not business executives. Congenially to their views and his own, and in contrast to any previous effort in this field since the Taft Commission, the Hoover Commission "thought of its project not only as a job of mobilizing information but also as a job of mobilizing influential leaders behind the idea of reorganization. . . . The Commission viewed its task from the outset largely as one of public relations . . . a much heralded project of mass data-gathering aimed at bringing support to the recommendations. . . ."[42] The reports, nineteen in all, were issued one at a time for maximum news coverage. They were usually short, with little elaboration of reasons. They were meant, like press releases, to be read by laymen. A Citizens' Committee was formed, and private funds were raised, to publicize them and promote action on the reports. They assumed the air of conventional wisdom. By a halo effect they stimulated the formation of "little Hoover Commissions" in many states, addressed to state government reorganizations.

The specific results of this monumental endeavor were impressive if not startling. The Commission listed some 277 distinct recommendations it made. Later the Citizens' Committee was able to count over 100 of these targets, little ones and big ones together, as battle trophies. Congress enacted, with modifications, several

---

[42] Emmerich, *supra* note 39, at 98.

major items on the agenda by ordinary legislation: the Military Unification Act, the State Department Reorganization Act, the establishment of the General Services Administration, the revised Classification Act, all in 1949. In addition the Reorganization Act of 1949 was adopted, under which President Truman submitted 35 reorganization plans over the next two years; 27 of these were sustained. Further recommendations, notably the switch to a performance-type budget presentation in 1950, were carried out by administrative action.

In the larger political sense of their functional effects on the American political system, the Commission's reports, which avoided like poison any mention of the Brownlow Committee, made the doctrines of that Committeee orthodox. They tended to strengthen President Truman's hand with Congress. And they effected no measurable savings in expenditures. In the light of the Commission's origins these results are paradoxical.

The latent ambiguity in the Commission's mission has already been noted. In a way, Hoover personified it. Having once been President, he had very definite notions, undimmed by the intervening years and events, about the need to strengthen the managerial capabilities of the office. As he put it in his letter transmitting to Congress the Commission's first report, *General Management of the Executive Branch:* "we must reorganize the executive branch to give it the simplicity of structure, the unity of purpose, and the clear line of executive authority that was originally intended under the Constitution."[43] If that was the mission, then the scope and scale of federal functions were not in issue.

But Hoover was equally convinced that the government was up to its neck in many enterprises it ought to get out of, the retrenchment of which would greatly reduce Treasury outlays, and so yield "savings," in his pre-Keynesian vocabulary. If the discovery and recommendation of such "savings"—beyond changes that would reduce overhead administrative costs—were the object, then the Commission had to pass judgment on the worth of a host of federal activities. A good deal of the time the Commission simply sustained the ambiguity by carrying water on both shoulders, as its enabling act had done. For example, the first report, after talk along the lines just quoted, concluded with a passage asserting in general terms that the savings from a thoroughgoing reorganization "can amount to billions."

A showdown occurred in the summer and autumn of 1948, as the presidential campaign began to intensify. It is revealing both as an explanation of the paradoxical outcome and as demonstrating a major limit to the utility of an advisory commission of this general type in this field. It emerged partly in the form of dissenting statements from certain commissioners, appended to particular reports, but chiefly in the way the Commission ignored recommendations from some of its task forces. The task forces on the Department of Agriculture and on federal-state rela-

---

[43] Commission on Organization of the Executive Branch, General Management of the Executive Branch, at viii (1948).

tions, for instance, and the Brookings report on welfare—especially the old-age-and-survivors insurance program—and most of all the Haskins and Sells report on lending agencies and federal business enterprises, all took their mandates to include substantive appraisals of underlying policies, and urged drastic federal withdrawals. At that juncture, if the Commission had adopted any of these recommendations to anything like the extent proposed, this would have amounted to a virtual endorsement of the Republican platform and the candidacy of Thomas E. Dewey. Even trying to take positions on these matters, as the watered-down Commission report on *Federal Business Enterprises* showed, split the Commission wide open.

Truman's electoral victory and the restoration of a Democratic majority in the House reinforced the lesson. The condition of bipartisan cooperation in a broad-scale reorganization effort was to take the existing scope and scale of government programs in controversial areas as given, and confine the mission to structural rearrangements. It is ironic that this fresh example of the utility, for some purposes, of maintaining a distinction between politics and administration should have come just at a time when academic students of public administration, breaking away from the older Goodnow tradition, were insisting on the inseparability of the two.

This is not to say that the Commission's recommendations were wholly neutral in impact, but only that in a situation of political contest over policy there was room only for reorganization proposals which did not raise that issue directly. The Commission's views plainly favored the President and department heads, within the executive branch; and as between Congress and the executive they favored the executive. This suggests a second lesson on the utility of a mixed commission. The inclusion of senators and congressmen in the Commission's membership may have been a price of securing the enabling act, to provide a balance of viewpoints on executive-legislative issues. At the least it was a device to contain conflicts and, by participation and immersion, to educate and animate the congressional members to work actively on behalf of the implementing legislation afterward.

Both expectations turned out to be illusions. The congressional members occupied midway positions on the scale of frequency of individual dissents recorded in the reports, and had little discernible influence on the recommendations. The Commission did not venture beyond its assigned province, so that its measures for strengthening institutions in the executive branch were not accompanied by any countervailing proposals for strengthening congressional oversight, such as the Brownlow Committee had offered.

As for the implementing legislation, the strategy of cooptation may have helped in the House, where the Commission's draft bill sailed through without serious difficulty. Not so in the Senate.[44] In the 81st Congress, assembling in 1949, Senator Aiken (R., Vt.) graduated out of the Committee on Expenditures, which had the bill in charge, and so was in no position to give it a boost. Senator McClellan (D.,

---

[44] *See* Heady, *The Reorganization Act of 1949*, 9 Pub. Ad. Rev. 165 (1949).

Ark.), now chairman of that committee, was in such a position and used it instead, first to block floor consideration of the House bill and then to hold up a conference agreement, until he had exacted two major concessions: a time limit on the President's authority to submit reorganization plans, and a veto by either chamber. He was unmoved either as a Democrat or as committee chairman by two formal messages from President Truman urging speedy passage. In retrospect it seems likely that the single-chamber veto, applicable to all plans, cost the executive more than it gained from the "clean bill" (without a list of exempted agencies) that the Commission set such store by.

In sum, the Commission succeeded in getting things moving and finding an area of agreement where conflict had prevailed. It generated more widespread favorable interest in the idea of reorganization than had been manifest before. Its reports led to extensive realignments of jurisdictions, and to a considerable strengthening of central institutions of direction and control. It made orthodox what had been rejected a decade earlier. But it did not escape political constraints, and its function was confirming rather than innovative.

4. The Second Hoover Commission, 1953-1955

If biptartisan composition and a balanced sharing of appointments were conditions necessary to the success of the first Hoover Commission, they were not sufficient, as the second commission showed. Constituted according to the same formula and having the same chairman, it nevertheless came to a very different end.

The election of President Eisenhower and the return of Republican majorities in both houses of Congress brought both a fresh impulse for reorganization proposals and apparently more propitious conditions for their favorable reception. His administration moved along two channels to that end. For immediate purposes the 1949 Act, then due to expire on April 1, was quickly extended; and the President, by his first Executive Order, named an Advisory Committee on Government Organization (of which, more presently). For longer-range purposes two mixed commissions were created by law in July, 1953. A 25-member Commission on Intergovernmental Relations was to reconsider the distribution of functions between the national government and the states. A 12-member Commission on Organization of the Executive Branch was given the same terms of reference as the one of the same name six years earlier. These commissions symbolized the resurgence of the conservative sentiments that had partly motivated the previous endeavor. Their memberships, again carefully balanced in categories, spanned a fair spectrum of opinion, but a majority in each had chiefly ideological aims, to turn the clock back on federal activities and spending. The Eisenhower Administration appears to have turned the two commissions loose, with ample funds, to see where they could get.

Not far, in this instance. It would extend this account unduly to trace the hilarious record of the Commission on Intergovernmental Relations, which was a victim of the changing official climate as the new administration confronted and became committed on a series of concrete issues long before this Commission had its say in 1955.[45] It wound up unable to agree on any single federal function it could recommend for abolition, and instead advocated the creation of one more piece of federal machinery, a monitoring staff in the Executive Office of the President to keep better track of evolving problems in federal-state relations.

The Second Hoover Commission reported in 1955 also, and fared no better. The Administration had sent up ten reorganization plans in 1953 and two more in 1954 and had seen them all sustained. Five of these, at least, raised significant issues: elevation of HEW to departmental status and authority for the Secretary of Agriculture over the internal structure of his department—both reversing previous defeats; further strengthening of the positions of the Secretary of Defense and Chairman of the Joint Chiefs; and reorganizations of the foreign aid and information agencies. Now came the Hoover report. The moderating internal constraints that had operated before were absent or diminished. Hoover either appeard to have learned little from the last round, or he took the occasion as a final opportunity, after many frustrations, to reach for his heart's desire. His task forces, liberated to comment on policy as well as on organization, did so freely. The Commission's report, too, indulged its chairman's well known policy views. Taking positions the Administration had passed by and could not endorse, it was read, perhaps with nostalgia, and firmly ignored— relegated to discussion in professional journals.[46] The near-blank record of reorganization plans submitted between 1955 and 1960—and not for want of Commission recommendations—is in the sharpest possible contrast with the outpourings in 1950.

It would exaggerate the Commission's importance, however, and be unfair as well, to charge it with major responsibility for the paucity of reorganization plans during Eisenhower's second term. The combination of Democratic majorities in Congress again after 1954 and waning interest on the part of the Administration counted for more in the outcome. The point to be made here is not only that a public commission is no panacea, but that without a stance of neutrality toward substantive policies its labors are at the mercy of shifting political alignments on which it has little influence. By the time this one got organized and completed its work the suppositions on which it proceeded had evaporated.

D. Presidential Task Forces

A third general alternative to a congressional committee or a public commission as a means of conducting a reorganization survey and formulating specific proposals

---

[45] COMMISSION ON INTERGOVERNMENTAL RELATIONS, REPORT (1955). All members signed the middle-of-the-road report. But two footnotes, *id.* at 59-60, carrying between them the signatures of ten of the 25 members, deplored the Supreme Court's 1937 decision that sustained the constitutionality of the Social Security Act, and the liberalization of the spending power, as having "fundamentally altered the balance of power designed by the architects of the Constitution."

[46] *See* Fesler, *Administrative Literature and the Second Hoover Commission Reports,* 51 AM. POL. SCI. REV. 135 (1957) for an acute critique.

is a presidential task force.[47] This course, whatever its disadvantages, tends to keep the reorganization ball in the President's court, so to speak, during the developmental stages of the process. From his standpoint it affords relative privacy, flexibility in adapting to changed conditions and control over both the content and timing of any published reports and recommendations. The first example of this type, though it does not closely resemble more recent models, was provided, as might be expected, by an activist President at odds with Congress, Theodore Roosevelt. It was entitled the Committee on Department Methods, and commonly known by the name of its chairman, Charles H. Keep, Assistant Secretary of the Treasury.

1. *The Keep Commission, 1905-1909*

President Roosevelt responded with characteristic enthusiasm to a proposal from Gifford Pinchot and James R. Garfield, members of his "tennis cabinet," for a study of the organization and operation of federal departments and agencies in Washington, with recommendations for their improvement. His letter of appointment, of June 2, 1905, named these two and three others like-minded, all officials of subcabinet rank, and went on at some length with precepts for their guidance.[48] The following year he asked the Congress for $25,000 for the employment of experts to assist the Committee, and was grudgingly allowed $5,000; the Committee later drew also on a $10,000 confidential fund at the disposal of the Secretary of the Interior, which Garfield had meanwhile become. The Committee was one of half a dozen such that Roosevelt employed to get action by independent executive initiative in various fields. He told its members that "I shall value the reports I receive largely . . . in proportion as they do not call for legislation."[49]

The Committee formed and utilized a dozen subcommittees, coopting for that purpose some 70 other officials, to work on special topics within their ken. These ranged over a diverse array of subjects and dealt with methods, since the Committee perforce took jurisdictions as given. Only one of its reports eventuated directly, though later, in legislation: the creation of the General Supply Committee—an ancestor of the present General Services Administration—a permanent interdepartmental agency located in the Treasury, to standardize and contract for common supplies.[50]

[47] A fourth, not pertinent here to the institutionalization of the presidency, is a bureaucratic mission, such as the Bureau of Efficiency had, 1916-1933, or as was given the General Accounting Office in the Legislative Reorganization Act of 1946, § 206, 60 Stat. 837.

[48] The most detailed account of the Committee and its work is by Kraines, *The President versus Congress: The Keep Commission, 1905-1909, First Comprehensive Presidential Inquiry into Administration*, 23 WEST. POL. Q. 5 (1970). *See also* Pinkett, *The Keep Commission, 1905-1909: A Rooseveltian Effort for Administrative Reform*, 52 J. AM. HIST. 299 (1965); WEBER, *supra* note 15, at 74-83; T. ROOSEVELT, AN AUTOBIOGRAPHY 368 (1913); G. PINCHOT, BREAKING NEW GROUND 296 (1947).

[49] Kraines, *supra* note 48, at 35, quoting the New York Times of March 24, 1906. He also recommended to Congress that the President "be given power to transfer any part of the work of a department to another department." *Id.* But this would have required legislation which was not in the cards.

[50] Act of July 17, 1910, ch. 297, § 4, 36 Stat. 531.

Two other proposals, for retirement allowances and position classifications and salary grades, marked early approaches to government-wide problems that would become subjects of legislation in the next generation—approaches that showed a considerable change in thinking about the treatment of government personnel from the harsh anti-employee attitudes plainly displayed in the Dockery-Cockrell studies. The Committee's expert on this subject, Herbert D. Brown, was thereby launched on a career with the Taft Commission, the Civil Service Commission and the Bureau of Efficiency, over the next two decades, as a leading authority on the improvement of administration; in those days the office of the chief executive provided no home for such a career.

Other subjects of the Committee's attention included the coordination of statistics, records management, government publications, accounting methods, transportation of government property and employees, interdepartmental telephone service, the need for an official gazette—realized in 1934 in the *Federal Register*—and the collection and publication of historical documents.

The Committee had scarcely gotten under way when the President handed it first one, and then, because he liked the Committee's handling of it, a second spot assignment of a quite different sort—to investigate a rumored bureaucratic scandal. The first involved the Public Printer and the award of a contract for typesetting machines; the second, the leaking and manipulation of cotton crop estimates to speculators. The Committee's inquiries and reports exposed the malefactors and their wrongdoings in these cases and so served the President's needs and brought public credit for the Committee as well, for its help in the housecleaning. But it seems doubtful that it could have continued in the capacity of an internal inspectorate and simultaneously have secured the cooperation at operating levels indispensable to its main function.

For the Committee aimed to make its impact on operations rather than on Congress or on public opinion. It prepared no overall report, and although 18 of its individual reports were published in one form or another, many more were not. Its most notable accomplishment may have been the introduction of double-entry bookkeeping into the Treasury. But it is in the nature of its concern with administrative methods that the results it achieved presently became invisible.

The Keep Commission was a presidential instrument, responsive to Roosevelt's temperament and the political situation at the time. It lasted as long as he was in office and no longer; it left no institutional residue in the executive office beyond the precedent that a President found a way of asserting responsibility for improving the efficiency of operations in the executive branch. When he dealt with sub-cabinet officials directly, he risked undercutting the positions of department heads. And when he took the initiative himself he provoked congressional jealousy. On the last day of his term, Congress added a rider to an appropriation, proposed by Chairman James A. Tawney (R., Minn.) of the House Appropriations Committee, aimed at the Keep Commission and others of that ilk. It forbade any future expenditure or detail of personnel "in connection with the work . . . of any commission, council, board, or other similar body, unless the creation of the same shall be or shall have been authorized by law. . . ."[51]

2. *The President's Advisory Committee on Government Organization, 1953, and Its Successors*

The post-World War II model of a presidential task force on reorganization was devised in the Eisenhower Administration and has commended itself, with modifications, to his successors. By his first Executive Order, President Eisenhower named an Advisory Committee on Government Organization consisting of Nelson A. Rockefeller, who had been active in the 1952 campaign, Arthur S. Flemming, who had been the minority member of the Civil Service Commission, and Milton Eisenhower, the President's brother. The Committee used a report developed at Temple University[52] and based on the Hoover Commission's unfinished agenda—President Robert L. Johnson of Temple had been chairman of the Citizens' Committee for the Hoover Report—and it also was a clearing point for suggestions from cabinet members and other sources. In this fashion the machinery was set up for changes that could be accomplished by reorganization plans.[53] The Committee worked to President Eisenhower's satisfaction during his first term and ran out of steam during his second.

President Kennedy turned to informal and, with one exception, unpublicized advisers for reorganization suggestions. The exception got him into one kind of trouble, and he took himself into another. Among the program planning projects undertaken during his 1960 campaign was a report by James M. Landis, former dean of the Harvard Law School and ex-chairman of the SEC, reviewing the problems of the independent regulatory commissions and their chronic backlogs.[54] Kennedy thought so well of it that he publicly commended it to Congress before his inauguration, and it went also to the American Bar Association. It inspired seven reorganization plans that he sent up early in 1961, each dealing with one of the commissions and prescribing the same medicine, similar to the first Hoover Commission's: let the President designate the commission's chairman, to serve at his pleasure in that capacity; let the chairman's hand be strengthened within the commission; and carry further the delegation of authority to individual members, panels or staff to dispose of cases in the commission's name, subject to discretionary review by the whole commission.

The Landis report had gone further in urging that cordinating offices be established in the Executive Office of the President to develop government-wide policies

---

[51] Act of March 4, 1909, ch. 299, § 9, 35 Stat. 1027.

[52] Afterward published as THE TEMPLE UNIVERSITY SURVEY OF FEDERAL REORGANIZATION (1953).

[53] D. EISENHOWER, MANDATE FOR CHANGE 133-35 (1963).

[54] SENATE JUDICIARY SUBCOMMITTEE ON ADMINISTRATIVE PRACTICE AND PROCEDURE, REPORT ON REGULATORY AGENCIES TO THE PRESIDENT-ELECT, 86th Cong., 2d Sess. (Comm. Print 1960).

for transportation, communications and energy, including relationships between the regulatory bodies and other agencies. Of the seven plans, only four were sustained. Those affecting the SEC, FCC, and NLRB, among the most politically sensitive of the regulatory agencies, were rejected. This outcome almost exactly paralleled President Truman's experience with his reorganization plans for the regulatory commissions in 1950. The Brownlow Committee's proposal in this field had fared worse; it died aborning. But the point here is not that Kennedy's adviser did not save him from coming a cropper in a course where others had faltered before him. Rather it is that the publicity he had given the Landis report, so far from carrying the day, had only increased his discomfiture in the event.

Kennedy's other trouble came from submitting reorganization plans—notably Plan 1 of 1962 to reverse a legislative defeat of the previous year and create a department of urban affairs—without showing them first to the Government Operations Committees. On this issue Senator McClellan held up the renewal of the Reorganization Act, when it expired in 1963, for over a year. Even a personal communication to the senator from the new President, Lyndon Johnson, on the heels of his first annual message, followed up by a written assurance of consultation from the Budget Bureau, the bill stalled for four months.[55] Consultation in advance is a perennial issue with far-reaching implications. Institutionalization of the process in this segment of policy, in the unlikely event it proved durable, would restrict the President more than the committee, since the initiative is his.

President Johnson improved on his two predecessors' reorganization records by sending up 17 plans in five years and seeing 16 of them sustained. In making his choices and formulating his strategy here, he kept entirely to informal and internal advice and unpublicized advisers—except when considering a single policy field only, as in the case of the postal reorganization proposed by the Kappel Commission.[56] For a start on a comprehensive review he enlisted the help of a group headed by Dean Don K. Price of Harvard, along with technical staff work from the Budget Bureau, in 1964, in devising his agenda and strategy for using the 1965 renewal of the reorganization act. His most comprehensive effort was the establishment in November, 1966, of a 7-man Task Force on Government Organization, to work altogether confidentially. It was headed by a private citizen, Ben W. Heineman, president of the Northwestern Railway, and included two officials, the Budget

---

[55] Acting Budget Director Elmer B. Staats on February 7, 1964, wrote carefully: "Please be assured of our intention to work closely with you and your committee concerning reorganization proposals and to take such other steps as may be necessary to improve communications between the executive branch and the Congress concerning reorganization plans. Through such cooperative efforts I am confident that it will be possible to eliminate or minimize the difficulties which you have identified." S. REP. No. 1057, 88th Cong., 2d Sess. 3 (1964).

[56] PRESIDENT'S COMMISSION ON POSTAL ORGANIZATION, TOWARDS POSTAL EXCELLENCE (1968). The essential problem for the President here was not what to do but how to stir enough support to overcome congressional and union opposition to a similar proposal made the previous year by his own Postmaster General, Lawrence F. O'Brien. *New York Times*, April 4, 1967, at 1, col. 1.

Director and the Secretary of Defense, three ex-officials, McGeorge Bundy, Kermit Gordon, and William Capron, and one academic, Herbert Kaufman of Yale.

This aggregation of talent and experience produced private reports to the President by the latter part of the summer in 1967 on some of the more intractable organizational problems—the coordination of anti-poverty programs and of economic policy, the future of HEW, the consolidation of regional administration, and others. But its work was largely aborted when the President decided not to run for re-election in 1968. Since nothing was published, only the strategy was lost.

President Nixon, shortly after securing a two-year renewal of the Reorganization Act, took a less secretive course than Johnson's. His approach relied more on businessmen but was plainly within the confidential task force pattern. By a press release of April 5, 1969, he appointed five members to an Advisory Council on Executive Organization headed by Roy L. Ash, President of Litton Industries. The others were George Baker, soon to retire as Dean of the Graduate School of Business Administration at Harvard; ex-Governor of Texas John B. Connally; Frederick R. Kappel, head of A.T.&T.; and Richard Paget, President of a well-known New York management consultant firm. A sixth was presently added, Walter N. Thayer, an investment banker and former proprietor of the *New York Herald-Tribune*.[57] The Council was to "deal with both immediate and long-range needs for organizational changes to make the Executive Branch a more effective instrument of public policy." The announcement went on to say:

> The Council will consider: (1) The organization of the Executive Branch as a whole in light of today's changing requirements of government; (2) Solutions to organizational problems which arise from among the 150-plus departments, offices, agencies and other separate Executive organizational units; and (3) The organizational relationships of the federal government to states and cities in carrying out the many domestic programs in which the federal government is involved.
>
> Although it is planned that staff assistance will be provided by the Budget Bureau's Office of Executive Management, the Council will have direct access to the President. Contacts with the Congress, the states and localities, and other interested entities will be handled through established government channels.
>
> The Council will work closely with the Office of Intergovernmental Relations established by the President under the supervision of the Vice President to serve as the liaison between state and local governments and the President . . . .[58]

The Council was given a budget of $930,000 for fiscal 1970 and expected to complete its work by the end of that calendar year.

In less than 12 months the Council's first product was unveiled, in the form of

[57] The Executive Director, Murray Comarow, who headed a staff of a score or more of professionals, had been with Booz, Allen and Hamilton, management consultants, and with the Federal Power Commission, and more recently the Executive Director of the Commission on Postal Organization appointed by President Johnson and chaired by Frederick Kappel.

[58] Office of the White House Press Secretary, Press Release, April 5, 1969.

Reorganization Plan 2 of 1970, which the President sent to Congress on March 12 and saw sustained by a bipartisan margin, 193 to 164, in the House against an adverse committee recommendation.[59] It established formally a cabinet-level Domestic Council and gave the Budget Bureau a boost in status by changing its name, creating some high-ranking positions in it and putting fresh emphasis on its managerial concerns—a boost the President reinforced by moving the Secretary of Labor, George P. Shultz, over to another cabinet seat as head of the Office of Management and Budget. The Ash Council also allowed press leaks to hoist trial balloons of reorganization proposals in other fields, including atomic energy, bank regulation, and the handling of environmental policies. As to the last of these, two more plans went up in July 1970, to create an independent Environmental Protection Agency with enforcement powers, and a National Oceanic and Atmospheric Administration with research missions, in the Commerce Department. But the Council made no general report and it remained within the President's discretion to decide what, if anything, to do with or about any of its recommendations to him.[60] For example, in his next State of the Union message, January 22, 1971 (after anticipatory soundings in the press a fortnight earlier), he drew on unpublished Council studies in proposing a sweeping consolidation of seven cabinet departments into four: Natural Resources, Human Resources, Community Development and Economic Development. The bold language of the message passed over the inconsistency of this appeal to hierarchy as a solution to problems of interdepartmental coordination with the Domestic Council solution adopted the previous year. But only three weeks after this seemingly quixotic gesture, the President cautiously released for "vigorous public discussion," without committing himself on it, a 125-page Ash Council report advocating the substitution of three single administrators for five of the regulatory commissions, with appeals from their decisions to a new 15-member administrative court. Although neither of these proposals was likely of enactment in 1971, the contrast in the methods of launching them was a vivid illustration of the options the President retained when the Ash Council disbanded.[61]

The Council's existence and broad mandate did not preclude the appointment of other groups to consider reorganization in particular fields. Just as President Johnson had named the Kappel Commission to examine separately the touchy subject of renovating the Post Office, President Nixon set up the Fitzhugh Commission to review the organization of the Department of Defense, a perennial target. Its controversial report was made public.[62]

---

[59] *See* authorities cited in note 7, *supra*.

[60] In testimony on Plan 2, Chairman Ash explained, without specifying, that his Council started by identifying nearly "100 organizational issues in the executive branch" and then gave priority to ten of these for detailed study. *Hearings on Reorganization Plan No. 2 of 1970 Before the House Subcomm. on Government Operations*, 91st Cong., 2d Sess. 15 (1970).

[61] N.Y. Times, Jan. 11, 1971, at 1, col. 5; Jan. 22, 1971, at 1, col. 7; and Feb. 12, 1971, at 1, col. 5.

[62] N.Y. Times, July 29, 1970, at 1, col. 8.

CONCLUSION

The foregoing review has distinguished three broad types of institutional approaches to comprehensive and official studies of executive branch reorganization, roughly associated with three overlapping time periods, and with basic shifts in the purpose and nature of the enterprise. Corresponding distinctions in institutionalization of the processes can be marked out.

In the first phase, lasting a half a century, the main purported object of the endeavor was "economy," to be realized chiefly by modernization of office methods; and the principal stakes were patronage. A further means of advancing the same general object was thought to be the elimination of "overlapping and duplication," by bringing together similar activities previously dispersed. The issue in this phase turned on the congressional claim—grounded in the second doctrine of 1789—of a monopoly prerogative over any decision, not only to change the organization of the executive branch, but even to undertake to study what changes might be desirable. This was the claim asserted in the Tawney Amendment, and rejected both by Theodore Roosevelt when he set up the Keep Commission and by Taft when he sought authorization for the Commission on Economy and Efficiency. The paradoxical observation that the President was more interested in legislation, while the Congress was more interested in administration, was made by Senator Jonathan P. Dolliver (R., Iowa) in opposing the creation of the Taft Commission:

> We have fallen upon times new and strange, when the frame, as well as the details, of legislation is perfected in the executive departments, and it looks as though this proposal for a commission were either an act of reciprocity or retaliation . . . by which Congress is about to say to the executive departments: "You attend to the preparation of bills for the Congress of the United States, and we will, as soon as possible, try to institute a modern system of bookkeeping for you."[63]

The congressional claim of monopoly rights in the search for economy was finally and formally abandoned in Section 1 of the Reorganization Act of 1939, which conferred on the President a permanent license to study the subject, with the help of the Budget Bureau. Partly, this may be attributed to the relative secular decline in the stakes of patronage. More directly, it was probably a result of the emergence of central managerial instruments—in the departments, and government-wide— better adapted to the purpose of effectuating detailed economies. The task had far outrun the capacities of either the President or Congress; it was delegated to administrative hands and the processes were pretty fully institutionalized there—saving a congressional prerogative for selective intervention.

The second approach, the resort to public commissions on reorganization be-

---

[63] 45 CONG. REC. 2159-60 (1910). *Cf.* Huntington, *Congressional Responses to the Twentieth Century,* in CONGRESS AND AMERICA'S FUTURE 22-25 (D. Truman ed. 1965); G. GALLOWAY, THE LEGISLATIVE PROCESS IN CONGRESS 166 (1955).

tween 1910 and 1955, failed to become institutionalized as a method of proceeding except when limited to specific policy fields. The circumstances of their creation differed markedly in each of the four instances reviewed here: they were *ad hoc* phenomena that set no pattern. Three of the four were done in by changed political alignments before their work was done. Except for the Brownlow Committee, it took them a couple of years to produce. The establishment of such a commission commits the Administration to try to take its work seriously; some prestige is lost if the effort comes to nothing. The relative detachment of a commission should enable it to speak bluntly and critically about offices and incumbents too close to the President for him to deal with candidly. The Taft and Brownlow commissions were redeemed by the educational value of the innovations they proposed, the fresh perspectives they introduced, which ultimately brought practical results. But these merits have not outweighed their risks in the eyes of presidents since the 1950's. Senator Abraham Ribicoff (D., Conn.), chairman of a Government Operations subcommittee, secured Senate passage in 1968, a campaign year, of a bill to establish a commission on the Hoover model. But the Budget Bureau opposed it and the House buried it.[64] It seems unlikely that a President will sponsor such a measure in the foreseeable future unless he is in deep trouble on other scores.

The relatively unpublicized task force method adopted by four successive Presidents since Truman is a logical outgrowth of the transformation in reorganization objectives that had already taken place. The Brownlow report in 1937 proclaimed that change in doctrine, from economy in operations to the need for strengthening the President's capacity to marshall and wield the far-flung resources of the executive branch. The first Hoover Commission gave this doctrine wider currency and greater legitimacy. It is a corollary, consonant with the first doctrine of 1789, that the President is entitled to avail himself of that method of formulating reorganization proposals which promises him the greatest degree of control over their form, content, and timing, since he has the most at stake.

It might be supposed that the principal beneficiary of a doctrine of presidential primacy would be the Budget Bureau and, accordingly, that the reorganization process would become as institutionalized as the formulation of the budget. The Bureau has had the legal authority for many years; it has had able people and has accumulated expertise. The technical intricacies of reorganizations—the legal niceties, the procedural precedents and case-law, the substantive disposition of funds, obligations, personnel, and so on—now comprise a formidable body of specialized knowledge, indispensable in making plans operational. The Bureau commands that knowledge. It also serves what it understands to be the interests of the presidency, and serves the incumbent President too, if it gets timely clues to his wishes. The Nixon Administration, in reconstituting the Office of Management and Budget, has

---

[64] *See Hearings on a Bill to Establish a Commission on the Organization and Management of the Executive Branch Before the Subcomm. on Executive Reorganization of the Senate Comm. on Government Operations*, 90th Cong., 2d Sess. (1968).

apparently tried to build a bureaucratic capability there that might make the task force device unnecessary in the future.

On the record since 1921, however, there are serious obstacles in the way of full reliance on that resource: the Bureau has been starved for appropriations itself; the interest of Presidents has been fluctuating and spasmodic; the Bureau's staff cannot very well reach up unless the President reaches down.[65] The virtue of the task force method is its flexibility in compensating for these handicaps and responding to the President's political assessments. The extent of the President's resort to that method is a measure of the limits he feels, or imposes, on the institutionalization of the process.

---

[65] Already in 1971, when the ink on Plan 2 of 1970 was hardly dry, the Domestic Council staff, reporting to its chairman, presidential assistant John Ehrlichman, had formed a subcommittee on organizational problems. It worked, at first unbeknownst to the Office of Management and Budget organizational staff, on, among other things, measures to give effect to the President's proposal to establish four super-departments.

SOCIAL ADVISERS, SOCIAL ACCOUNTING, AND THE PRESIDENCY

WALTER F. MONDALE*

On September 10, 1970, the United States Senate passed S. 5, the Full Opportunity and National Goals and Priorities Act. Among other things, the bill would have established a Council of Social Advisers in the Executive Office of the President.[1]

The bill was not acted on by the House. However, Senate passage represents significant progress for this measure, which did not even emerge from committee when it was first proposed in 1967 as S. 843.[2] I have re-introduced the bill in the Ninety-second Congress, again as S. 5.

I

THE EXECUTIVE OFFICE OF THE PRESIDENT

One might wonder why a United States Senator is so concerned about a structural innovation in the President's office, but I believe that a review of the case for such a Council and of the precedents regarding Executive Office structure will show that Congressional impetus for this is both well-founded and appropriate

In the twenty-five years since the end of World War II, the Executive Office of the President has undergone radical structural change. This is not readily recognized, perhaps because of the staying power of the two best-known, general-purpose staff units, namely the White House Office and the Bureau of the Budget (now the Office of Management and Budget). Yet these are the only two present units which were in the Executive Office in 1945.

It is also little realized that today's Executive Office contains sixteen separate units, in contrast with four at the end of 1945, and that eleven of the present constituent units have been established or significantly altered in the past ten years.[3] So the

---

* United States Senator from Minnesota.

[1] S. 5, 91st Cong., 2d Sess. § 103 (1970). As originally introduced, the bill would also have established a Congressional Joint Committee on the Social Report, but this provision was deleted. See 116 CONG. REC. S15,163 (daily ed. Sept. 10, 1970). Provision for a Congressional Office of Goals and Priorities Analysis was added in Committee. S. 5, § 202. These latter provisions are not discussed in this article, which is intended to focus on the more directly presidential issues.

[2] S. 843, 90th Cong., 1st Sess. (1967). The hearings on this bill were published in three parts in 1968. See Hearings on S. 843 Before the Subcomm. on Government Research of the Senate Comm. on Government Operations, 90th Cong., 1st Sess. (1968). Among those participating in these hearings were Dr. Bertram M. Gross, a Political Science Professor, and Joseph Kraft, a journalist, who were early advocates of a Council of Social Advisers.

[3] The White House Office and the Office of Management and Budget, as Executive office units, date back to 1939. Since then the following additions have been made: Council of Economic Advisers (1946); National Security Council (1949); National Aeronautics and Space Council (1961); Office of Emergency Preparedness (1961); Office of Science and Technology (1962); Office of Special Representative for Trade Negotiations (1963); Office of Consumer Affairs (1964); Office of Economic Opportunity (1964); National Council on Marine Resources and Engineering Development (1966); Office of the Vice Pres-

structure of the Office is quite fluid and, increasingly, specialized. It is against this background that the proposal to establish yet another unit—a Council of Social Advisers—must be evaluated.

II

What a Council of Social Advisers Would Do

With the steady evolution of the Executive Office's composition, it seems clear that the question is not *whether* we should consider establishing new units in the Executive Office but rather, which ones, and when. Under my proposal, the Council of Social Advisers (CSA) would be composed of three of the nation's most gifted and respected social analysts (appointed by the President and confirmed by the Senate) and staffed by a number of America's brightest young social scientists. The CSA would be responsible for monitoring, on an on-going basis, specific and actual conditions in the country which affect the "social opportunity" of our people. Developing a system of "social indicators" would be a principal task of the Council.[4]

A chief objective of such an agency would be to enlarge the chances each of our citizens has to develop his potential to the fullest. That is why I have called the proposal the "Full Opportunity Act." Indeed, the bill stipulates, really for the first time in our history, "the opportunity to live in decency and dignity"[5] as a national goal for all of our citizens.

The bill also provides for an annual report of the President on the nation's social status. Requiring the President to report annually on such areas as education, health, housing, alienation, political participation, personal security, and social mobility would do far more than assure the publication of CSA findings and recommendations: It would guarantee such societal knowledge visibility of the sort that only presidential involvement can generate.

It has been asked whether the state of the art in social accounting and the state of the art in the social sciences warrant the formalization in statute of social accounting and reporting requirements. Much of America's turmoil in the 1960's grew out of massive frustration at continuing social unfulfillment. That frustration mysteriously eluded the attention of decisionmakers, in both the public and private sectors, until the time for defusing the bomb had all but slipped away. Tragically, that should never have been the case. For in truth, the real conditions of explosive neighborhoods in Watts, Detroit, Newark, and elsewhere were known—and their implications understood—by a variety of social scientists who not only possessed such publicly-useful knowledge but published it as well.

ident (1969); Office of Intergovernmental Relations (1969); Council on Environmental Quality (1970); Office of Telecommunications Policy (1970); and Domestic Council (1970).

[4] *See especially* Social Indicators (R. Bauer ed. 1966) for a comprehensive review of the concept of social indicators and social accounting.

[5] S. 5, 91st Cong., 2d Sess. § 101 (1970).

To our collective sorrow, most of those studies remained buried in the forbidding pages of the scholarly journals of a dozen or more academic disciplines,
ranging from anthropology to political science. One can only imagine how different
the tumultuous decade just ended might have been had there existed then the sort
of mechanism for monitoring and reporting social conditions I am proposing.

Thus it becomes clear that the social sciences do have something to contribute
to the process of rationalizing public policymaking. The social sciences have
demonstrated in recent years both a rediscovered interest in social problem-solving
and a dedication to the development of research tools which serve this end.

During the three years that my proposal has been before the Congress, the
objective of social reporting has been widely accepted. Both the Johnson and Nixon
Administrations have based their opposition on the structural changes proposed
by the bill, but they have pledged themselves to further the development of social
accounting. In fact, the Department of Health, Education, and Welfare produced in January 1969 a document entitled *Toward a Social Report*.[6] As rudi-
mentary as this pilot effort was, it illustrates that we can begin whenever we are
ready.[7]

In the four years since I first introduced the "Full Opportunity Act," a number
of individuals and study groups have determined that it is time to establish a
Council of Social Advisers and to provide for an annual Social Report. For
example, in October 1969 the Behavioral and Social Sciences Survey Committee of
the National Academy of Sciences—Social Science Research Council recommended the
preparation of an annual social report, initially outside of the government but
with the aid of federal funds.[8] The Committee also recommended the subsequent
establishment of a Council of Social Advisers. In December 1969, the National
Commission on the Causes and Prevention of Violence also recommended that
consideration be given to the establishment of such a council and to the preparation
of a social report.[9]

III

NEED FOR A SOCIAL ACCOUNTING SYSTEM

A second point which must be made was strongly underscored by the hearings
held on the CSA proposal in both the Ninetieth and Ninety-first Congresses. Put
succinctly, hunch, intuition, and good intentions have been the heavy artillery of

---

[6] U.S. DEP'T OF HEALTH, EDUCATION, AND WELFARE, TOWARD A SOCIAL REPORT (1969).

[7] The hearings on S. 5 contain testimony and an extensive bibliographic section documenting more
fully the state of the art in social accounting. *See Hearings on S. 5 Before the Special Subcomm. on
Evaluation of Social Programs of the Senate Comm. on Labor and Public Welfare*, 91st Cong., 1st &
2d Sess. (1970).

[8] NATIONAL ACADEMY OF SCIENCES AND SOCIAL SCIENCE RESEARCH COUNCIL, THE BEHAVIORAL AND
SOCIAL SCIENCES: OUTLOOK AND NEEDS (1970).

[9] TO ESTABLISH JUSTICE, TO INSURE DOMESTIC TRANQUILITY, FINAL REPORT OF THE NATIONAL COM-
MISSION ON THE CAUSES AND PREVENTION OF VIOLENCE 272 (1969).

social problem-solvers, to a far greater extent than anyone has recognized. This point was made most forcefully in the testimony of Mr. Joseph A. Califano, Jr., principal domestic policy assistant in the Johnson White House (and now a supporter of S. 5) who observed, at a December 1969 hearing:

> The disturbing truth is that the basis of recommendations by an American Cabinet officer on whether to begin, eliminate or expand vast social programs more nearly resembles the intuitive judgment of a benevolent tribal chief in remote Africa than the elaborate sophisticated data with which the Secretary of Defense supports a major new weapons system.[10]

He also related the experience he had when, in 1965, the Department of Health, Education, and Welfare did not even know the composition of welfare rolls. There was—and still is—the myth that there are vast numbers of able-bodied men receiving welfare.

When the welfare data were finally obtained, almost *two years* later, we learned that of the 7.3 million then on welfare:

—3.5 million were children
—2.1 million were women over 65
—700,000 were handicapped or blind
—900,000 were mothers of the children
—100,000 were males who were incapacitated beyond any ability to work or be trained
—and 50,000, less than one-tenth of one per cent, were males who could possibly be called "able-bodied."[11]

Despite such experiences, the Johnson Administration believed that sufficient progress in social accounting could be made through the existing executive structures. It pointed particularly to the Bureau of the Budget, the Council of Economic Advisers, and the Department of Health, Education, and Welfare. It also thought the Program Planning and Budgeting System, which it had initiated in 1965, would greatly improve analysis of social programs by the operating agencies and the presidential staff.

It is true that efforts to predict and evaluate the effects of social programs have expanded greatly. But we are already suffering from the fact that such efforts are scattered and unconnected.

When the Nixon Administration first assumed office in 1969, it found an elaborate review of the cost-effectiveness of various Economic Opportunity Act programs, which the General Accounting Office had prepared on order of the Congress. Somewhere in the midst of the study were data which ultimately proved disastrous to the Job Corps. The GAO figures showed that the annual cost for

---

[10] Statement of Joseph A. Califano, Jr., in *Hearings on S. 5, supra* note 7, at 204.
[11] *Id.* at 209-10.

training a Job Corps enrollee ranged between $6000 and $8000. They also showed that only sixty-five per cent of participants could be classed as successful.

The central difficulty, from a policy point of view, was one which unfortunately occupied little if any of the time or attention of those who ultimately decided the fate of the Job Corps. Questions there were that deserved to be asked and answered:

Is it really such an outrage to spend $3000 to $4000 for six months' training of an urban youngster with a wretchedly deprived background and no future but one most likely to be devoted to crime or waste?

What would it cost society to keep such a person in prison or on welfare?

Given the difficulty of the problem, is a sixty-five per cent success rate really poor, or is it possibly a great achievement?

Most importantly, what other programs were there to use which would offer a higher success rate, a lower cost, or both?

What future might have awaited the Job Corps had questions such as these been asked and answered can only be left to conjecture. For in due course some 17,000 youngsters who had found new hope in the Job Corps fell under the axe of an unusually cruel system of social accounting. Indeed, several months later, the Administration was unable even to locate almost one-half of these young people, though it had promised to transfer them all to other manpower programs.

The danger of piecemeal social accounting was underscored when a number of us in Congress asked for data which would permit a comparative analysis of the Job Corps with a variety of other manpower programs favored by the Administration. Several weeks later the GAO, following repeated congressional inquiries, produced a table which featured the number "2." This was a footnote which said that the data were "not available."

Subsequent experience with alternative manpower programs suggests that the Job Corps was, and is, relatively effective after all. For example, it turned out that there were *no* placement data on the JOBS program, which was initially favored by the Administration. Later, we learned that this was one of the poorest manpower programs, with a success rate of only thirty to fifty per cent. So it would seem that a partial system of social accounting permits, or perhaps encourages, unwise decisions. Now that we have gone so far in measurement and evaluation, I think we dare not stop.

IV

Need for Structural Change

Surely it was at least in partial recognition of this decision-making deficiency in the American political system that, less than six months after having assumed office, President Nixon created a National Goals Research Staff (NGRS) on July 12, 1969.[12] Physically and organizationally located within the White House

---

[12] Only three days earlier, the Bureau of the Budget had opposed S. 5 on behalf of the Administra-

itself, the NGRS was from the outset over-shadowed by the larger political imperatives which confronted the Administration. Overseeing the work of the NGRS was but one of several responsibilities of a member of the White House staff, Mr. Leonard Garment.

The NGRS was commissioned originally to undertake a comprehensive review of the nation's objectives in the years immediately ahead and to prepare a report each year on the Fourth of July. Ultimately it produced a first, and final, compilation of potential problems which could come to plague the American people.[13] So disturbingly wanting was the report that the *New York Times* observed editorially that it represented a "disappointing evasion of responsibility."[14] Moreover, the *Times* editorial continued,

> The 169-page report, plus appendices, which was a year in the making, sets forth neither goals nor priorities. "The Staff did not have a goal-setting function," the report contends. If not, this White House task force was either misnamed or misdirected, or both.[15]

As is so frequently the case with organizational changes not based on statute, the NGRS effort aborted at some critical juncture. Those not privy to the pressures which played upon that small group may never know with certainty either the reason for the project's demise or the point at which it came. Still the experience of the NGRS may be instructive.

The point to be made is simply that the Nixon Administration's early efforts to achieve improved social policymaking have not succeeded. In disbanding the NGRS, the White House announced that its work would be carried on by the new Domestic Council. Thus we have seen two administrations rely, at one time or another, on the Budget Bureau, the Council of Economic Advisers, the Department of Health, Education, and Welfare, a new National Goals Research Staff, and a new Domestic Council to do a job which both agreed needs doing. So the relevant question is, when will such disparate and disconnected impulses be gotten together into some sort of comprehensive, systematic enterprise which has a decent chance for perseverance and productivity?

I am convinced that the day will not dawn when such irrational policy judgments as that involved in the Job Corps illustration are no longer made until America is provided with a new statutorily-mandated governmental structure. This structure must be capable of synthesizing our knowledge in the social area and proceeding directly to obliterate current gaps in that knowledge. Surely the unhappy experience of the NGRS underscores the need for a status which assures

---

tion, principally on the grounds that a new structure was not needed and would only be duplicative. *See* Statement of Maurice Mann, Assistant Director, Bureau of the Budget, in *id.* at 144-45.

[13] Toward Balanced Growth: Quantity with Quality, Report of the National Goals Research Staff (1970).

[14] *What Goals?*, N.Y. Times, July 21, 1970, at 34, col. 1.

[15] *Id.*

continuity. And no good can come from continuing to make decisions based on the chance availability of unconnected social measurements and evaluations.

So critical is the range of social problems confronting our country today that we can no longer afford the idle luxury of what John Gardner has so eloquently and tellingly termed "stumbling into the future." With a gunstock full of notches commemorating such disastrous undertakings as that of the NGRS, now is the time to target our hopes for improved social policymaking in one direction and one direction only. I believe that the creation of some sort of mechanism capable of comprehensively analyzing social conditions in this country, and reporting factually on those conditions to the President, the Congress, and the country, is the direction in which we now must move. We have already invested tremendous amounts of energy, talent, and money in cost-benefit analysis, experimentation with planning-programming-budgeting systems, and a wide variety of program evaluation techniques. Is it not now appropriate to move unhesitatingly toward a more sophisticated level of institutionalized structures competent to the task and responsible for performing it?

V

THE COUNCIL, THE CONGRESS, AND THE PRESIDENT

Some observers, who agree that we need a system of social accounting and that a new statutory structure is the only way to bring it about, nevertheless harbor one further concern. What chance, they ask, is there that even a council created by statute could effectively do all of these things which need doing so urgently if it is unwanted by the President?

Surely no one would suggest that the conclusions and recommendations in the annual social report prepared by a Council of Social Advisers for the President and the Congress would run counter to the thinking of the President or his Administration. Yet, such a report would necessarily contain data and analysis which might lead other commentators to different conclusions.

Mr. Charles Schultze, former Director of the Bureau of the Budget has said:

> The United States budget is not the document of an executive whose decisions are law, nor of a prime minister whose party must support him or bring down the government. It is, rather, a set of proposals to the Congress for action on appropriations and tax measures. Precisely because it must advocate the course recommended by the President, the budget cannot emphasize the difficulty of the choices made. It records the President's decisions, but it does not identify the close ones. Alternatives that were serious contenders for adoption but were finally rejected are seldom if ever mentioned. In some cases, programs generally recognized as ineffective or of low priority are debated but finally left unchanged because all participants in the debate realize how few are the lances a President can afford to break against politically impregnable targets. Thus, the

budget is a document designed to persuade an independent Congress rather than to analyze policy alternatives.[16]

Even if we had reason to believe that a comprehensive system of social accounting would be promptly initiated by the executive branch, without a statutory requirement, there would be a sound basis for legislation. The Congress also must have access to such information. Prestigious members of a statutory council, subject to Senate confirmation and available to testify before congressional committees on their findings, would assure the Congress and the public of the required quality and visibility of their work. Further, the tension between the council members and the Congress should elevate the level of analysis in the same way that our understanding of economics has been enhanced through the hearings on the *Economic Report*.

There is ample precedent, since the Second World War, for the establishment of specialized councils which (*a*) were essentially foisted on given administrations and (*b*) have proved to be meritorious additions to the federal government's structure, notwithstanding initial executive opposition.

Certainly the Council of Economic Advisers, created by the Employment Act of 1946,[17] supports this thesis. Similarly, the National Security Council, established in 1947,[18] and the Council on Environmental Quality,[19] set up only a year ago, came to occupy respected positions even within administrations which initially opposed them. The Nixon Administration, for example, opposed incipient congressional efforts to highlight the ecological crisis by a statutory prescription for top-level presidential and congressional advice. Yet when signing into law the measure creating the new Council, the President heralded the action as one opening a new decade of the environment, and he has used it widely and effectively since then.

History compels the conclusion that Presidents use, in varying degree, all of the statutorily-created structures in the executive branch. Moreover, they tend to use most vigorously and trustingly those bodies which draw esteem and respect both to themselves and their President. Thus it may safely be concluded that a Council of Social Advisers which performed satisfactorily its mission of measuring and monitoring and reporting on social conditions in America would, far from meeting perpetual presidential resistance and rancor, come in time to enjoy a position of trust and respect. From such a position it could reasonably be anticipated that the Council could began to elevate social policymaking in America to new levels of sophistication.

CONCLUSION

The principal concern of this essay has been the interrelationship between a

---

[16] C. SCHULTZE ET AL., SETTING NATIONAL PRIORITIES 4 (1970).
[17] Ch. 33, 60 Stat. 23.
[18] National Security Act of 1947, ch. 343, 61 Stat. 495.
[19] National Environmental Policy Act of 1969, 83 Stat. 852.

proposed federal mechanism for improving social policymaking and the office of President of the United States. Is there some possibility that even a valuable new council would contribute to overburdening him with specialized advisory units?

I believe a Council of Social Advisers, charged with the responsibility for advancing and asserting existing knowledge of real social facts about this society, should serve to integrate, coordinate, and systematize the now dissident and discordant efforts of social planners and evaluators wherever they may be located within the federal government.

Moreover, the CSA should, in operation, synthesize advisory inputs which now compete for individual, isolated attention, thus reducing the cumulative advice-receiving burden of the President. Additionally, in synthesizing available information, the CSA would be speaking to the President—and to the Congress and the country—in a voice which, while a blend of many voices, would still be coherent.

Finally, I believe that we shall never begin to end our hopeless method of making social policy decisions of the most sensitive sort on the basis of hunch, intuition, and good intentions until we move in the direction pointed to by this legislative proposal. The enactment of legislation creating a comprehensive advisory role in the social policy area will, I believe, radically alter not only the process by which decisionmakers choose, but ultimately the choices which are made.

When President Nixon established the National Goals Research Staff in July 1969, he stated that the report to be prepared by the unit should "serve as a focus for the kind of lively widespread public discussion that deserves to go into decisions affecting our common future."[20] The document which ultimately emanated from the NGRS could not begin to serve the critical focusing function the President had envisioned for it. After a round of newspaper comments, it disappeared from view. No congressional committee held hearings on it. A Council of Social Advisers, speaking social facts to the American people in a clear and coherent voice, could provide the kind of focus the President asked for.

When, finally, such a Council is created—as I think is very likely—it will be a most fitting recognition of the firm resolve of our people to govern themselves rightly and intelligently and of the efforts of many, along the way, to make a start toward the objective so well stated by Abraham Lincoln: "If we could first know where we are, and whither we are tending, we could better judge what to do, and how to do it."[21]

---

[20] 5 WEEKLY COMP. PRES. DOC. 982, 984 (1969).

[21] Address delivered by Abraham Lincoln Before the Republican State Convention, Springfield, Ill., June 16, 1858, in 3 COMPLETE WORKS OF ABRAHAM LINCOLN 1 (J. Nicolay & J. Hay eds. 1905).

THE PRESIDENCY AND MANAGEMENT IMPROVEMENT

Marver H. Bernstein*

In its final report of December, 1952, the President's Advisory Committee on Management concluded that there was "no single, sure-fire, and practicable panacea to guarantee the improvement of management in the Federal Government. The Federal establishment is so varied that no uniform program would be feasible or desirable. Rather, the aim should be to keep unrelenting pressure on administrators to devise and adopt programs suited to the tasks under their jurisdictions."[1]

What is needed to improve federal management, the Committee asserted, are the following ingredients: a chief that "cares about getting a job done," adequate machinery and staff, a management system that produces results, and systematic review and appraisal of performance. The story of management improvement in federal government is mainly an account of how successive efforts since 1921 to improve the quality of federal management have failed or have fallen far short of their objectives.

I

The Initial Programs for Management Improvement

The basic statutory authority for management improvement is found in the Budget and Accounting Act of 1921, which provides in section 209 that the Bureau of the Budget, when directed by the President, shall make studies of departments and agencies to enable the President to determine what changes shall be made in their organization, activities, methods of business, appropriations, assignment of functions, and regrouping of services. During the 1920's and 1930's there were less than 100 positions in the Bureau, and little attention was given to management. In 1937, the President's Committee on Administrative Management made a major effort to grapple with problems of organization and management in the executive branch. The Committee proposed to fix responsibility on the President to take the initiative in improving management in the departments and agencies and devised the reorganization plan as the method of reorganization. In the Committee's judgment, it was essential that central executive direction pursue "day after day and year after year, in season and out of season, the task of cutting costs, of improving the service, and of raising the standards of performance."[2]

In 1939, the Bureau of the Budget was transferred from the Treasury Depart-

---

* Professor of Politics and Public Affairs, Princeton University.

[1] President's Advisory Committee on Management, Report to the President, at 18 (1952).

[2] President's Committee on Administrative Management, Report with General Studies, at 45 (1937).

ment to the newly created Executive Office of the President, and a new Division of Administrative Management within the Bureau was directed "to conduct *research* in the development of improved plans of administrative management, and to *advise* the executive departments and agencies of the Government with respect to improved administrative organization and practice," and "to aid the President to bring about more efficient and economical conduct of Government services."[3] As civilian agencies of economic mobilization were created during the period of 1939-1944, the Division of Administrative Management was assigned the tasks of reviewing their budgetary requirements as well as their problems of organization and management. In other areas, the Division did relatively simple things to promote better administrative performance.

As the Bureau became more fully aware of the efforts of the War and Navy Departments in 1942 and 1943 to recruit experts in management from consulting firms and from industry, it decided to mount a program to develop higher managerial skills in the civilian agencies. A Management Improvement Branch under Lawrence Hoelscher was established to conduct research on accounting systems, budget formulation, and the paper work side of personnel management. The Branch intended to provide leadership in stimulating agencies to improve their practices. From the experience of the War Depatrment, it designed a work simplification program for testing in civilian agencies. In the mid-forties, as it gained more experience, it prepared management bulletins on such topics as work measurement, property control, telephone service, and the preparation of budget justifications. And it conducted training courses for federal agencies on organization and management and on budget formulation and execution. These activities attempted to meet the serious lack of adequately trained professionals in specific managerial posts and to advance the state of the management art by investing in research.

In the period 1946-1948, the Division of Administrative Management had a staff of about 55 professionals. But in 1948-49, heavy budget slashes cut deeply into the Management Improvement Branch, leaving intact only the group working on financial management and the joint Treasury-Bureau-General Accounting Office program in financial management that was launched in 1948.

The report of the Hoover Commission in 1949 proposed to deal with management improvement mainly through the process of reorganization. It focused attention on proposals for structural realignment in the executive branch and had little to say specifically about management improvement. The report did, however, stimulate President Truman to embark on a management improvement program in July 1949, when he issued an executive order directing department and agency heads to review their programs, provide periodic and systematic appraisals of operations, identify opportunities to improve performance, install improvements, and report periodically

---

[3] Establishing the Divisions of the Executive Office of the President and Defining Their Functions and Duties, Exec. Order No. 8248, 3 C.F.R. 576 (Comp. 1938-43).

to the Budget Bureau "on the progress made in establishing management improvement programs and the results achieved therefrom."[4] The Bureau was directed to review agency plans for management improvement, advise and assist federal agencies, exchange information with them, and report to the President. In addition, the order created the Advisory Committee on Management Improvement consisting of twelve members (five federal officials and seven private citizens) to assist the President in developing a government-wide program for management improvement.

In October, 1949, Congress provided legislative support in the Classification Act of 1949 by directing each department to make a systematic review of its operations in accordance with the directions of the Bureau of the Budget. To emphasize even more its concern for federal management, Congress enacted the Budget and Accounting Procedures Act of 1950 which authorizes and directs the President through the Bureau of the Budget to evaluate and develop improved plans for the organization, coordination, and management of the executive branch to achieve more efficiency and economy.[5]

II

THE INFLUENCE OF THE BUREAU OF THE BUDGET IN THE MIDDLE YEARS

On January 31, 1950, the Bureau issued Circular A-8, *Agency Responsibility Under the President's Management Program*, calling for annual reports by the agencies on their progress in improving the quality of management. Thus was started a flow of paper from management analysts in the agencies to the Bureau that proved to be essentially worthless in meeting the objective of stimulating aggressive efforts to improve administrative performance. After Korea, the Bureau's limited staff for management improvement was able to conduct only a paper review of trivia accumulated from agency reports that the Advisory Committee on Management described as "evidently the product of departmental staff report writers rather than the unburdenings of operators concerned with the future of their operations."[6] In June, 1951, the Bureau tried to revitalize the reporting process by emphasizing the responsibility of agency heads for management improvement and by reducing the reporting requirements, but these measures had little beneficial effect.

Under Circular A-8, the Bureau was directed to carry out four activities:

(a) issue guides to assist agencies in developing effective review systems;
(b) evaluate the review systems of the agencies and the adequacy of actions taken by them to achieve potential improvements;
(c) maintain working relationships with the agencies to assist them on a day-to-day basis in improving their managerial effectiveness; and
(d) submit reports to the Budget Director and the President as required.

---

[4] To Provide for Continuing Action to Improve the Management of the Executive Branch of the Government, Exec. Order No. 10072, 3 C.F.R. 277, § 1 (Comp. 1949-53). For a review of actions 1950 (mimeo).

[5] Budget and Accounting Procedures Act of 1950, 31 U.S.C. § 104 (1964).

[6] PRESIDENT'S ADVISORY COMMITTEE ON MANAGEMENT, *supra* note 1, at 17.

In practice the first and third activities proved to be the key ones. The Bureau's staff was cut again in 1950, and it was unable to do more.

This formidable battery of legislative and executive documents produced little constructive action. The effectiveness of the Advisory Committee depended almost entirely upon continuous presidential pressure on agency heads. At first, President Truman closed the two-day, bi-monthly meetings of the Committee by reviewing management problems with the agency head in order to impress him with the importance the President attached to management improvement. According to plan, the Committee dealt with four major agencies in each bi-monthly session, giving a half day to each. The Budget Bureau's staff instructed the chief management assistant to each agency head to brief his boss on his philosophy of management, what he is doing to improve management, what staff he has to help him, what major problems of management he has solved, what problems he is working on currently, and what management problems are caused by factors beyond his control. This rather straight-forward approach usually had devastating effects. Many agency heads were forced to pull materials together from scratch. In the charitable opinion of the Committee, some agency heads "were informed and informative, displaying a broad grasp of the affairs committed to their hands, while others revealed a concept of management as in a pigeonhole apart, concerned only with housekeeping details."[7]

The Committee's focus on management improvement was halted by the Korean War and Truman's decision to have the Committee confine its attention to problems of economic mobilization. Before it terminated in December, 1952, it issued a report with four recommendations designed to improve federal management:

(a) Congress should give the President permanent reorganization authority;
(b) the President should maintain unrelenting pressure on executives for management improvement;
(c) federal agencies should strengthen management staff facilities at all administrative levels; and
(d) the executive branch should inaugurate an executive development program.

The last proposal was finally adopted in 1970 when President Nixon's Reorganization Plan No. 2 of 1970 became effective.

Throughout its report, the Committee underlined the need for continuing, conscientious attention by executives to management improvement. At the same time, the Committee seemed fully aware of the forces militating against such concern: the diffusion of governing authority, the absence of clear program objectives, diffused legislative activity, high turnover among key executives, and sharp swings in goal orientations. "These uncertainties," it stated, "do not encourage sustained and concentrated attention to management problems."[8] Generally the Committee applauded the approach of the Bureau of the Budget, noting that it had shied away from

---

[7] *Id.*
[8] *Id.* at 4.

rigid controls and had emphasized stimulation of agency interest in management improvement. The Committee's recommendation of a special fund for the use of the President in financing major management studies was adopted by Congress, which established a no-year appropriation for this purpose. These funds were used to finance 26 studies from 1953 to 1960.

In 1951, President Truman hoped to reduce government employment by imposing personnel ceilings on individual agencies. Because of the opposition of the Bureau to ceilings, a program was adopted to promote better utilization of manpower. Under Circular A-44, which was issued jointly with the Civil Service Commission in June, 1951, the Bureau, in cooperation with the Civil Service Commission, was directed to make studies of agency operations in order to achieve better manpower utilization. But with a staff cut to about 22, the Bureau was in a very weak position to undertake its own studies or to secure the concerted cooperation of agency staffs in developing programs to achieve better use of agency personnel.

From 1953 to 1959, with a staff of approximately 23 to 29 in the Bureau's Office of Management and Organization, special attention to management improvement activities was discontinued, although the Bureau continued to give emphasis to the joint program in financial management. Some effort was made to encourage federal employees to promote better management by authorizing schemes of incentive awards for employees.[9] President Eisenhower looked primarily to bankers and accountants for leadership in the Budget Bureau. The Administration's interest in economy was stronger than its concern for improving management, and the Bureau was expected to set an example for the executive branch in economical use of personnel. Thus in a period in which management technology was developing at an extremely rapid pace, the resources that the presidency might call upon for leadership in improving federal management were minimal. Even the Second Hoover Commission, reporting in 1955, took little interest in these matters. Although it recommended that the Bureau expand its managerial functions, it was almost completely silent on the problems of departmental management.

From 1953 to 1959, the dominant force in management improvement was the Rockefeller Committee, whose studies were focused mainly on problems of structure and organization. The Office of Management and Organization in the Bureau provided some staff work for the Committee. Four areas of policy were given special and air traffic control and navigation. In the first three, cabinet committees were charged with responsibility for preparing policy recommendations. In the fourth treatment: telecommunications, water resources and power, railroad transportation, area, Bureau staff worked with the Rockefeller Committee to produce proposals that influenced changes in the organization of the Federal Aviation Agency in 1958.

---

[9] Employee awards were authorized by Act of Oct. 28, 1949, ch. 782, §§ 1001-03, 63 Stat. 954, 971. A new legal basis was provided by the Act of Sept. 1, 1954, ch. 1208, § 304, 68 Stat. 1173. The Budget Bureau set forth its instructions to the agencies for the administration of these programs in various supplements to Circular A-8.

Nelson Rockefeller had become Under Secretary of the Department of Health, Education, and Welfare in 1953. In the course of organizing the newly created department, he clashed with the Bureau of the Budget over matters relating to structure and management. He seemed to conclude that the Bureau would not be able to provide leadership in management improvement because of its preoccupation with budget analysis and budget cutting. He proposed a reorganization of the Executive Office of the President that abolished the Bureau of the Budget and created a new Office of Executive Management, in which management functions would be assigned higher priority. The proposal was seriously considered in the White House, but in the end it was dropped because Rockefeller insisted on abolition of the Bureau of the Budget. In the history of management improvement in the federal government, the significance of the Rockefeller proposal lies in its conviction that the Bureau was unable to provide sustained leadership in the field of management improvement. This view was picked up again during the consideration of Reorganization Plan No. 2 of 1970, which designated the Bureau as the Office of Management and Budget and emphasized the President's need for substantially enhanced staff capability in areas of executive management, including improvement of organization, information, and management systems.

In 1959, partly in reaction to the Rockefeller attack, the Budget Director concluded that "more emphasis should be placed on Bureau leadership in the field of management improvement throughout the executive branch."[10] In that year the Bureau appointed an Interagency Council on Management Improvement to advise it on the improvement of federal management.

In a speech on May 17, 1960, Elmer B. Staats, then Deputy Director of the Budget, outlined five prinicples to guide the government's role in management improvement:

(a) Management improvement is primarily the responsibility of the individual agencies.

(b) "The President must set the tone and the pace by requiring that agency heads devote real attention to the struggle to reduce red tape, waste, duplication, and still perform their role with timeliness and satisfaction to the Congress and the public."

(c) The Budget Bureau should provide a central clearing house for ideas and information about management and act as a catalyst in problem solving. It should be expert in finding the answers to managerial problems.

(d) Full interagency support is needed to permit the Bureau to reactivate its role in management improvement.

(e) The ability to sustain a central service for management improvement depends on the ability of that service to produce results.[11]

---

[10] BUREAU OF THE BUDGET, MANAGEMENT IMPROVEMENT IN THE EXECUTIVE BRANCH, A PROGRESS REPORT 2 (1961).

[11] The Bureau's Future Role in Management Improvement, Address by Elmer B. Staats, Deputy Dir. of the Budget, May 17, 1960.

Accordingly, in 1960 the Bureau requested 18 additional professional positions, 10 of which were to be used to provide more assistance to agencies in applying improved managerial practices. When Congress approved a small amount of additional staffing in the fall of 1960, a Management Services Branch was created to meet the need for central leadership and assistance to the agencies. The Bureau immediately invited 25 agencies to join with it to identify the significant steps taken in recent years to strengthen agency management and the opportunities for future improvement. The limited results of this inventory are summarized in the Bureau's report of May 1961.[12] The report included a final section on techniques of management improvement, embracing work simplification, automatic data processing, and techniques of systematic analysis, such as the engineered approach to production and planning problems and such statistical techniques as scientific sampling and operations research.

Perhaps the most constructive contribution of the Bureau in the period 1960-1965 was the mounting of courses to train budget and management analysts in improved techniques. The Management Services Branch in the Office of Management and Organization began to develop materials for training purposes in 1960, working closely with the U.S. Army Management Engineering Training Agency (AMETA), which had been training army personnel in the use of management techniques. Since the Agency had better training materials and courses than the Branch could develop quickly, it made full use of the Agency courses. For five years it sponsored 8 to 10 courses for federal personnel on automatic data processing, procedural analysis, operations research, statistical quality control, engineering economics for decision making, and budget formulation and execution. The training courses were teminated in 1965 as the current demand for trained personnel was satisfied. These training courses competed somewhat with new training programs of the Civil Service Commission, but the Bureau justified its activity as an effective way to fulfill its responsibility to provide leadership in developing management skills. The Bureau resumed special training activity in 1970 under the Joint Financial Management Program.

As a consequence of the renewed effort beginning in 1959 to provide better leadership for improving management, the Bureau's staff assigned to administrative management increased slowly. From a total of 26 full-time management analysts in 1955, the staff increased to 29 by 1960, 41 by 1965, and 49 by 1970, just slightly above the staff of 46 in 1950.[13] While the proportionate increase in professional staff was substantial over a twenty-year period, improvement of management had remained a relatively marginal concern of the Bureau of the Budget.

---

[12] BUREAU OF THE BUDGET, *supra* note 10.

[13] *Hearings on Reorganization Plan No. 2 of 1970 Before the Subcomm. on Exec. and Legis. Reorganization of the House Comm. on Gov't Operations*, 91st Cong., 2d Sess. 124 (1970).

III

RECENT EFFORTS AT MANAGEMENT IMPROVEMENT

President Kennedy seemed to have little interest in professional management and in the managerial problems of the executive branch. He could not accept as reasonable the continuing growth in federal employment, however, and consequently became interested in manpower utilization as an alternative to the imposition of manpower ceilings. The manpower approach led in turn to some interest in reviewing the internal operations of various agencies. From 1961 to 1963, the Office of Management and Organization in the Bureau focused its limited resources on automatic data processing, work measurement, cost reduction, and manpower utilization. In the Johnson Administration, these concerns were followed by productivity measurement and the "war on waste," an up-dated model of cost reduction, and the introduction of PPBS (performance-planning-budgeting system) throughout the executive branch. The Bureau moved rapidly from one program of management improvement to another, each with its own rhetoric, style, and temporary commitment to a new fashionable tactic of administrative reform. While each program had its own set of biases, collectively they had two characteristics in common. They shared a reluctance to become involved in making substantive judgments about the value and performance of programs, and they stimulated most staffs of management analysts in the agencies to make routine inquiries, unimaginative analyses, and minor recommendations for the improvement of management.

Early in 1962, the Bureau organized a conference on work measurement.[14] In October of 1962, the President issued a memorandum to agency heads setting forth a program to improve the utilization of manpower.[15] The goal was to reduce the number of employees needed to carry out essential government programs. In the same year, the Bureau asked five agencies to join it in an experimental project to develop productivity measures for these agencies as a whole or for major components.[16] The Bureau's aim was to develop productivity indices as a tool for managers to use in determining appropriate courses of action in the operation of federal agencies. The study, which was completed in 1964, is probably the most impressive document in the field of management improvement produced during the Kennedy-Johnson years.[17] It devised valid measures of productivity for four of the five participating agencies and concluded that "in all likelihood measurement of productivity is feasible in a considerable number of other organizations . . . where the nature of the service produced by the organization offers reasonable prospects

[14] See BUREAU OF THE BUDGET, PROGRESS IN MEASURING WORK (1962).

[15] Improving Manpower Controls and Utilization in the Executive Branch, Presidential Memo. (Oct. 11, 1962).

[16] The agencies included the Treasury Department, the Veterans Administration, the Post Office Department, the Federal Aviation Agency, and the Department of the Interior.

[17] BUREAU OF THE BUDGET, MEASURING PRODUCTIVITY OF FEDERAL GOVERNMENT ORGANIZATIONS (1964).

of its quantitative description."[18] More generally the study stressed the leadership role of administrators in the drive to improve managerial effectiveness. It concluded:

> Recently there has been increased emphasis at the highest level of the United States Government on the economy and efficiency of Government operations and on the need for proper criteria to measure progress. Since improving the efficiency of Government operations involves, of course, raising of Government productivity, productivity measurement, by providing strategic data, can contribute to these objectives. Yet in the final analysis, productivity measurement can contribute to better management only if the measures are developed and interpreted with complete objectivity, and positive and imaginative action is taken by responsible management to achieve improvements.[19]

During 1962 and 1963, the Bureau made an effort to establish a central reference file of materials relating to management improvement. The effort never succeeded because the agencies failed to submit sufficient material on the development and use of various tools and techniques of management to build a worthwhile collection.

In 1963, the Bureau embarked on a drive to reduce costs through better management. In an unpretentious report it outlined the main possibilities for improving federal management, including automatic data processing, manpower utilization, incentive awards, management of property and supplies, financial management, new approaches for managing complex programs, uses of statistics, and management of field activities.[20]

President Kennedy's program for improving federal management tended to emphasize three elements:

(a) placement of responsibility for manpower control and utilization in each agency head;

(b) establishment in each agency of systematic methods for discovering better uses of manpower; and

(c) research in methods of increasing productivity.

As already noted, progress was made toward instituting relevant research, but significant improvements in management were achieved in only a handful of agencies, despite the clearer designation of agency heads as the executives responsible for improving agency management.

During 1964, President Johnson continued the emphasis on cost reduction. In an award ceremony in Washington in December, he honored 30 federal employees who were cited for their personal contributions to this drive. The President dramatized the drive as his "war on waste" and publicized the substantial savings allegedly resulting from the systematic effort to reduce costs. For example, the Department of Defense reported in October, 1964, that in the fiscal year 1964 it had

---

[18] *Id.* at 16.

[19] *Id.* at 18.

[20] BUREAU OF THE BUDGET, COST REDUCTION THROUGH BETTER MANAGEMENT IN THE FEDERAL GOVERNMENT (1963).

saved $2.8 billion and in November it identified 95 obsolete, unneeded facilities to be consolidated, reduced, or closed, claiming ultimate savings of almost half a billion dollars a year. A 1965 report bearing the title, War on Waste, credits the Administration with a high degree of "managerial prudence" in its effort to get "a dollar's value for a dollar spent."[21] Costs were reduced, according to the report, by controls over hiring; tighter control of files, overtime, travel, and communication; improved procurement, contracting, supply, and space utilization; use of excess facilities instead of new procurement; automation, improved equipment, and advanced technology; streamlined organization; elimination of unnecessary work; and better methods of operation.

In 1965 the focus of management improvement shifted from cost reduction to systematic analyses for budget preparation and program evaluation (PPBS), and economists replaced management and budget analysts as the key professionals.

During 1969, President Nixon focused his interest in management improvement on increased productivity and manpower utilization as ways of combating excessive employment. In line with his memorandum on this subject to the heads of agencies on February 17, 1969, which he reiterated in his statement of July 22, 1969, the Bureau undertook to develop better means of estimating and justifying requests for personnel. In April, 1970, it issued the first in a series of Executive Management Bulletins on the use of statistical procedures for justifying manpower requirements in relation to planned work. It contained no mandatory provisions for the use of statistical techniques but made each agency responsible for deciding which of the available techniques were best suited for its use.[22]

The management analysis staff of the Bureau, now designated the Office of Executive Management, worked primarily on two problems closely related to the interests of the Nixon Administration: the rationalization of the regional office structures of several federal agencies and the reduction in the time required to process applications for federal grants-in-aid. In these projects the Bureau provided leadership and assistance to the federal agencies involved, principally the Department of Health, Education, and Welfare and the Department of Housing and Urban Development.

In February, 1970, two important steps were taken to promote better management. First, the President established the Advisory Council on Management Improvement comprised of ten executives from private life "to recommend improved methods and procedures that can be introduced to sharpen the efficiency of Government operations."[23] Second, the Budget Director issued a revised Circular A-44 on Feb. 16, 1970, establishing a formal government-wide management improvement

---

[21] BUREAU OF THE BUDGET, WAR ON WASTE: COST REDUCTION THROUGH BETTER MANAGEMENT (1965).

[22] BUREAU OF THE BUDGET, EXECUTIVE MANAGEMENT BULLETIN: ANALYZING MANPOWER REQUIREMENTS USING STATISTICAL ESTIMATES (1970).

[23] Establishing the President's Advisory Council on Management Improvement, Exec. Order No. 11509, quoted in the White House press release of Feb. 11, 1970.

program. Perhaps the principal feature of the new program is the emphasis it gives to the goal of management effectiveness instead of dollars saved. Agency heads are directed to undertake systematic reviews of agency programs in order to identify "persistent problem areas of high level priority" and give concentrated attention to resolving these problems.[24] The cost-reduction program is strengthened by requiring agency heads to fix at the beginning of each fiscal year a monetary goal of savings expected to be realized from new and improved management actions, together with subgoals for major activities or organizational units. Acceptable ways to measure monetary savings and to validate them are set forth in some detail for the first time. The Bureau is directed also to develop an "idea interchange" for distributing information on management improvement to all agencies.

The revised Circular A-44 instructs each agency to employ a variety of techniques to stimulate employees to seek ways to improve management. In addition a new system of presidential awards is created to honor exceptional achievement in reducing costs or improving operating effectiveness. The Bureau is directed to choose a common area of government-wide operations for periodic study. Examples are records management and printing and reproduction. Finally each agency is directed to file an annual management improvement report, due on September 30.

On March 12, 1970, President Nixon submitted to Congress Reorganization Plan No. 2 of 1970, which redesignated the Bureau of the Budget as the Office of Management and Budget.[25] In supporting the plan, the President stated:

> Improving the management processes of the President's own office . . . is a key element in improving the management of the entire Executive Branch, and in strengthening the authority of its Departments and agencies.[26]

The President emphasized the need for a substantially enhanced institutional capability in the general area of executive management, including program evaluation and coordination, improvement of organization of the executive branch, information and management systems, and development of executive talent. It appeared, therefore, that one of the principal purposes of the reorganization was to equip the presidency with better instruments for purposes of improving the management of the executive branch. Together with the Domestic Council, the Office of Management and Budget began life on July 1, 1970. It is too early to speculate about its effectiveness as the President's agent of management improvement.

IV

EVALUATION OF THE FEDERAL EFFORT

The history of management improvement in the federal government is a story of inflated rhetoric, shifting emphasis from one fashionable managerial skill to

[24] Establishment of a Management Improvement Program Applicable to All Government Operations, Bureau of the Budget, Circular Revised A-44, § 3, at 2, Feb. 16, 1970 (mimeo.).

[25] H.R. Doc. No. 91-275, 91st Cong., 2d Sess. (1970).

[26] Id.

another, and a relatively low level of professional achievement. In recent administrations, each President has proclaimed the importance of improving the management of federal programs administered by the executive branch, but at the same time he has been unable to give more than a low order of priority to government-wide programs of management improvement. No President has been able to identify any significant political capital that might be made out of efforts to improve management except for the conservative purpose of economizing or reducing costs. Even when Presidents have wanted to stress the improvement of management, they have been forced to concentrate on more important problems.

The fitfull task of the Bureau of the Budget has been to provide moral leadership and to encourage the departments and agencies to become more sensitive to managerial problems and to undertake studies to promote better management. Since 1950, the Bureau has never had more than a corporal's guard to deal with problems of management.

In federal experience, management improvement has been weak in motivation, purpose, and achievement primarily because it has been accorded very low status by political and career executives. There appear to be few incentives for these executives to focus their concerns and resources on efforts to improve the management of programs they administer. Several conditions help to account for the low status of management improvement. As all reports on the subject assert, nothing less than leadership from the top has the possibility of creating an enviroment conducive to improvement of managerial practices. Senior political and career executives have drastically limited time to devote to these matters. Because they cannot deny the soundness of more effective management in the public interest, they tend to rely on occasional gestures toward better management, expressed in the accepted rhetoric of managerial reform, emphasizing a currently fashionable concept or tool, such as ADP, productivity measurement, manpower utilization, or cost reduction. As long as political payoffs for management improvement remain dubious and illusive, executive commitment seldom rises above lip service.

Another condition of executive leadership in the federal establishment is the brief tenure of secretaries and agency heads and their top staffs compared to the lead time, sustained effort, and investments in staff that are required to bring about significant improvements in management. Affirmative results are not likely to emerge in the short run, which is the time frame in which public executives function. They also tend to be crisis-oriented and can hardly resist the apparent need to assign available manpower to emergency or high-priority tasks. Management improvement, therefore, is most likely to be a deferable, residual concern that cannot compete for executive commitment against the demands of substantive programs and insistent policy issues.

Cost reduction, the most persistent focus of management improvement, tends to penalize agencies and programs that are performing relatively well. In order to highlight improvements in management, normally it is necessary to demonstrate waste and inefficiencies and to pinpoint responsibility for bad management. At the very least an executive must admit that a program or function is not working well and the administration is perhaps belatedly trying to undertake some appropriate remedial action. Even when savings result from better management, it is usually very difficult to arrange to use such savings for high priority programs in the same agency. Not only do executives lack incentives to improve the management of their programs, but they are likely to encounter built-in penalties if they attempt to bring about improvements.

As the Bureau of the Budget noted in its study of producivity measurement, the appraisal of administrative performance is very difficult and suspect unless the objectives of government programs are identified and clarified. Yet, if offices responsible for management improvement become involved in making value judgments about goals and missions, they are likely to be charged with interference with the responsibilities of executives.

The standing of management improvement has also been seriously undermined by the common tendency to exaggerate the usefulness of various tools and skills employed by analysts. New management tools have been oversold, propagandized, and undermined by overexpectations and by insufficient attention to the specific operating problems and situations of individual agencies. Moreover, it has been very difficult to document persuasively the savings that result from improvements in management. Claims of savings of the magnitude of a half billion dollars or more are apt to be regarded with derisive disbelief. In most cases, it is unlikely that savings resulting from concerted efforts to improve management will have any significant impact on the agency's budget or on the national budget.

Lastly, it is hard to find instances in which clientele groups have encouraged agencies to improve the quality of their management. Often disclosures by agency personnel of ineffective administrative operations or serious deficiencies in program performance may also cast doubt on the propriety of the behavior of private parties or the soundness of policies and actions that support clientele interests. Agency employees who are able to document findings of poor management and excessive costs are often unrewarded by their agency heads and may in fact be penalized for their misplaced zeal and bad judgment by reassignment, demotion, or forced resignation.

This analysis ascribes the weakness of presidential efforts to stimulate improved management to the lack of appropriate incentives in the political and administrative setting of federal administration. Paul Appleby noted a quarter of a century ago that leadership of the public is usually associated with marked individuality. In filling executive positions, the President ideally should strike a balance between a capacity for institutional leadership and a capacity for administrative management. But we have developed no theory that explains how professionalized administration is made compatible with the politics of democracy. An agency head is expected to be both political executive and administrative manager; yet the two capacities seldom go together well. As an exercise in administrative morality, periodic presidential exhortation of public executives to increase productivity and become more efficient will undoubtedly continue. But it is not likely to rise above the level of marginal achievement without much more sophisticated emphasis on executive recruitment and development and the creation of incentives that encourage and reward managerial performance.

THE BUDGET BUREAU THAT WAS: THOUGHTS ON THE RISE, DECLINE, AND FUTURE OF A PRESIDENTIAL AGENCY

ALLEN SCHICK*

On July 1, 1970, during its fiftieth year, the United States Bureau of the Budget nominally ceased to exist. Its function, personnel, and traditions were transferred to the Office of Management and Budget, a new unit within the Executive Office of the President with a potentially broader mission than its predecessor carried.[1] From the point of view of bureaucratic continuity, the line of authority established in the Budget and Accounting Act of 1921 has been perpetuated. But on the premise that organizations ordinarily are restructured only after they have declined, not at the peak of their capabilities, this article discusses the inadequacies which led to the decease of the Bureau, once the premier institution in the President's Office. And on the presumption that reorganizations rarely work out exactly as intended, we will examine the prospects for the Office of Management and Budget.

It is difficult to make a case that the Bureau was inadequate for its various roles, for it always was graced with a favorable public image. Periodically, the Bureau was featured in the media as a valiant guardian of the purse, its directors as embattled enemies of spend-lust bureaucrats, its examiners as men working without honor or acclaim to combat the predatory wiles of federal agencies. The Bureau's image was enhanced by the absence of serious scandal or impropriety; even when there were visible shortcomings in the budget process (such as the gross underestimation of the costs of the Vietnam War and the miscalculation of the 1971 budget deficit), the Bureau managed to escape severe opprobrium. This sheltered existence was due in good part to the Bureau's presidential mission and cloistered mode of operation. Only a portion of the Bureau's reality was open to public view, and in a town that often seems to thrive on a fishbowl existence, the Bureau was spared close scrutiny. Few leaks emanated from the Bureau and not many newsmen or scholars penetrated its curtain of secrecy and bureaucratic routines. Most journal articles relate to the directorship of Harold Smith (1939-1945), a period during which the Bureau became the central management arm of the federal government.[2] There is almost nothing in the public record concerning the opera-

---

* The Brookings Institution.

[1] Technically, the functions of the Bureau of the Budget were transferred to the President, who by Executive Order, delegated them to the Office of Management and Budget. Exec. Order No. 11,541, 3 C.F.R. 10,737 (Supp. 1970). It is anticipated that in the future certain administrative duties will be transferred to other federal agencies.

[2] See Pearson, *The Budget Bureau: From Routine Business to General Staff*, 3 PUB. AD. REV. 126 (1943); Marx, *The Bureau of the Budget: Its Evolution and Present Role*, 34 AM. POL. SCI. REV. 653, 869 (1945).

tions of the Bureau during the 1960's, a decade of unheralded but significant changes in the relations between the Bureau and the White House.

Nevertheless, there have been signs of a decline in the stature, if not the performance, of the Budget Bureau. Just as its location in the Executive Office Building, situated next door to the White House, once was an indication of the Bureau's eminence as a presidential institution, the recent removal of major portions of the Bureau to a less prestigious address signalled its decline relative to other presidential staffs. On certain matters, such as program planning and administrative reorganization, the Bureau's role has been subordinated, with White House aides and task forces taking the lion's share of the action. The attempt in the mid-1960's to establish a Planning-Programming-Budget System manifested a conviction among top Bureau officials that the existing budgetary practices were inadequate, but the only limited application of PPBS bespoke the inability of the Bureau to significantly overhaul its own or the bureaucracy's budget traditions. In 1967, a presidential task force found grave defects in the central administrative apparatus, and it proposed the bolstering of the Bureau's program development capabilities and the creation of a separate White House unit to coordinate federal programs.[3] In the same year, the Bureau undertook an evaluation of its operations, and some changes were made in its internal structure.[4] Finally, in 1970, the President's Advisory Council on Executive Organization proposed and the President implemented the establishment of a new Domestic Council and the conversion of the Bureau into the Office of Management and Budget.

All these developments point to, but do not prove, a slippage in the perceived ability of the Bureau to discharge the functions it had acquired over the past half century. Of course, the decline of the Bureau may be a case in which expectations and demands—both of which climbed sharply in the 1960's—rose faster than performance, rather than an outright drop in competence. Yet perceptions of inadequacy can be every bit as damaging as objective measures of performance. Furthermore, the inadequacy of the Bureau must be seen in terms of its presidential mission. Perhaps the Bureau merited its reputation as the best-informed institution in Washington, and one indispensable to the President, but this does not mean that in terms of presidential requirements it was good enough or as good as it once had been. Finally, the reader will be misguided if he interprets "inadequate" to mean "unsuccessful." By most measures, the Bureau continued to be successful in its last years. Whether or not it was adequate is the concern of this article.

---

[3] The recommendations of the Heineman Task Force (named after its chairman, Ben Heineman) have never been made public, and no action was taken on them by President Johnson.

[4] *See* United States Bureau of the Budget, The Work of the Steering Group on Evaluation of the Bureau of the Budget, A Staff Summary (1967) [hereinafter cited as Steering Group].

I

THE USES OF THE BUDGET BUREAU

During its existence, the Bureau was successful when it possessed a near monopoly in the exercise of a particular function deemed vital to presidential interests. This condition prevailed during the early years of the Bureau when it served as an instrument of presidential control over agency spending, and during later periods when the Bureau gained pre-eminence in administrative management and legislative clearance. In recent times, however, the Bureau lost its role as a unique supplier of presidential services and its functions no longer were as germane to the President as they once had been. To understand why and in what sense the Bureau was eclipsed, it is necessary to look at its several major functions in terms of their utility to the President and the position of the Bureau vis-à-vis other performers of the same functions. This rise and decline of the Bureau pertains to the three key roles it has played: central control of federal spending, leadership in administrative management, and program planning for the President. In terms of all three of these functions, the Bureau was less effectively positioned in the 1960's than it had been during earlier periods.

A. The Use of the Budget Power

The Budget Bureau always exercised a virtual monopoly as the central budget review agency of the federal government. It seldom possessed exclusive use of that power because from time to time other presidental staffs intervened in the budget process, sometimes even overriding the judgments and procedures of the Bureau. Nevertheless, central budget review for the President was the number one aim in the creation of the Bureau and this function always was the core of its power. Yet the function was put to different uses by the nine Presidents served by the Bureau. While no President can afford to ignore or withdraw from the budget process, budgeting has become less useful to the President than it once was. In fact, the budget process tends to operate as a constraint on presidential power rather than as an opportunity for the development and assertion of presidential policies and priorities. Accordingly, contemporary Presidents may find it to their advantage to spend comparatively little time on budget matters and to insulate themselves from the process. In preparation of his 1971 budget, President Nixon is reported to have invested approximately 40 hours and to have been displeased by what he regarded as an unproductive use of so much of his time. Among the changes wrought by the establishment of the Office of Management and Budget is the interposition of an additional layer between the President and the budget director and two new layers between the examinations divisions and the White House. These moves attest to the decline of the budget process as an instrument of presidential power and, concomitantly, a decline in the status of the agency which superintends that process.

From the start, the budget process was operated in a way that restricted its utility for presidential policy making. The 1921 Budget and Accounting Act did not change the manner in which agencies prepared their budgets but interposed the President and the Budget Bureau between the spending agencies and congressional committees. Just as they had for more than a century, agencies continued to prepare their estimates with freedom to ask for whatever they wanted, and without much guidance or constraint from the President. The President entered the budget process after the agencies had formulated their requests, and he was authorized to make his own spending recommendations to Congress. This division of budgetary labors gave policy initiative to the agencies and spending control to the President. As long as he was actively involved as a budget cutter and was willing to abjure a policy development role, the President was well served by a budget process and a Bureau which functioned almost exclusively as agents of spending control. This course of action was precisely the one taken by the Budget Bureau in its inaugural year under Charles Dawes and was the dominant role of the Bureau until the New Deal effected radical changes in federal programs and expenditures. Dawes dedicated the Bureau to the "routine business" of economy and efficiency, involving his small staff in the minutiae of budget execution and separating the budget routines from the policy operations of the government. Dawes understood that his new organization would succeed only if it secured presidential support by achieving its presidential mission. Without the President, the Budget Bureau "would be as dead as a locomotive without water and coal."[5] In an era when economy and efficiency were the bywords of American politics, Dawes succeeded in winning presidential support by producing immediate and deep cuts in federal spending, thereby demonstrating the utility and potency of the new budget process. Perhaps from a contemporary perspective it is difficult to comprehend a President so heavily engaged in economy and efficiency, but the 1920's were different times, and perforce, so too were the uses to which budgeting was put. However, by structuring the budget process in a way that confined the President and the Bureau to a budget-cutting role, Dawes and his successors left a legacy which to this day constrains the policy-making usefulness of the budget process.

The coming of the New Deal rendered budget-cutting secondary, and in some ways contrary, to presidential interests. At a time that the President was promoting expansionist programs, continued use of the budget process to hold down spending would have hindered the President's policy goals. Accordingly, much of the control apparatus built during the 1920's (including the Business Organization of the Government, the Coordinating Service, and the Bureau of Efficiency) fell into disuse and was dismantled. The Bureau withdrew from detailed budget execution, so that "except for apportionment, budget is regarded as a responsibility

---

[5] C. DAWES, THE FIRST YEAR OF THE BUDGET OF THE UNITED STATES, at x (1923).

of departmental and agency management."[6] The apportionment process was turned into a mechanism for the assertion of presidential policy preferences on particular matters. By impounding funds appropriated contrary to his wishes, the Bureau enabled the President to partly offset his lack of an item veto and to contravene congressional intent and bureaucratic pressures.

The abandonment of close spending control did not spell the depreciation of the Bureau as a presidential institution because it was coupled with the acquisition of new assignments, in the area of legislative clearance and administrative management, which were vital to the President and over which the Bureau held a virtual monopoly. But though these new roles enabled the Bureau to enhance its position in the Executive Office, they did not reverse the decline in the usefulness of budgeting for the President. As we have explained, except in special circumstances, the President no longer operates as the controller of agency spending. Annual increases in federal expenditures no longer are regarded as signs of impotence or inefficiency, and no stigma attaches to a President who recommends budget totals appreciably higher than the previous year's. Quite the contrary, since the New Deal a rising budget has been interpreted as evidence of vigorous presidential leadership in national affairs and of the entrance of the federal government into new responsibilities. Each year the President's budget points to spending increases as indications of the goals and accomplishments of his administration. With some exceptions (such as President Johnson's first budget for fiscal 1965), recent Presidents have centered their attention on budget totals and on a small number of program initiatives, leaving the details of the budget, including many important policy questions, to be worked out by the Budget Bureau. This limited presidential involvement has been facilitated by the enlarged role of the budget as an instrument of fiscal policy. Inasmuch as fiscal policy concerns budget aggregates, a President who gives primacy to this approach has grounds for making his overall budget decisions somewhat independently of the particular program choices and costs that constitute his budget. Thus in switching to the "full employment" definition of budgetary balance for his 1972 budget, President Nixon made some early decisions on the acceptable range of budget aggregates and he subsequently gives less attention than in the preceding year to the details of particular programs.

The withdrawal of the President from detailed superintendence of the budget process has coincided with the entrenchment of the incremental rules and strategies described by Aaron Wildavsky in *The Politics of the Budgetary Process*.[7] By means of incrementalism, budgeting has been bent to a purpose that is virtually the opposite of what was intended originally. Rather than operating as a presidential weapon against agency spending pressures, the budget process enables agencies to mobilize support for their activities and expenditures and to push for an ex-

---

[6] J. BURKHEAD, GOVERNMENT BUDGETING 354 (1956).
[7] A. WILDAVSKY, THE POLITICS OF THE BUDGETARY PROCESS (1964).

panded base. Under incremental rules, the spending base—what agencies were authorized to do and spend last year—escapes rigorous presidential or Budget Bureau scrutiny, with the consequence that the President is locked into the spending commitments made in the past, and he possesses effective control over only a small fraction of the budget. When he tries to cut the base—to eliminate the tea tasters or to reduce impacted school aid—the President often is unable to overcome congression or bureaucratic opposition. Most Presidents, therefore, have been content to accept the base (which grows from year to year) as uncontrollable. This means that a President who wants to redirect federal programs and priorities finds himself constrained by the many mandatories and pressures written into the budget, and he is tempted to work through nonbudgetary channels to achieve his program objectives. Faced with a budget that is an agglomeration of his predecessors' legacies, a President may decide to get through legislation what he cannot buy through his budget. That is, he may propose program starts with low buy-in costs as a means of evading the constraints of the budget, thereby assuring that the budget will continue to remain beyond his control in future years.

Thus the implications of incrementalism for relations between the President and the Budget Bureau were far reaching. First, the Bureau was the bearer of bad news, informing the President that most of his opportunities had been mortgaged by prior commitments or by agency spending demands. It is not surprising for the President, under such circumstances, to keep some distance between himself and his budget process. Second, the President may strive to circumvent the budget process and its constraints through his legislative program. As we will explain later, he probably will draw on the staff and skills of the Budget Bureau, but not on the Bureau as an institution. Third, the President will concentrate his interests on the spending aggregates and on select policy issues, but he will not be much concerned with the budget process or with the routines of the Bureau.

The Budget Bureau never abandoned completely its budget-cutting ethic, though it generally abided by the norms of incrementalism and only feebly cut into the spending base. Increasingly, Bureau personnel became involved in presidential policy formulation, sometimes on detail to special task forces, occasionally (as in the genesis of the antipoverty program) as forceful advocates for particular approaches. But this left the Bureau with a serious ambivalence concerning its budget role: no longer fully a budget cutter, but not quite a program planner, the budgeter had to operate under conflicting norms and pressures. PPBS and the reorganization plan which terminated the Bureau represented somewhat divergent ways of coping with this ambivalence: the former would have united budgeting and presidential program planning; the latter established separate institutions for budgeting and programming. Both approaches recognized that budgeting had lost its pivotal position for the presidency.

B. Legislative Clearance and Program Development

The second central function performed by the Bureau was program planning for the President, through the legislative clearance process and by means of ad hoc arrangements. Richard Neustadt has described how legislative clearance began modestly in the Harding Administration, but through a series of accretions became a leading mechanism for shaping the President's program. Neustadt suggests that this process gravitated to the Budget Bureau because "there are no other work-flows so compelling of decision *on a constantly recurrent basis*—except, of course, those in the budget process."[8] Neustadt's account ends during the Eisenhower years when White House staffs were small by comparison with their present size, and the Bureau was operating without a potent rival. In later years, this position was attenuated by the growth of an independent White House capability to which the Bureau became subservient.

Legislative clearance was inaugurated in the Bureau's first year simply as a means of buttressing its new spending controls. The initial regulations dealt only with legislative proposals "the effect of which would be to create a charge upon the public treasury or commit the Government to obligations which later require appropriations to meet them."[9] Until the New Deal, legislative clearance was limited to this negative use, to deter agencies from securing via legislation what they could not obtain through budgetary channels. But just as it impelled a redirection of the budget process, the New Deal broadened the scope of legislative clearance by eliminating the distinction between fiscal and nonfiscal matters and prescribing that all legislative proposals must be cleared through the Budget Bureau to determine whether they are in accord with the President's program. Significantly, the clearance machinery laid virtually dormant during the first two years of Roosevelt's Administration; "the most important legislative proposals were not submitted either to the Budget Bureau or to the National Emergency Council."[10] To have required that all legislation be cleared through the Budget Bureau undoubtedly would have slowed the flow of program proposals to Congress.

In revitalizing and expanding the clearance process, Roosevelt was reacting to the increasingly independent and uncoordinated legislative initiatives taken by the departments. Roosevelt viewed central clearance as a means of enabling his agents in the Budget Bureau to keep track of, and oppose or thwart when necessary, the many proposals sent to Congress by the departments. Thus even as he amplified its scope, Roosevelt retained the negative orientation of the clearance process. The President "intended to protect not just his budget, but his prerogatives, his freedom of action, and his choice of policies, in an era of fast-growing govern-

---

[8] Neustadt, *Presidency and Legislation; Planning the President's Program*, 34 Am. Pol. Sci. Rev. 1021 (1955).

[9] United States Bureau of the Budget, Circular 49 (Dec. 19, 1921).

[10] Pearson, *supra* note 2, at 139. The National Emergency Council was an interagency, Cabinet-level group that functioned during the early years of the New Deal and was abolished in 1939.

ment and of determined presidential leadership."[11] In fact, much of the clearance effort was devoted to enrolled bills awaiting presidential action.

The clearance process underwent further expansion during the Truman presidency when it was converted into a mechanism for the preparation of the President's legislative program. "The emphasis of central clearance had been negative; it was to be made positive. It had interpreted policies and programs where it found them; it was to help create them. It has relied on Bureau staff resources; it was to draw instead on the expanding Executive Office as a whole."[12] This enlarged process involved both the solicitation of departmental legislative proposals in conjunction with the annual call for estimates and the preparation of a comprehensive program for presentation to Congress. Legislative clearance was the the routinization of the President's leadership in program formulation, a role which was legitimized by the New Deal and retained (albeit less vigorously) by President Eisenhower when he returned the White House to the Republicans in 1952.

While the clearance process was continued in the 1960's, its scope and importance diminished significantly. The role of the Budget Bureau shrunk in consequence to the emergence of separate legislative liaison and policy staffs in the White House, and the highly routinized clearance machinery was shunted to a subordinate position. On the most important matters, the Bureau's legislative reference unit was bypassed altogether, drawn in as only one of several participants but without a lead role, or put to work under the direction of White House aides. In short, although the forms of legislative clearance remained unchanged, and Bureau personnel continued to be active in policy development, the initiative passed from the Bureau to the White House.

In Truman's time, the Bureau gained eminence in program planning and central clearance because it had no peer as the supplier of data and expertise and was eager to work in tandem with a small White House staff. The central wartime staff (the Office of War Mobilization and Reconversion) had been disbanded, the President was striving to build a record in the face of determined congressional opposition, and Budget Director James Webb liberally offered his legislative reference staff for presidential use, breaking "precedent by making his subordinates available to White House aides, on their terms, for their purposes."[13] In effect, the legislative reference group was co-opted by the White House, though it retained its official identity within the Bureau. Under President Eisenhower, the Bureau continued to maintain its pivotal position because it satisfied two needs that confronted the new inexperienced administration: "the need for facts about the past to help project decisions for the future, and the need for caution in commitments

---

[11] Neustadt, *Presidency and Legislation, The Growth of Central Clearance*, 38 AM. POL. SCI. REV. 650 (1954).

[12] *Id.* at 660.

[13] *Id.*

until homework has been done."[14] But in retaining its presidential role, "the Budget's clearance operations were dependent, now more than ever, on guidance from the President and access to him, by and through his White House aides."[15]

The clearance and program planning system which was elaborated during the 1940's and 1950's was downgraded during the 1960's. President Kennedy dismantled much of the coordination machinery established by his predecessor and he preferred to work with White House intimates on major policy issues, drawing the staff of the Bureau into the informal process as the need arose. Kennedy had his Sorensen, Johnson his Califano, and Nixon his Ehrlichman to oversee and pull together the presidential policy-making apparatus. On the basis of interviews in Washington, Robert S. Gilmour reports "the opinion is widespread that the White House has taken over from Management and Budget on legislative matters of 'any real importance.' "[16] When President Johnson's 1967 task force on government organization examined the inadequacies of the President's policy-making institutions, it proposed the creation of a new unit divorced from the legislative reference operations. And, of course, the 1970 reorganization of the Executive Office provided for a Domestic Council as the President's policy staff functioning independently of the legislative reference machinery.

Undoubtedly, the decline of the routinized clearance process was due in part to the personal styles of Presidents Kennedy and Johnson and to their preferences for working closely and informally through White House assistants. Once the new policy staffs were installed in the White House, the Bureau lost its monopoly and the leverage which it provided. Compared to the President's own men, it was difficult for the Bureau to speak authoritatively in the name of the President or to respond swiftly to the President's policy directives. But the decline in the Bureau's program planning role also was due to inherent limitations in the central clearance process. As it became entrenched in its routines, legislative clearance came to be the procedure for the disposition of the thousands of legislative items not commanding presidential attention, with the White House handling the major items and articulating the President's priorities. The programs which went through the clearance machinery were departmental programs, not the President's own initiatives. Despite its enlarged scope, legislative clearance always had been more appropriate for overseeing the departments than for formulating new programs, and it never quite outgrew the negative orientation with which it had been originated. Thus, the clearance process had not been a suitable instrument for recent Presidents who wanted to carve their own program goals independent of the departments. Moreover, the clearance process in the Bureau never was able to cope with bursts of legislative and program activity. The clearance staff always has been

---

[14] *Id.*

[15] *Id.* at 665.

[16] Robert S. Gilmour, *Central Legislative Clearance: A Revised Perspective*, 31 PUB. AD. REV. 156 (1971).

too small—about a dozen professionals—to monitor the congressional hopper and also formulate policies for the President.

Even during the heyday of legislative clearance, there had been some questioning of the Bureau's capability to function as the President's policy arm. Arthur Maass in a 1953 article pointed to potential conflicts between the staff's and the client's perspectives and he called for the establishment of a new presidential unit that would not be bound to the traditions and limitations of the Bureau. While this proposal was not realized until 1970, it received informal recognition in buildup of the White House staff in the 1960's. The 1947 precedent of detailing Bureau personnel to White House assignments became the standard operating procedure of the 1960's. However, the result was the demoralization, and possibly also the debilitation, of the Bureau as an institution. By the close of the decade, it was generally recognized by observers of the presidency that the central policy machinery was in need of repair; frenetic improvisations were no substitute for careful policy research and follow-through on program initiatives.

C. Administrative Management

Leadership in administrative improvement was conferred upon the Bureau by section 209 of the Budget and Accounting Act of 1921, but it was only with the issuance of Executive Order 8248 in 1939 and the rapid expansion of its staff that the Bureau actively assumed this role.[17] A Division of Administrative Management was formed, and it attracted some of the best young talent in public administration, including a number of persons who were to become postwar leaders in American political science. In 1943, a field service was added to carry the ideology and methods of administrative reform to federal operations across the country. At its peak, Administrative Management was the second largest unit in the Bureau, and it functioned as an in-house consulting service for the federal bureaucracy. The Division conducted hundreds of administrative surveys and it aided the War Department to convert from a peacetime to a wartime footing. According to contemporary accounts, the Bureau's work in administrative management was perhaps the main factor in the Bureau's prominence during its first years in the Executive Office.[18]

The Bureau came to leadership in administrative management with a big headstart over all other presidential agencies. "Of the entire President's office, only the Budget Bureau had any sort of detailed knowledge of federal organiza-

---

[17] Executive Order 8248 directed the Budget Bureau "to keep the President informed of the progress of activities by agencies of the Government with respect to work proposed, work actually initiated, and work completed, together with the relative timing of work between the several agencies of the Government; all to the end that the work programs of the several agencies of the executive branch of the Government may be coordinated and that the monies appropriated by the Congress may be expended in the most economical manner possible to prevent overlapping and duplication of effort." Exec. Order No. 8248, 3 C.F.R. 217 (Supp. 1939).

[18] See Marx, supra note 2, at 887-92.

tion."[19] The Bureau also enjoyed a favored position vis-à-vis most federal departments which (with some notable exceptions such as Agriculture) did not yet possess management staffs of their own and were willing to turn to the Bureau for advice and guidance. The entrance of the Bureau into administrative management came at a most opportune time. The program development phase of the New Deal had ended and left in its wake a sprawl of new and vastly expanded federal agencies. There was a need for administrative improvement comparable to the program innovations that had been made. By 1937, Roosevelt sensed that the task at hand was to make the new programs work, and to work well, and to provide presidential leadership in the management of the federal establishment. He set up the President's Committee on Administrative Management and its recommendations led to the creation of the Executive Office and the expanded role of the Budget Bureau. "The administrative research functions," it reported, "are practically undeveloped; it is in this respect that the Bureau has missed its greatest opportunity."[20] The new emphasis on administrative management was in accord with the orientation of Budget Director Harold Smith who frequently spoke and wrote of the Bureau from a management point of view.[21] The rise of administrative management also was abetted by the release of the budget process from the control orientation which had prevailed earlier and by the ability of the Bureau to multiply its staff (from 45 when the President's Committee reported to 564 only seven years later). Finally, the rise of administrative management came at a time when public administration was at a peak in the United States, and the Bureau effectively cashed in on this prominence.

The decline of administrative management occurred over a period of years and was not the consequence of any particular event. After World War II, administrative management was downgraded in the Bureau, and the authorized strength of this Division was cut sharply. In 1952, as part of a general reorganization of the Bureau, the Division was replaced by an Office of Management and Organization, and in the following year the field service was terminated. Increasingly, the President turned to alternative organizations, such as the two Hoover Commissions, for overall leadership in administrative reform and to handle major reorganizations, while the Bureau was consigned routine administrative matters of low presidential concern. Federal agencies began to develop their own management staffs and they had less need for the Bureau's services. In addition the growing numbers of management consulting firms were competitors to the Bureau, and most agencies apparently preferred to go outside to supplement their own resources. Of considerable relevance to the decline of administrative manage-

---

[19] Pearson, *supra* note 2.

[20] PRESIDENT'S COMMITTEE ON ADMINISTRATIVE MANAGEMENT, REPORT WITH SPECIAL STUDIES 16 (1937) [hereinafter cited as PRESIDENT'S COMMITTEE].

[21] A number of Mr. Smith's articles and addresses were published in H. SMITH, THE MANAGEMENT OF YOUR GOVERNMENT (1945).

ment was the postwar shift in public administration from a reformist discipline beholden to the norms of efficiency and committed to the improvement of government operations to a diffuse field in search of new scientific foundations. Many public administrators came away from their wartime experiences rejecting the administrative dogmas that had been handed down to them, and disengagement from practical administrative affairs became a widespread means of accommodation to their own uncertainties. The net effect was to sever administrative management from the discipline in which it had been molded.

As the traditional concerns of administrative management receded from presidential attention, the administrative experts in the Bureau were left without a White House interest in their services. Meanwhile, the Bureau did not successfully make the transition to the new administrative problems that were reaching the President's desk. These pertained to the management of programs cutting across departmental and governmental lines. Here was an area in need of coordination for none of the provisional coordinating mechanisms set up by the President (the Office of Emergency Planning, and the Vice-President's office in the intergovernmental field; lead and convenor machinery in the interdepartmental field) were doing the job well enough. Nor was the Bureau. It was impeded by several factors: its own inability to reorient the Office of Management and Organization; Congressional rejection of attempts to re-establish a field service; the reluctance of agencies to solicit or bow to intervention by the Bureau; and the high political stakes inherent in interdepartmental and intergovernmental problem solving.

By the middle of the 1960's, the administrative management group was, in the words of a working paper prepared for the Bureau's 1967 self-study, "A depressed area . . . which has been looking too long at the same problems and has gone stale."[22] The Steering Group found that the Bureau had difficulty in obtaining and retaining capable management personnel, and that "agencies have moved well ahead of the Bureau in organization and management and new developments have not come from the Bureau." The chief aim of the subsequent reorganization of the Bureau was to revitalize its capacity to deal with intergovernmental and interdepartmental problems. An Office of Executive Management was formed, old-time management people were encouraged to leave, and new men were brought in. Creation of the Office of Management and Budget (as the name suggests) is a further effort to restore the Bureau to leadership in administrative management.

Thus, at the time of its demise, the Bureau had lost its presidential position in the three major functions it had previously acquired. Of course, many other functions had gravitated to the Bureau over the years. Of these, two warrant brief comment. Under the Federal Reports Act of 1942, the Bureau had the potential

---

[22] This and all subsequent quotes that are not attributed to source are from the unpublished minutes and working papers of the Steering Group. These documents are held in the Library of the Office of Management and Budget.

to become not only the clearinghouse for forms and surveys issued by federal agencies but also the overseer of the information systems operated by the agencies. The Bureau never sought to achieve this potential, and it settled for a narrow role in statistical policy that was peripheral to its broader budgetary and management functions. The second function—fiscal policy—was born in the early years of the Keynesian Revolution when the Bureau established a small fiscal analysis unit that had the potential to become one of its most vital operations. However, this potential died on the vine with the transfer of fiscal analysis to the new Council of Economic Advisors in 1946.

Charged with many functions, some of which were at cross purposes and none of which commanded the highest presidential attention, the Budget Bureau became a clustering of hard-working and reasonably well-informed individuals struggling to accommodate their many assignments and diversions to the inelasticities of the clock and calendar. Individually, Bureau personnel often performed brilliantly, but the Bureau lacked a "clear sense of purpose and direction"; its staff was "not pulling together."

II

THE BUREAU AS A PRESIDENTIAL INSTITUTION

Shortly after he was appointed the first budget director, Charles Dawes recorded in his diary that he had once told the President: "if I could take any office I would not want the position of Secretary of the Treasury, but that of an assistant secretary to the President."[23] During his one-year stint as director, Dawes constantly kept this preferred role uppermost in his mind as he carefully laid precedents for perpetuating the Bureau as a presidential institution. Although the Bureau was lodged in the Treasury Department, Dawes fostered the myth that it operated solely "by direction of the President." Dawes' conception of the Bureau and its director were shared by President Roosevelt's Committee on Administrative Management. The Committee rejected the recommendation of A. E. Buck, its eminent consultant on budgeting, that the Bureau be made an integral portion of the Treasury Department in order that there be a single agency with full responsibility for the financial policies of the national government. The astute members of the Committee preceived that far greater than the need for fiscal coordination was the need for a presidential agency with comprehensive superintendence over federal administration. Accordingly it urged that the Bureau be restructured "to serve in various ways as the agent of the President," and that the budget director "be relieved to the greatest possible extent from the minor details of administration. He should be released for duties of maximum importance to the President."[24]

---

[23] C. DAWES, *supra* note 5, at 46.
[24] PRESIDENT'S COMMITTEE, *supra* note 20, at 17.

By the mid-1960's, the conception of the budget director's role held by Dawes and the President's Committee had been realized, but not their conception of the presidential mission of the Bureau. "In recent years, the director has become more and more a White House assistant," a finding which was supported by the steering group's research. Between 1962 and 1966, the portion of the items signed by the director that went to the President nearly doubled, from twenty to thirty-eight per cent. In terms of workload, the volume of correspondence to the President shot up from 293 items in 1962 to 642 items just four years later.[25] Wearing his second hat, the director pulled other Budget men into the frenzy of presidential policy-making, but this role laid bare one inadequacy of the Bureau and gave rise to another. It revealed the unpreparedness of the Bureau to serve as a presidential institution, and it barred the director from giving adequate attention to the management of his own organization.

The unpublished minutes and papers of the steering group candidly discussed the Bureau's infirmity to perform in a presidential role. The Bureau was inhibited by its traditional style, "the doctrine that the Bureau serves an abstraction called the 'Presidency' rather than individual Presidents." Many staff members resisted their intensive contacts with White House operators "as not being in keeping with the traditions and professionalism of the Bureau." The failure of the Bureau to tool up for a presidential role placed "an inordinate burden on the director. He has no institutionalized resources to which he can turn. He finds himself spending a great deal of time handling specific requests [from the White House] and in integrating the various pieces of information from inside and outside the Bureau."

The Bureau's failure to orient itself to the service of the President was due largely to its institutional status. As it became the institutionalized presidency, the Bureau became separated from the President. With a 500-man complement, the Bureau was just too large and too remote to be the President's own. It had so many things to do of middling or low presidential concern, and though he could impress Bureau men into his service for short-term projects, the President could not get the Bureau to assign its staff to full-time presidential work. William Carey who saw the White House from his position as Assistant Director of the Budget writes:

> Lyndon Johnson spent the better part of a year badgering the Budget Director to assign "five of the best men you have" to drag advance information out of the agencies about impending decisions and actions . . . but the Budget Bureau never came anywhere near satisfying him because its own radar system was not tuned finely enough.[26]

An institutionalized Bureau could serve every President with fidelity, but it

---

[25] STEERING GROUP, *supra* note 4, at 3-3, and working papers prepared for the Steering Group.
[26] Carey, *Presidential Staffing in the Sixties and Seventies*, 29 PUB. AD. REV. 453 (1969).

could effectively serve only a caretaker President. It could not be quick or responsive enough for an activist President who wants to keep a tight hold over program initiatives. The Bureau had "a negative, critical style, rather than a positive, creative one"; many old-timers who had internalized the norms of spending control could not adjust to the "go-go" posture of the New Frontier and Great Society. Over a period of decades, the Bureau had become a rigidified institution, suffering from what Herbert Kaufman has termed the "natural history of organizations." The routines of budgeting and legislative clearance, to mention only the two most important ones, had been solidified by years of tradition-building and practice, and were not easily changeable. It was a labyrinthian task to make even minor modifications in the procedures for budget preparation and review, and in fact, few changes were made in this process pursuant to PPBS.

The President could not combat these ridigities through his power of appointment or by taking advantage of staff turnover within the Bureau. President Harding had made the Bureau his own by creating an entirely new organization; FDR accomplished almost the same thing by multiplying the Bureau's staff tenfold. In the 1960's, an incoming President had authority to appoint a handful of the Bureau policy-leaders and by tradition most of these (the deputy director, some of the assistant directors, and the division chiefs) came up through the ranks rather than from outside. Nor could the President depend on ordinary attrition to free slots for new men. Contrary to popular impression, there was considerable immobility in the Bureau, especially in its upper ranks. Fully two-thirds of the supervisory officials had been in the Bureau sixteen years or longer,[27] a statistic that suggests the difficulty of remaking the Bureau in the President's image.

The capability of the Bureau to function effectively in a presidential role was impaired by the close identification of many examiners with the agencies they were assigned to review. There are strong incentives for examiners to maintain favorable relations with their agencies; they depend on the agencies for a steady flow of data, as well as for judgments on the value of particular programs. While their contacts with White House staff are sporadic and often curt, examiners have continuing, personal contacts with their agency counterparts. The examiners are well-informed on the wants and preferences of their agencies; often they must work without specific policy guidance from the President's men. Examiners frequently hold the same agency assignments for a number of years and are called upon to review the very programs they once had a hand in formulating. Career advancement for many examiners is via transfer to agencies with which favorable relations had been forged. While outright sweetheart relations are rare, many examiners are forceful protectors of their agencies' interests. When PPBS was started, they protected the agencies against efforts by analysts to probe more rigorously into the worthwhileness of federal programs. And they regularly protected

---

[27] STEERING GROUP, *supra* note 4, at 6-4.

their agencies during Director's Review (conducted by the Bureau at which final sub-presidential decisions are made) which is structured as a sort of adversary confrontation between the examinations divisions which defend their budget recommendations and the budget director who presides as the guardian of the President's interests.

The conversion of the budget director into a White House assistant and the failure of the examiners to manifest a presidential perspective engendered serious problems in the management of the Bureau. In the words of the Steering Group,

> the quality and individual competence of budget directors . . . has been so great that Bureau stature in the view of the President and Congress probably never has been higher. Paradoxically, the institution has suffered internally because of inattention to day-to-day management.

The cost of prolonged inattention to the management of the Bureau was manifold. Because there was no one short of the director (and his deputy) to tend to the operations of the Bureau, the staff often had to work without adequate or timely feedback and without guidance from above. The morale of the Bureau suffered, and so did its capability to respond to presidential needs. Another problem was the difficulty of effectuating changes in the Bureau without active support and direction from the top. Had the director been able to give attention to the implications of PPBS for his own agency and to the modifications that should have been made in budget practices, PPBS would have had a much better chance for success. But although the director was committed to the principles of PPBS, he was able to apply only minimal pressure on the examinations divisions, and he never took the necessary steps to tool up the Bureau for PPBS. The result was that the Bureau required more PPBS material from the departments than it could handle, and the departments readily perceived that the Bureau was not practicing what it was preaching.

Perhaps the most costly problem was the inability of the director to transfer his presidential role to the Bureau as a whole. In his service to the President, the director was divorced from his staff, and much of the Bureau's presidential work was done with only limited utilization of the staff. By giving attention to internal management, the director might have been able to harness the Bureau more effectively to a presidential mission, but that might have rendered him less available to advise the President.

The 1967 Steering Group proposed to remedy these problems by: (1) establishing a new high-level position for internal management; (2) bringing the assistant directors into managerial roles; and (3) delegating a greater portion of the workload to the divisions. The 1970 reorganization went a big step further. In effect, it severed the director of the Office of Management and Budget from the daily operations of his agency. The director is available to serve as a presidential advisor (his office is in the White House) and to draw on the resources of OMB as the need arises. He has two deputies to handle the management and budget components of this new conglomerate, and he does not preside at Director's Review of the Budget.

Despite the difficulties of maintaining itself as a presidential agency, the Bureau has wanted to hold on to that role. Power, status, and tradition have something to do with this obstinance, but also the conviction that the Bureau is best suited to serve the President. Thus from the report of the Steering Committee: "The Bureau is the only office to which the President and the White House Staff can turn for a composite perspective and Government-wide substantive knowledge of operating programs," and, "The Bureau is the only Executive Office which provides the White House on [sic] across-the-board familiarity with Federal programs."[28] The effectiveness with which this case can be made depends on whether the President has alternatives to the Bureau. In 1967, he did not; today he does.

III

THE PRESIDENT GETS HELP

The President has much more help than he had thirty-five years ago when the Brownlow Committee thought that he could be sufficiently served by six assistants with a passion for anonymity. Yet the President still needs help, not merely additional assistants, but new institutions to get the job done.

It is worth considering why the burdens of the President have so far outgrown the resources he already commands. The answer comes in three parts pertaining to the policy role of the President, his relations with the executive departments, and the intergovernmental character of many federal programs.

A. Policy Leadership

Over the past four decades, the role of the President in program planning has become institutionalized, but he has not acquired additional resources commensurate with this expanded responsibility. At first, he was adequately served by the Bureau's central clearance machinery, then he added staff to the White House, and in the 1960's he relied on close associates and special task forces.[29] In terms of legislative productivity, the ad hoc arrangements seemed to be effective, with Congress enacting record numbers of new programs in 1964 and 1965. Paradoxically, however, the Great Society left in its wake the widespread belief that the central policy machinery of the federal government was in disrepair. The new programs had barely begun and they were already stirring a host of operational problems that pointed to deficiencies in design and execution. White House and Budget Bureau insiders perceived that they had failed to look far enough to the future or to relate their plans to the realities of program implementation. Alternatives had not been carefully examined; cost and effectiveness had not been accurate-

---

[28] *Id.* at 1-9, 3-4.
[29] *See* Thomas & Wolman, *The Presidency and Policy Formulation: The Task Force Device*, 29 PUB. AD. REV. 459 (1969).

ly calculated. Brain-storming might have been an appropriate method for gathering a bushelful of legislative proposals, but it could not substitute for thorough policy analysis. William Carey stated the problem candidly:

> The Presidency is in trouble on several counts. Its policy analysis resources are shallow and improvised. Its planning capabilities are overstrained. It has no built-in facility for assessing changing social trends and revising priorities.[30]

In recent years, there have been countless proposals for some new presidential policy staff. In a paper prepared for President Johnson's Task Force on Government Organization, Rufus Miles called for an "Office of Policy Studies" to do the advance intelligence work for the President. The Task Force itself proposed a new program development unit within the Budget Bureau. President Nixon created a Domestic Council within the White House Office to direct program planning for the President. It is difficult to weigh the portent of the Domestic Council for the Office of Management and Budget. On paper, OMB has been cut off from the policy-making business. President Nixon's reorganization message stipulated a clear division of labor between the Council and OMB:

> The Domestic Council will be primarily concerned with *what* we do; the office of Management and Budget will be primarily concerned with *how* we do it and how *well* we do it.[31]

If the words mean what they say, the President declared that the successor to the Bureau of the Budget could not overcome the limitations on a policy role that had beset the Bureau, and he therefore had to seek relief in an entirely new body.

Immediately after the reorganization was cleared through (or more accurately, not vetoed by) Congress, journalists began to weave speculations centering around the likelihood that John Ehrlichman would become the czar of federal domestic policy, assuming a position comparable to Henry Kissinger's in the national security field. But the appointment of George Schultz as director of the Office of Management and Budget altered the prospects substantially. Ehrlichman's Domestic Council has not grown to its predicted staff size and Schultz seems to be at least his coequal in matters of presidential policy making. Schultz, however, has disengaged himself from the daily operations of OMB. Though he had the final say on most budget appeals from the agencies, it is too early to ascertain whether the rank he has achieved in the presidential firmament will extend to his underlings in Management and Budget. It is possible that if Schultz gains in White House stature, the bearers of the Budget Bureau's tradition will suffer still further decline.

B. Operational Leadership

The second problem area for the President has been program coordination. In

---

[30] Carey, *supra* note 26, at 457.

[31] Reorganization Message of President Richard Nixon to Congress, Mar. 12, 1970 [hereinafter referred to as Reorganization Message].

recent times, the job of the President grew so burdensome because he could not—or did not want to—rely on his departments. Operational matters which might have been settled at departmental levels were taken over by White House intervenors who were impatient for results and distrusted the slow-moving bureaucracy. Two reasons can be offered for the intervention of White House men in what otherwise might have been handled by the departments themselves. First, the federal government was faced with an increasing amount of interdepartmental business. The simple matter of placing a single-stop service center in a neighborhood involved the participation of three or more federal agencies. Second, in the eyes of White House operators, the departments could not be trusted to do the job themselves. The head of a department was beholden to his own bureaucracy and could not function as a loyal agent of the President. The authors of a 1960 study put it this way: "Operations are too important to be left entirely to the executive agencies."[32]

The notion that the agencies cannot be trusted is not shared by many who have seen the government from a departmental perspective. Robert Wood who frequently felt the heavy hand of Budget Bureau and White House intervention during his years near and at the top of HUD points to problems created by an unwillingness to let the agencies do the job: "Decisions tend to be reviewed and reviewed; and operational delays increase accordingly. . . . Operational matters flow to the top—as central staffs become engrossed in subduing outlying bureaucracies—and policy-making emerges at the bottom."[33] Wood proposes to relieve the presidency of its unnecessary burden by restoring department heads to positions of operational leadership in their respective jurisdictions. He argues that secretaries could be the President's men if only they were not hamstrung by other men who claim exclusive right to speak in the name of the President. Wood foresees department heads modeled along the McNamara pattern. The stronger they are allowed to become, the more they will be independent of their own bureaucracies, and the more capable therefore to serve the President.

Wood's version of departmental leadership is embodied in one aspect of the 1970 reorganization, but rejected in two others. The Domestic Council is a Cabinet-level body capable of representing the views of the departments to the President and of superintending the execution of presidential policy. This feature of the Domestic Council was highlighted by President Nixon in his reorganization message. The President took the position that establishment of the Council would mean more delegation of authority to the departments. The Domestic Council "will provide a structure through which departmental initiatives can be more fully considered, and expert advice from the departments and agencies more fully utilized."[34]

---

[32] J. COFFEY & V. ROCK, THE PRESIDENTIAL STAFF 77 (1960).
[33] Wood, *When Government Works*, THE PUBLIC INTEREST, Winter, 1970, 39, 42.
[34] Reorganization Message, *supra* note 31.

There are other features to the reorganization plan, however, that portend continuing intervention. First, the Domestic Council can go the way of the National Security Council and supersede the departments in their own spheres of operations. Thus far, this has not happened, partly because Ehrlichman has not built up his staff to the large size anticipated at the time of reorganization. But the potential is there for the President to seize should he become dissatisfied with the operational performance of the departments. Second, the Office of Management and Budget has been given an expanded mandate to operate as program coordinator. Here, too, additional staff is a prerequisite for full assumption of the power, but there are preliminary indications that OMB men have increased their intervention in departmental affairs.

C. Intergovernmental Leadership

A third presidential burden derives from the growth of the federal role in intergovernmental affairs. The legacy of the Great Society was several hundred additional grant-in-aid programs, and the attendant difficulties of meshing together the disjointed activities of Washington, the states, and the local governments. The President has been drawn into the intergovernmental thicket for the same reason that he has become involved in interdepartmental matters; no single department has full jurisdiction and the President cannot rely on the departments for effective program delivery. An additional factor operates in the intergovernmental sphere; the President must deal with political leaders who are not always willing to accept the decisions of the President's administrative subordinates in the executive departments.

Unless there is a massive scaling down of federal grants programs or a shift to unrestricted grants, the prospects are for an escalation of presidential attention to the relations between federal agencies and inferior political jurisdictions. Both the Domestic Council and the Office of Management and Budget have stand-by capability for intervention in particular instances when the President wishes to assert his presence and for protracted monitoring of stubborn intergovernmental issues. We can expect "flying feds" to play trouble-shooting roles in behalf of the President and to overleap departments in the negotiation of intergovernmental bargains.

IV

AULD LANG SYNE

The Budget Bureau that was is not the Office of Management and Budget that will be. OMB will not be able to match its predecessor's position because it does not possess the monopoly held by the Budget Bureau over key presidential functions. The Domestic Council, however varied its experience will be under different Presidents, will be a rival of Management and Budget for all of the great functions once housed in the Bureau. However, this does not mean that OMB should be written off as a major instrument of the Presidency. To be sure, the Bureau was downgraded by the 1970 reorganization, and the budget component of OMB was diminished in relation to the management work. But Management and Budget still will possess the longest institutional memory in the President's office and all future Presidents will rely on it for a variety of important chores.

To future historians, the Budget Bureau will have been another chapter in the story of the presidency. But perhaps we should bid farewell to the Bureau with the words of William Carey:

> If this is to be the year of lighting for the Domestic Council, it ought not be the year of eclipse for the Bureau of the Budget, because we will not see its like again.[35]

---

[35] Carey, *Reorganization Plan No. 2*, 30 PUB. AD. REV. 634 (1970).

PRESIDENTIAL ADVICE AND INFORMATION: POLICY AND PROGRAM FORMULATION

Norman C. Thomas*

The "Hickel letter" incident of May, 1970, occurring in the context of the movement of American forces into Cambodia and the campus crises that precipitated and followed the killing of four Kent State University students by National Guard troops, raised in dramatic fashion the questions that are asked about every national administration in time of trouble. "Who sees the President?" "To whom does he listen?" "Is the President isolated?" "What are his sources and means of obtaining information?" Although not nearly so widely publicized, similar and related questions concerned the members of two subcommittees of the House of Representatives as they conducted hearings in the Spring of 1970 on presidential advisory committees and on President Nixon's proposed Reorganization Plan No. 2 of 1970, to restructure significantly the Executive Office of the President.[1] These concerns reflect the general recognition among observers of and participants in high level national politics that responsive presidential policy leadership is as dependent upon the formal and informal processes whereby the President obtains advice and information as it is upon his personal characteristics such as political style and tactics. Academicians have understood the institutional as well as the personal dimension of presidential leadership for some time,[2] but it often tends to be overlooked by sophisticated observers and is not recognized by the public. Undoubtedly, this condition exists because of the extent to which the mass media have personalized politics and, more importantly, because personal traits and characteristics have always offered simpler and more visible explanations of presidential behavior. It is easier for the analyst to develop and for the public to understand explanations that focus on the individual who occupies the White House than it is to wrestle with the complex questions of where ideas come from and how they are translated into policies that lead to operating programs of action.[3]

---

* Professor of Political Science, Duke University; Author, CONGRESS: POLITICS AND PRACTICE (1964); RULE 9: POLITICS, ADMINISTRATION, AND CIVIL RIGHTS (1966).

[1] Hearings on Presidential Advisory Committees Before the Subcomm. of the House Comm. on Government Operations, 91st Cong., 2d Sess. (Mar. 12, 17, 19, 1970) [hereinafter cited as Presidential Advisory Committees]; Hearings on Reorganization Plan No. 2 Before the Subcomm. of the House Comm. on Government Operations, 91st Cong., 2d Sess. (Apr. 28, 30 & May 5, 1970) [hereinafter cited as Reorganization Plan No. 2].

[2] See, e.g., P. APPLEBY, POLICY AND ADMINISTRATION 113 (1949); Seligman, Developments in the Presidency and the Conception of Political Leadership, 20 AM. SOCIO. REV. 706 (1955); Seligman, Presidential Leadership: The Inner Circle and Institutionalization, 18 J. POL. 410 (1956); J. BURNS, PRESIDENTIAL GOVERNMENT ch. IV (1965); Cronin & Greenberg, Introduction to THE PRESIDENTIAL ADVISORY SYSTEM xii-xx (T. Cronin & S. Greenberg eds. 1969).

[3] Cf. Cronin & Greenberg, supra note 2, at xic; Yarmolinsky, Ideas into Programs, THE PUBLIC INTEREST, Winter 1966, at 70.

In this paper I will examine the formal and informal advisory and informational devices that modern Presidents employ in the formulation of policies and programs.[4] My primary concern is with information inputs to presidential decision-making processes and with the conversion of those inputs to policy choices. The questions that will guide the analysis include: (1) What are the President's major sources of information and advice? (2) What kinds of people tend to become presidential advisors? (3) What are the limitations of the various advisory mechanisms? (4) What are the advantages of the different mechanisms? (5) What kinds of relationships exist between the President and his advisory system? (6) What are the characteristics of a viable advisory system? (7) What trends and developments are emerging in the patterns of advising, informing, and assisting the President with respect to his policy-making responsibilities?

I

PRESIDENTIAL COUNSELLING: AN OVERVIEW

A. Staffing the Presidency

Since the late 1930's, Presidents, their principal assistants, and students of the presidency have regarded as axiomatic the presidential dependence on advice and information and the need for assistance in securing and utilizing them. The Brownlow Committee Report of 1937, the Reorganization Act of 1939 which established the Executive Office of the President, the Employment Act of 1946 which created the Council of Economic Advisers, the reports of the two Hoover Commissions in 1949 and 1955, the development of an elaborate formal staff under President Eisen- however, the use of informal and *ad hoc* study groups, task forces, and committees by Presidents Kennedy and Johnson, and, most recently, President Nixon's creation of the Domestic Council are manifestations of the continuing effort to respond to the presidential need for assistance. That effort is often referred to in governmental circles as "staffing" while academically it has been encompassed within the broader and more ambiguous term "institutionalization."

According to William D. Carey, a former Assistant Director of the Budget who spent 25 years with the Bureau of the Budget, staffing should assist the President with respect to policy analysis, communications, outreach, and command and control.[5] In the process of policy and program formulation as distinguished from implementation,[6] policy analysis, communication, and outreach are of more direct importance than

---

[4] Thomas E. Cronin, in his contribution to this symposium, explores the exchange system that the President relies upon for the implementation and monitoring of programs.

[5] Carey, *Presidential Staffing in the Sixties and Seventies*, 29 PUB. AD. REV. 450 (1969).

[6] The distinction between formulation and implementation made in this symposium is one of convenience rather than theoretical conviction. It is not my intention to reinstitute the ancient politics-administration dichotomy. There is quite obviously a continual overlapping of formulative and implementing actions in all policy areas as events move in parallel as well as in series with continual feedback from prior actions affecting future decisions. But there does exist a temporal sequence in presidential policy leadership and I have chosen to recognize it in order to deal more extensively with the subject and,

the operational problems of command and control that lie at the center of policy implementation. Staffing for policy and program formulation has varied from the Roosevelt to the Nixon Administrations along a continuum of structural formality ranging from the elaborate staff arrangements favored by President Eisenhower to the free-wheeling administrative chaos that characterized the early years of the New Deal under President Roosevelt.[7] The determination of an administration's position on that continuum is a matter of subjective judgment that rests on several factors: the President's desire to innovate; the frequency and duration of policy crises; the necessity and desire for secrecy in presidential decision-making; the President's leadership style; the President's personal relations with his immediate staff, his principal subordinates, and congressional leaders; the President's administrative orientation—his preference for systematized or random procedures, written memoranda or oral briefs, etc.; and the President's priority ranking among the great quantity of matters pressing on him for attention.

While I have not attempted to operationalize these factors so as to permit a quantitative measurement of recent presidential administrations, I will explore qualitatively their possible relationships with the degree of structural formality that might be anticipated in the presidency. It seems quite apparent that a President seeking to develop new policy departures will tend to prefer flexible staffing arrangements. This was the case with Presidents Roosevelt, Kennedy, and Johnson, all of whom were innovation-minded, but not with Eisenhower or Nixon, who both tended to favor improvement and refinement (some might say consolidation) of existing policies and programs.[8] The President who seeks to change policies more than incrementally finds it helpful and necessary to obtain a steady flow of ideas, suggestions, and information from a wide range of sources outside as well as within the government.[9] His emphasis is likely to be more on the scope and variety rather than the precision and detail of his policy intelligence. He is more apt to run the risk that his decisions may be based on less than a comprehensive analysis of the situation than to risk missing a promising new proposal that could lead to a breakthrough. However, the costs of the structural flexibility required by an innovative President can be substantial in terms of the lack of coordinated effort and the erosion of policy control. Activist Presidents have tolerated chaotic advisory

---

secondly, to distinguish more clearly between the types of advice and information sought, the sources of such knowledge, and the uses made of it in the principal stages of the presidential policy process.

[7] See R. NEUSTADT, PRESIDENTIAL POWER (1960); A. SCHLESINGER, JR., THE COMING OF THE NEW DEAL chs. 32-33 (1959); K. CLARK & L. LEGERE, THE PRESIDENT AND THE MANAGEMENT OF NATIONAL SECURITY (1969); Neustadt, *Approaches to Staffing the Presidency: Notes on FDR and JFK*, 57 AM. POL. SCI. REV. 855 (1963).

[8] I am aware of the innovativeness of the Family Assistance Program that President Nixon proposed in 1969. The major domestic policy orientation of the Nixon Administration is not activist, however. At most it can be characterized as mildly reformist or restorative.

[9] For a discussion of President Johnson's efforts to expand the sources of policy proposals beyond the traditional devices of agency submissions and clientele group suggestions see Leuchtenberg, *The Genesis of the Great Society*, THE REPORTER, April 21, 1966, at 36-39; Thomas & Wolman, *The Presidency and Policy Formulation: The Task Force Device*, 29 PUB. AD. REV. 459 (1969).

processes and have often received sloppy if not shoddy advice.[10] Policy crises can also affect staffing arrangements. A low incidence and short duration of crises tends to favor the growth of formalized staffing. As long as information can be obtained and processed routinely, formal arrangements can serve the President quite effectively. Crisis conditions, however, have a way of forcing the development of special temporary devices to deal with the particular situation.[11] Information is needed quickly; there is no time for carefully prepared analyses embodied in position papers. Persons not normally in the formal policy-making structure may be needed for advice and consultation. The pace of events is so rapid that decisions must be reached without the usual process of checking and approval. These and similar considerations lead to flexible staffing arrangements. Of course, recurrent crises are now a fact of our national political life,—"emergencies in policy with politics as usual," Neustadt wrote over ten years ago[12]—and to a degree they can be handled through predetermined routines. But to the extent that each crisis presents a unique threat to the nation and to the President it will call forth a special set of arrangements to deal with it. The more crises that arise, the more the President will require flexible devices to meet them.

Staffing arrangements are also a product of presidential personality and temperament. A President who has a penchant for secrecy and surprise, like Johnson or Roosevelt, finds flexible arrangements much more suitable than formal ones. Also, some Presidents—e.g., Roosevelt and Kennedy—are more free wheeling and less bureaucratically oriented than others in their approach to administrative tasks.

Finally, to the extent that national security policy matters intrude upon domestic politics formal staffing arrangements tend to be favored over informal. The handling of national security policy lends itself more readily to systematic intelligence gathering and evaluation and to structured decision-making than do domestic affairs. The opportunity for internal maneuvering and bargaining is greatly reduced in situations affecting national security. The need for consensus behind the President's course of action is a powerful stimulus to close ranks. This facilitates formalization. In addition, the sheer volume of information that must be processed in the national security policy realm requires a considerable amount of systematization. Also, since most Presidents find they must devote the bulk of their time and attention to national security policy, and some prefer to do so anyway, there are strong pressures toward formalized staffing.

It should be apparent, however, that not all of these factors work with the

---

[10] *Cf.* D. MOYNIHAN, MAXIMUM FEASIBLE MISUNDERSTANDING (1969).

[11] The Cuban missile crisis of 1962 is an excellent case in point. President Kennedy dealt with the extremely grave challenge through the vehicle of a temporary "executive committee" consisting of key Cabinet and sub-cabinet officials, top-ranking military officers, and members of his staff. He did not reinstitute this body for any subsequent crisis. *See* A. SCHLESINGER, JR., A THOUSAND DAYS chs. 30, 31 (1965); T. SORENSEN, KENNEDY ch. 24 (1965); E. ABEL, THE MISSILE CRISIS (1966); Allison, *Conceptual Models and the Cuban Missile Crisis*, 63 AM. POL. SCI. REV. 689 (1969).

[12] R. NEUSTADT, *supra* note 7, at 191 (1960).

same intensity, and that they may work against each other in any given presidency. For example, Kennedy's strong foreign policy orientation, a formalizing influence, was apparently overcome by the steady flow of crises and by anti-formal personal preferences and traits. Thus, it is difficult to estimate precisely the degree of structural formality in recent administrations. It is possible on the basis of scholarly studies, however, to locate them in a rough ordering that gives some idea of relative formalization.[13]

FIGURE 1

FORMALIZATION OF STAFFING ARRANGEMENTS IN MODERN
PRESIDENTIAL ADMINISTRATIONS

Roosevelt	Kennedy	Johnson	Truman	Nixon	Eisenhower
Highly Informal		Mixed			Highly Formal

The intervals between the Administrations are proximate and some may quarrel with the position of the Johnson and Truman Administrations near the middle of the scale. Yet it can be said with some confidence that the Roosevelt and Eisenhower Administrations mark the opposite extremities of the continuum, that the Kennedy and Nixon Administrations are next in the degree of staffing informality and formality respectively, and that the Johnson and Truman Administrations do fall in the midsection with the former tending toward somewhat more informality.

The consequences of the level of staffing formalization are mixed. Both highly formal and extremely informal arrangements have accompanying costs and benefits for the President who adopts them.[14] The principal advantage claimed for formally structured policy formulation lies in the comprehensive codification of decisions which results in increased presidential control of the bureaucracy and provides a basis for common understanding of policy goals and programs. It is also argued that a formal approach results in the more systematic, careful decisional processes that are essential to the management of large bureaucracies. The primary costs of formalization are asserted to be the loss of flexibility of action, premature closure of policy options, and the ultimate triumph of technique over purpose. It should be emphasized that no President will adopt a completely formal or informal approach to staffing. There is a considerable built-in tendency to formalization in the structures and routines of the component elements of the Executive Office, e.g., the budgetary process, that

[13] See the previously cited works of Neustadt, *supra* note 7, Clark & Legere, *supra* note 7, Thomas & Wolman, *supra* note 9; Neustadt's important articles on central clearance and presidential program planning, *Presidency and Legislation: The Growth of Central Clearance*, 48 Am. Pol. Sci. Rev. 641 (1954), and *Presidency and Legislation: Planning the President's Program*, 49 Am. Pol. Sci. Rev. 980 (1955); Semple, *Nixon 1: Major Reshuffle at White House*, New York Times, June 14, 1970, § 4, at 1, col. 1; *Reorganization Plan No. 2, supra* note 1.

[14] This discussion follows K. Clark & L. Legere, *supra* note 7, at 25-28, 217-18.

cannot be abandoned for both practical and legal reasons. Likewise, there is such a continual flow of crises and new problems that no amount of systematic contingency planning or routinization can obviate the necessity for at least occasional resort to *ad hoc* policy guidance. But within fairly broad parameters a President may secure advice and information in a variety of ways. As noted above, much depends on the President's interests and style, but since it is not possible to measure let alone predict those qualities with any degree of confidence, I will focus the analysis that follows on the control of staffing for policy formulation through structural forms and institutionalized procedures.

B. Information and Advisers in the Government Context

Advising Presidents is complicated by the nature of the information process in government. That process has been characterized as "institutionalized self-deception."[15] This condition arises from two factors: the hierarchical structure of bureaucracy and the adversary nature of American politics. The men in the higher echelons require information—facts and arguments—to defend themselves against attack. Their subordinates and their staffs undertake to provide it to them. In order to serve their chiefs and to protect themselves, advisers and information sources inside the government tend to make their presentations in the most favorable light possible. The result is that "a kind of propitiatory optimism creeps into government reports"[16] and "what is taken to be true, therefore, is what it is politically desirable to believe."[17] It is incumbent on top officials, Frankel concludes, to recognize this flaw in governmental communications and to develop corrective instruments that will introduce a measure of skepticism to the decision-making process sufficient to insure more balanced judgments. One of the most effective and widely utilized correctives is seeking advice from outsiders, particularly from the so-called "experts." This practice also has its limitations, however.

Outside advisers, especially intellectuals and/or technical experts, encounter substantial difficulties in attempting to challenge the criteria that are the basis of existing policies. True, they bring to their task prestige, extensive information, intensive experience, and perspectives grounded more in theory and first principles than pragmatic compromises with perceived reality. But these assets are fragile and are accompanied by liabilities. Laski has warned that in the political realm, expertise runs the danger of sacrificing "the insight of common sense to the intensity of experience."[18] Since experts often lack humility and broad perspective, Laski argues that they can only make a valuable contribution to government if they can manage to

---

[15] C. FRANKEL, HIGH ON FOGGY BOTTOM 80 (1969). Frankel, a distinguished philosopher, served from July 1965, until December 1967, as Assistant Secretary of State for Cultural Affairs. This discussion draws upon his incisive account of his bureaucratic experience.

[16] *Id.* at 83.

[17] *Id.* at 88.

[18] Laski, *The Limitations of the Expert*, in THE INTELLECTUALS 167 (G. De Huszer ed. 1960).

relate their judgments to the values and aspirations of the public. Also, experts should take care not to oversell their advice. This is perhaps particularly applicable to social scientists whose theories and understanding of human behavior are limited—in spite of extensive information and sophisticated research. Yet, in an effort not to appear incompetent when asked for advice, they will often make recommendations that are either unrealistic or politically infeasible when the wiser course of action would be merely to suggest what common sense dictates. Kissinger, in a perceptive discussion,[19] asserts that the central problem that the intellectual faces when called upon for advice is that his contribution is invoked and utilized in terms of bureau-cratically determined criteria. He thus finds that he may be providing information that becomes the basis for endorsing and legitimizing existing policies rather than serving as the basis for judgment regarding the efficacy of those and alternative policies. In addition, the intellectual must be careful not to formulate his contribu-tion so abstractly as to destroy its value to the political leaders who requested it. The challenge to the intellectual whose expertise is invoked is, therefore, to reconcile "two loyalties: to the organization that employs him and to values which transcend the bureaucratic framework and provide his basic motivation."[20] Most of all, the in-tellectual who serves the government must retain his independence and his dis-interestedness. It is no easy task to accomplish, but the effort must be made as long as the advice of intellectuals and experts is essential to effective leadership in policy formulation.

The information process in government is also complicated in its efforts to in-corporate expertise effectively by the extensive reliance placed upon committees as vehicles for coordinating advice, synthesizing information, and framing proposals. Kissinger states that reliance on committees arises from the lack of substantive competence by high-level political executives.[21] As policy is identified with committee consensus it loses any sense of direction and becomes a matter of adjustment to the lowest common denominator. Committees, asserts Kissinger, emphasize conversation and fluency rather than reflectiveness and creativeness. They tend to suppress dis-agreement in the quest for consensus which most often favors the familiarity of the status quo. In their normal functioning, committees, whether they are composed of government officials or outside experts, are subject to substantial weaknesses. They cannot provide top leaders with the sense of purpose that will enable those officials to make effective use of the committee system. So far it has not been possible to de-velop a presidential advisory and information system that overcomes the limitations of governmental information processes, including the defects of committees. This analysis of presidential staffing devices will consider their potential for resolving such problems.

---

[19] H. KISSINGER, THE NECESSITY FOR CHOICE ch. 8 (1960).
[20] Id. at 353.
[21] Id. at 343. See his discussion of committees and their defects, id. at 344-47.

II

THE VARIOUS ADVISORY MECHANISMS

The President obtains advice and information from the presidency itself, the executive branch, Congress, and the public. The utilization and evaluation of this "intelligence" is accomplished through four principal mechanisms: the Cabinet and its appurtenant committees, the Office of Management and Budget, the White House staff, and a variety of presidential advisory groups including task forces, councils, commissions, conferences, and committees.[22] These advisory devices are not arrayed in a neat series of concentric institutional rings around the President. There is often overlap between the channels of the devices so that information flows from one to the other or it may be simultaneously processed by two or more of them. The utilization of specific advisory mechanisms is in part a function of their proximity to the President, but it is also determined by his relationships with individual advisers and their access to him. Although this analysis of advisory mechanisms has an institutional focus, it is undertaken with a recognition of the importance of individual interaction between the President and his advisers.

A. The Cabinet

The advent of a new national administration is always heralded by extensive speculation concerning the composition of the Cabinet. This speculation usually centers on leading members of the President's party, but it takes into consideration certain criteria of appointment designed to give the Cabinet a broadly representative character. For example, the Secretary of the Interior is traditionally a Westerner, Agriculture goes to a farm state figure, the Attorney General must be a lawyer, and Commerce and Treasury are usually filled by men from the business community. Not infrequently the President-elect has announced his determination to utilize the collective talents of his Cabinet, which of course will include "the best men the nation has to offer," in the conduct of his administration. The Cabinet, it is promised, will become a meaningful instrument of leadership and not a ceremonial organ with little functional value. By implication the previous administration failed to utilize the Cabinet's great potential as an advisory council for high-level policy formulation. With equally predictable frequency, the new President finds after no more than a few months in office that the Cabinet is hardly a suitable vehicle for collective decision-making. Its value, as a collectivity, is more symbolic than operational; as an institutional embodiment of the representational scope of the administration rather than an instrument of collective choice.

The problem that Presidents encounter when they attempt to utilize the Cabinet is that it is a far more suitable means of consolidating and extending political strength than of advising with respect to policy development. It is an aggregation

---

[22] This typology of advisory mechanisms follows that suggested by Cronin & Greenberg, *supra* note 2, at xvii-xviii.

of highest level presidential advisers, but not a viable high-level advisory group. This condition is a consequence and reflection of the "pluralistic conditions of departmental growth and of Cabinet appointment."[23] Cabinet departments developed over time to perform a variety of functions in response to the felt needs of many divergent groups. This pattern of growth encouraged the departments to act more or less independently of each other. The selection of Cabinet members on the basis of geographic and clientele interests encourages in Cabinet members a particularistic loyalty to their subordinates and to their clientele groups that competes with loyalty to the President. This conflict of loyalties works against the formation of any informal sense of mutual responsibility. But without a "sense of corporate unity and common purpose,"[24] the Cabinet's potential as an advisory body cannot be realized.

The President can, and frequently does attempt to build support through individual Cabinet members and their departments. But even this use of the Cabinet is limited by the conflict of loyalties. To the extent that Presidents choose Cabinet members who will be unbending in their fealty to him, they risk weakening the supportive potential of the appointments. The departmental pressures that impinge on Cabinet members are so strong, however, that they "may make even a personal supporter act as the President's 'natural enemy' when he heads a major department."[25] The resignation of Health, Education and Welfare Secretary Robert Finch in May, 1970 provides a contemporary illustration of this old problem. A close personal friend and long-time political associate of President Nixon, Finch experienced great difficulty in reconciling his intense personal loyalty to the President with the expectations of the HEW bureaucracy and the demands of its clientele. His seventeen month tenure as Secretary was marked by his refusal to exploit his relationship with the President on behalf of his departmental constituency and that constituency's consequent disenchantment with him. When Finch left the Cabinet it was to assume a position on the White House staff as a counsellor to the President that was more compatible with their special relationship.

The Finch case raises the question of the degree to which it is possible for Cabinet members to be the President's men.[26] While no President can tolerate a Cabinet in which all members regularly choose departmental over presidential interests, it is also true that unquestioning loyalty to the President is equally dysfunctional. What is called for is a Cabinet-presidential relationship that is "at once highly autonomous and deeply responsive."[27]

The unsuitability of the Cabinet as an advisory mechanism does not mean, however, that the President is not dependent on his department heads for advice. But

---

[23] R. FENNO, THE PRESIDENT'S CABINET 131 (1959).

[24] Id. at 132.

[25] D. TRUMAN, THE GOVERNMENTAL PROCESS 406 (1951).

[26] Cf. M. BUNDY, THE STRENGTH OF GOVERNMENT 37-40 (1968).

[27] Id. at 38. See also T. SORENSEN, DECISION-MAKING IN THE WHITE HOUSE 68-70 (1963).

the advice and political assistance which Cabinet members can provide must come from them as individual political actors of considerable standing. As the head of a large bureaucracy with substantial information gathering and evaluating capabilities, with at least some independent sources of power, the Cabinet member has resources that are valuable to the President. They can be utilized in various ways. Cabinet members are usually consulted extensively regarding the development of presidential policies in their areas of activity. They participate in the development of legislative proposals for their departments[28] and in deliberations that lead to the formulation of the President's legislative proposals. Frequently Cabinet members serve on inter-departmental committees and task forces that formulate policies and resolve differences between agencies. Also, depending on their departments, Cabinet members serve on either the National Security Council or the newly established Domestic Council.[29]

There is, then, a substantial amount of unified presidential policy control over departments and agencies, but it is not achieved through the Cabinet. It arises through the use of other instruments and through direct relationships between the President and individual Cabinet members. In this latter regard, the Cabinet official often acts as a broker between the President and his staff and the bureaucracy and its clientele. Occasionally a Cabinet member may become a close confidant of the President on policy matters that range beyond the jurisdiction of his own department. In such instances, mutual respect and attraction permit the Cabinet member to be more than a formal adviser. The cases of Attorneys General Robert Kennedy in his brother's Administration and John Mitchell in the Nixon Administration illustrate this type of relationship. In all cases, however, a Cabinet member is only as important as the President wants him to be. The influential men in the Cabinet will shift depending on presidential preferences and values and external circumstances.

In the final analysis, it is necessary to look at devices below and beyond the Cabinet to understand fully the dynamics of presidential intelligence for policy formulation. Cabinet members are major participants in the policy-making process in their roles as heads of executive departments and by virtue of individual personal and political resources and not as members of a group of top level advisers. But the Cabinet member is more than a presidential staff resource or personal adviser.[30] He is the principal political executive in his particular policy arena. In this capacity he often speaks for the administration. Neustadt's remarks on the role of the Secretary of State are particularly instructive regarding the situation of the Cabinet member:

> The Secretary has work of his own, resources of his own, vistas of his own. He is in business under his own name and in his name powers are exercised, decisions

---

[28] See Neustadt, *Presidency and Legislation: Planning the President's Program, supra* note 13; Neustadt, *Presidency and Legislation: The Growth of Central Clearance, supra* note 13.

[29] See the discussion at 554 *infra*.

[30] *See Testimony of Richard Neustadt Before the Senate Subcommittee on National Security Staffing and Operations*, in THE PRESIDENCY 511 (A. Wildavsky ed. 1969).

taken. Therefore he can press his personal authority, his own opinion, his adviser's
role, wherever he sees fit across the whole contemporary reach of foreign relations
. . . his status and the tasks of his Department give him every right to raise his
voice where, when and as he chooses.[31]

The Cabinet member draws much of his advisory strength from his departmental
responsibilities; yet he cannot devote himself too extensively to running his department, else important policy choices will be made with little input from him.

The inefficacy of the Cabinet as a formal advisory mechanism and as a policy-
making body does not obviate the need for collective action at some point in the
process. Differences in perspective and objectives are bound to exist between agencies.
Somewhere, not too far removed from the President, there must be a means of
identifying alternatives, clarifying goals, and settling upon compatible courses of
action. In short, policy coordination is necessary. Given the phenomena of depart-
mentalism and of social and political pluralism, that coordination can only be
secured through committees or through routinized procedures. It cannot be obtained
by presidential fiat.

Cabinet-level committees for policy-making and policy coordination include those
appointed to deal with a specific subject or problem, such as the Cabinet committees on
economic policy and on environmental quality, and formal policy councils like the
National Security Council (NSC) that are established by law or executive order
and that operate with sizeable staff support. The most widely utilized means of
securing coordination, however, is the interagency committee which generally operates
at the sub-cabinet and agency head level.

Cabinet committees can be an effective means of handling a specific situation or
policy problem. They can focus attention on it quickly and have flexibility in developing situations. But they are limited by other demands and claims made on their
members. If Cabinet committees are provided with supportive staffs of significant
size they quickly tend to become routinized operations and to lose the sense of
urgency and the flexibility that justified their initial establishment. Cabinet committees that acquire permanent status tend to lose their high initial visibility and
also their capacity to hold the attention of their members. They become one of many
groups operating in the presidential arena. The committee that President Nixon
established to facilitate school desegregation illustrates the problems encountered by
a continuing Cabinet-level committee. The committee was chaired by the Vice
President and included the Attorney General, the Secretary of HEW, and a number
of subordinate officials. Because desegregation involves unsettled questions of constitutional interpretation and is a highly sensitive issue, the committee has not been
able to develop a uniform national policy. Presidential statements on the subject have
reflected the differing approaches of the Justice Department and HEW. Continuing
controversy has forced the committee into the background.

---

[31] *Id.* at 522-23.

B. The National Security Council

An important institutional participant in the presidential advisory system is the National Security Council, a body which "constitutes the most ambitious effort yet made to coordinate policy on the Cabinet level."[32] Since its establishment the NSC has been both central and peripheral to the formulation of national security policy. A review of the uses that Presidents have made of the NSC reveals the alternative ways of allocating responsibility for policy planning and coordination in this crucial area.

President Truman saw the NSC, which was established by the National Security Act of 1947, as a necessary facility for study, analysis, and the development of policy recommendations. Truman did not, however, regard it as a policy-making body. He was concerned lest the NSC encroach on his constitutional powers and thus he did not meet with it until the Korean war began. Even with its increased activity and status after that point, the NSC was no more than a convenient staffing mechanism with a limited policy-making role.

In sharp contrast, President Eisenhower expanded the NSC into a comprehensive policy system. He regarded the council as a top level forum for vigorous discussion of carefully prepared policy papers. These NSC discussions contained statements of divergent interpretations and approaches and ultimately produced resolutions of the issues. The NSC was, in Eisenhower's view, a corporate body of advisers rather than a group of departmental and agency spokesmen. He chaired NSC meetings and led discussions of papers prepared by the Planning Board, one of the two staff arms of the Council. The other staff unit, the Operations Coordinating Board, concerned itself with problems of policy implementation. After a subject had been raised for NSC consideration by anyone from the President on down in the system, an analysis would be conducted under the direction of the Planning Board and involving the agency with the major interest in it. Eventually a policy paper would come before the council for discussion and action. Once approved, NSC policy actions were sent to the departments and agencies for execution under the direction of the Operations Coordinating Board. The process has been described as a "policy hill" with the NSC at the summit and policies moving up the formulative side through the Planning Board and down the implementation side through the Operations Coordinating Board to the departments.[33] The NSC also dealt with current policy matters, although smaller groups of officials usually handled important issues.

President Eisenhower's NSC staff system imposed a comprehensive framework of order on all aspects of national security affairs. Its defenders argued that it insured that the President would receive all relevant information and points of view, that it

---

[32] Hammond, *The National Security Council as a Device for Interdepartmental Coordination: An Interpretation and Appraisal*, 54 AM. POL. SCI. REV. 899 (1960). *See also* Falk, *The National Security Council Under Truman, Eisenhower and Kennedy*, 79 POL. SCI. Q. 403 (1964); K. CLARK & L. LEGERE, *supra* note 7, at chs. 4-5. This discussion draws upon these sources.

[33] *See* Cutler, *The Development of the National Security Council*, 34 FOREIGN AFFAIRS 442 (1956). *See also* R. CUTLER, NO TIME FOR REST (1966). Cutler was President Eisenhower's Special Assistant for National Security Affairs.

provided a reservoir of policy guidance, and that it afforded rational coordination of policy formulation and execution. Its critics charged that the system was so ponderous that it was incapable of responding effectively to emergencies or of developing new policy departures. It was asserted that the NSC system rigidified an incremental approach in a policy arena where flexibility was of great value. Furthermore, the critics claimed, the system purchased consensus at the price of ambiguity. Differences were said to be papered over with vague policy statements that had no value as guides to action.

The alleged defects of President Eisenhower's NSC system were highlighted in a senatorial inquiry conducted by Senator Henry M. Jackson (D-Wash.) during 1960 and 1961.[34] The Jackson subcommittee made a series of proposals that would have "deinstitutionalized" the system. It recommended that the Council be a smaller group, limited in membership to top officials and meeting only to advise on critical issues and problems. The support staffs would be abolished and their functions reassigned. Finally, the subcommittee suggested that the Secretary of State take the lead in formulating national security policy and that coordination of policy implementation be accomplished by an action officer or an informal interdepartmental committee.

President Kennedy, acting along the lines proposed by the Jackson committee, proceeded to dismantle most of the Eisenhower NSC system. All that remained was the statutory council consisting of the President, Vice President, the Secretaries of State and Defense, and the Director of the Office of Emergency Planning, and a small staff headed by McGeorge Bundy, the Special Assistant for National Security Affairs. The Council was but one of many ways of solving problems and President Kennedy consulted its members more often individually than collectively. The NSC staff became involved in various activities and was a major source of information for the President. It worked closely with the bureaucracy, the Bureau of the Budget, and the Office of Science and Technology. Its principal task was to identify and manage issues. When it became apparent that the State Department was unable to assume the major responsibility for initiating and coordinating national security policy, the NSC staff assumed much of that important role.

The NSC itself was primarily used to consider long term policy problems that could be dealt with through planning. The NSC staff worked more directly for the President than for the Council. It concentrated on the action oriented processes that President Kennedy's approach to foreign affairs required. The Eisenhower distinction between planning and operations was abolished in favor of a commitment to action with policy serving as the rationale.

The abrupt transition from the Kennedy to the Johnson Administration was marked by the new President's desire to minimize the shock of the assassination.

---

[34] SUBCOMM. ON NATIONAL POLICY MACHINERY OF THE SENATE COMM. ON GOVERNMENT OPERATIONS, 86TH CONG., 2d SESS., ORGANIZING FOR NATIONAL SECURITY (Comm. Print 1960).

Gradually a distinctive Johnson pattern emerged. It was characterized by the President's reduced dependence on the national security staff in dealing with the bureaucracy and by increased reliance on the State Department for policy coordination. The NSC met fairly often, but rarely to consider major current issues. More important to presidential policy formulation were weekly luncheon meetings, held on Tuesdays, of the President and selected top officials. These informal gatherings served as vehicles for making key decisions, receiving advice, and establishing policy guidance. The informality of the meetings permitted an extensive interchange of viewpoints and stimulated a flow of information, but they were defective in that items often arose without advance staff work and no record of decisions was kept.

The Johnson presidency was one in which the President received a heavy flow of information through personal contacts and written memoranda. His responses, usually transmitted verbally by the Special Assistant for National Security or the NSC staff, served as guidelines for the bureaucracy. But there was no mechanism for locating issues and centralizing their management. The President disposed of most issues on the basis of memoranda processed by the Special Assistant. Decisions were made after discussions with a wide range of individuals in and outside of the government. There was, however, "no predictable pattern to such consultation . . . . At the end a decision emerged."[35]

In order to reduce the need for the NSC staff to function as an *ad hoc* interdepartmental coordinator, President Johnson delegated to the Secretary of State, in National Security Action Memorandum 341 of March 1966, responsibility for "over-all direction, coordination, and supervision of interdepartmental activities." The vehicles for accomplishing this mission were the Senior Interdepartmental Group (SIG) headed by the Undersecretary of State and Interdepartmental Regional Groups (IRG's) headed by assistant secretaries of state. The operational consequences of this system were not as intended. Whenever the President or the NSC staff assumed control, as they did with respect to most critical issues, "the existence of the system was of little significance."[36]

President Johnson's approach to national security policy had two distinguished characteristics—informality and heavy reliance on the NSC staff under the direction of the Special Assistant. The NSC staff was not actively involved in policy initiation, however. What it did was act as an intermediary and brokerage agent for the President, offering advice and providing support when required. The President retained much direct power over national security matters in his own hands, leaving largely to chance and his personal resources the formulation of coherent and rationally interrelated policies.

It is somewhat premature to speak with certainty about the Nixon Administration's arrangements for managing national security policy. President Nixon appears

---

[35] K. CLARK & L. LEGERE, *supra* note 7, at 95.
[36] *Id.* at 103.

to have concluded that a substantial National Security Council staff under the direction of his Special Assistant, Henry Kissinger, and the reestablishment of the formal NSC system are both necessary. The Kissinger staff, considerably expanded and more formalized than its predecessors, plays a major role in coordinating interdepartmental policy planning. The NSC has been reactivated as "the principal forum for presidential consideration of foreign policy issues."[37] The NSC met 37 times in 1969 and considered over 20 major problems. It operates in a manner similar to the Eisenhower NSC only without the formal staff units. Initial policy analyses are prepared by Interdepartmental Groups chaired by an assistant secretary of state. (These resemble the IRG's of the Johnson Administration.) Then an interagency review group of senior officials, which is chaired by Kissinger, examines the papers "to insure that the issues, options, and views are presented fully and fairly."[38] Finally, the matter under consideration is presented to the President and the NSC.

Nixon's NSC system seeks to involve all relevant agencies in a process that insures that the President and the Council have all the available pertinent information. It obtains a measure of flexibility through special interagency groups, such as the Verification Panel in the area of strategic arms limitation and the Vietnam Special Studies Group. It makes provision for crisis planning and management through a special group of high officials, the Washington Special Actions Group.

The Nixon NSC system combines White House and departmentally centered control of policy formulation through use of both a sizeable NSC staff and interagency groups. It relies on systematic formal procedures but seeks to retain flexibility through special committees. Most significantly, according to the President, it is built upon a realistic appraisal of the tasks that it faces.[39]

C. The Domestic Council

As Wildavsky has observed, there are two presidencies, one concerned with national security policy, the other with domestic affairs.[40] Substantial differences distinguish the two policy realms. In national security policy, events often move at a rapid pace with potentially grave consequences. Very little that happens can be dismissed as inconsequential and actions may be irreversible once taken. In domestic affairs, policy decisions are usually incremental adjustments in previous courses of action. Major policy changes occur only infrequently and then only after prolonged pressure and deliberations or in periods of crisis. Most domestic policy decisions are reversible; if they fail to meet the pragmatic test of results, something else will be tried. Another difference involves presidential control over

---

[37] Report by President Nixon to the Congress, U.S. Foreign Policy for the 1970's: A New Strategy for Peace, in 116 CONG. REC. H927 (daily ed. Feb. 18, 1970) [hereinafter cited as Report by President Nixon].

[38] Id.

[39] Id. at H928.

[40] Wildavsky, The Two Presidencies, TRANS-ACTION, December, 1966, at 7. This discussion draws on Wildavsky's excellent analysis.

policy. As a matter of constitutional and practical necessity Presidents have greater discretion in national security matters. There are fewer rivals for policy control and the ability of those rivals to obtain and use information is much less than in domestic affairs. The range of options and competitors is much broader in the domestic realm where interest groups and Congress possess greater capacity to bargain with the President. Wildavsky calculates that in the period 1948-64, positive congressional responses to presidential initiatives were almost twice as great in national security matters as in domestic affairs.[41]

The differences between the two policy realms have resulted in contrasting staffing patterns. National security policy formulation has transpired with the benefit of the elaborate intelligence capabilities of the Central Intelligence Agency and the armed services and with the support of the NSC and its staff. There has been no comparable formalization of structure and process in the domestic arena. Coordination of policy formulation has been a responsibility of many agents: the Bureau of the Budget, the Council of Economic Advisers, the Office of Science and Technology, and more recently, the councils on rural and urban affairs, as well as devices such as interagency task forces, the concept of a lead agency, and reliance on individual presidential assistants. There has been an informal and often unsystematic approach to policy formulation as compared with the national security policy arena. To the extent that there has been a coordinating force, it has been provided by the budget bureau. But the Bureau was never intended to function as a top level policy council that considered proposals for action after careful staffing had been completed. Rather, it was a staff agency with about 500 career professionals that cleared legislation drafted in the bureaucracy, analyzed proposals emanating from the departments, agencies, and other sources, and prepared the budget. All this was done with a view to maintaining the integrity of the President's overall program.

The pattern of domestic policy coordination has varied between administrations. For example, President Johnson utilized a small staff headed by Joseph A. Califano, a presidential assistant. President Kennedy assigned responsibility to a group of his White House staff aides with special assignments to his brother. Under President Eisenhower, Sherman Adams, acting in the manner of a military chief of staff, personally directed the process of domestic policy coordination. President Nixon, after a year in office and on recommendation from his Advisory Council on Executive Organization, established the Domestic Council through Reorganization Plan No. 2 of 1970. The Domestic Council is composed of the President, the Vice President, the Attorney General, the Secretaries of Agriculture, Commerce, HEW, HUD, Interior, Labor, Transportation, and Treasury, and other officials as may be deemed appropriate on an *ad hoc* basis. The Council is to have a staff of professional

---

[41] *Id.* at 8.

experts[42] and is headed by a presidential assistant whom the President designates as its executive director.

At this writing, the Domestic Council is still establishing its procedures and recruiting its staff. The pattern of its operations is not sufficiently clear to permit a description, let alone an analysis, to be made. However, the rationale for the Council and the Administration's expectations for it were made quite explicit in the House hearings on the reorganization plan.[43] According to Roy L. Ash, the chairman of the Advisory Council on Executive Reorganization,[44] the major organizational premise was that presidential staff functions for policy and program formulation should be separated from those for program implementation and administration. This reaffirmation of the old politics-administration dichotomy,[45] which academicians had thoroughly discredited by the early 1950's,[46] rested on the belief that it was "unsound" to have the same organization perform both functions because different kinds of information, skills, and attitudes are required for each and because policy formulation requires a longer time perspective and is less subject to daily pressures than implementation is.[47] Such a formal separation of functions characterized the NSC system under President Eisenhower, but it had not previously been employed in presidential staffing for domestic affairs. Its effectiveness remains to be demonstrated. It does recognize the increased necessity for effective program evaluation and the complexities of program implementation.

The Ash commission envisioned the Domestic Council as "a way to bring together under one roof many, but not necessarily all, of the sources for developing domestic policy."[48] It is intended to provide a more effective means than reliance on interagency task forces and informal contact by the White House staff of bringing necessary information and opinions to the President and of resolving interagency disputes. The Domestic Council formalizes previous arrangements which, according to the Ash commission, were random and haphazard. The staff will gather information, analyze issues, and present the Council with opposing lines of reasoning.

---

[42] At this writing the staff consists mostly of Republican political activists rather than social scientists and other specialists.

[43] *Reorganization Plan No. 2, supra* note 1.

[44] The council was established on April 5, 1969. Mr. Ash, the President of Litton Industries, served as its only chairman. It has commonly been referred to as the Ash Commission.

[45] The development of the analytical distinction between politics and administration is attributed to Woodrow Wilson and Frank J. Goodnow. *See* Wilson, *The Study of Administration*, 2 POL. SCI. Q. 197 (1897); F. GOODNOW, POLITICS AND ADMINISTRATION (1900). The relationship of the dichotomy to American administrative scholarship is carefully explored in D. WALDO, THE ADMINISTRATIVE STATE ch. 7 (1948).

[46] *See* Friedrich, *Public Policy and the Nature of Administrative Responsibility*, in 1 PUBLIC POLICY (C. Friedrich ed. 1950); Kingsley, *Political Ends and Administrative Means*, 5 PUB. AD. REV. 375 (1943); W. ANDERSON, RESEARCH IN PUBLIC ADMINISTRATION 106 (1945); P. APPLEBY, *supra* note 2; Long, *Power and Administration*, 9 PUB. AD. REV. 257 (1949); Long, *Bureaucracy and Constitutionalism*, 46 AM. POL. SCI. REV. 808 (1952); Long, *Public Policy and Administration: The Goals of Rationality and Responsibility*, 15 PUB. AD. REV. 22 (1954).

[47] See the testimony of Roy L. Ash, *Reorganization Plan No. 2, supra* note 1, at 9-10.

[48] *Id.* at 10.

The task of the staff will be to make certain that policy alternatives have been fully presented so that the President and the Council can make informed, rational choices. It is anticipated that the President and the Council will act with a "common data base" developed by the staff.[49] The Ash commission realized that Presidents will vary in their utilization of the Domestic Council. Its expectation was, however, that the Council will prove to be a useful managerial tool that increases the President's control over policy formulation and reduces somewhat the time required to achieve it.

The establishment of a domestic analogue to the NSC raises several questions. Although the Domestic Council staff is supposedly to refrain from reconciling any issues in its analyses, is it realistic to expect that the staff will not have a major substantive impact on policy? Such an impact can perhaps be minimized if recruitment is on professional grounds. But the pressures to insist on political criteria will be great if not overpowering. The establishment of a technical career staff comparable to that of the former Bureau of the Budget seems unlikely. One of the advantages of the Bureau was its devotion to the needs of the presidency. This was made possible, at least in part, by its separation from the political pressures of the White House. The Domestic Council—if it is to be the high-level forum for discussion, debate, and ultimate policy determination that its creators envision—will operate in closer proximity to the President. It will necessarily have a highly political staff. Can this staff provide a continuing institutional memory for domestic affairs?

A second set of questions pertain to the Domestic Council's relationships with other presidential staff units, with the bureaucracy, and with Congress. At the reorganization hearings, Representative Chet Holifield (D-Calif.) argued that the Council would become a barrier between the President and the new Office of Management and Budget (OMB). This would downgrade the OMB, Holifield reasoned, since the policy functions formerly exercised by the budget bureau would be performed by the Council staff. Furthermore, Holifield feared, that staff will be unavailable to Congress and yet be able to affect the decisions of the OMB.[50] The question of congressional-Domestic Council staff relations remains to be determined. The role of the OMB in policy formulation does appear likely to be substantially reduced. The OMB will no longer participate in formulating legislative proposals and following them through. The useful feedback of program results and knowledge of program defects that enabled the budget bureau's program divisions to help the bureaucracy develop amendments to existing legislation and to formulate new legislative proposals will be channeled to a different policy staff. Raymond Saulnier, who served as chairman of the Council of Economic Advisers (CEA) during the Eisenhower Administration, raised objections at the hearings to the absence of the Budget Director and the Chairman of the CEA from the Council's statutory mem-

---

[49] *Id.* at 55.
[50] *Id.* at 43.

bership.[51] He argued that this would deprive the Domestic Council of the "intimate knowledge of budget resources and demands" and the CEA's special competence in economic matters. He recommended that the CEA be assigned responsibility for staffing Domestic Council agenda items in its area. Whether the importance of the OBM, CEA, and other staff units will be lessened is an unanswered question. Their status may be jeopardized by the new arrangement, but it is too early to make such a judgment.

Finally, it is unclear how the existence of the Domestic Council will affect interagency relations and agency access to the President. The department heads will undoubtedly have access to him through the Council and also directly as in the past. But their subordinates will not have these points of contact. Agency heads and subcabinet officers will have to deal with the Council staff on matters involving policy formulation and with the OMB on matters of budget and policy implementation. To the extent that the OMB retains its former policy formulation roles, there will be duplication of effort (with the risk of considerable confusion) and the rationale for the reorganization will be defeated. There is also a question regarding access to the White House. In the Johnson and Kennedy Administrations, presidential assistants served as points of contact for agencies and interest groups and acted as brokers between the White House, the bureaucracy, Congress, and the attentive public. For example, Douglass Cater was President Johnson's liaison man for educational policy. Even after two years of the Nixon presidency, there is still (in early 1971) great uncertainty regarding the points of contact. The Domestic Council may increase rather than reduce the communication gap between the White House and the bureaucracy, especially below the Cabinet level. The Council and its staff may isolate the President rather than bring him closer to the operational problems of domestic politics as intended.

The Domestic Council is, then, a major but uncertain factor in presidential policy formulation. Ideally it will prove to be an effective staffing arrangement that permits the administration to arrive at the "best solution after weighing carefully all viable choices."[52] On the other hand, it could become a rigidified policy control structure that impedes initiative, blocks alternatives, stifles originality, and is incapable of quick, flexible responses.[53] The best guess is that its performance will fall between these two stools.[54]

D. Office of Management and Budget

Since presidential-bureaucratic relations through the instrumentality of the former

---

[51] Id. at 32-34. Supporters of the reorganization plan responded that the Chairman of the CEA and the Budget Director would be included on the Council at the President's discretion.

[52] HOUSE COMM. ON GOVERNMENT OPERATIONS, DISAPPROVING REORGANIZATION PLAN NO. 2 OF 1970, H.R. REP. No. 1066, 91st Cong., 2d Sess. 23 (1970).

[53] Id. at 21.

[54] Cf. Carey, Reorganization Plan No. 2: Remarks by William D. Carey, 30 PUB. AD. REV. 631 (1970).

Bureau of the Budget (BOB) are the subject of another paper in this symposium,[55] I will not dwell at length on the role of this major presidential staff unit in policy formulation. As every student of American government learns in the introductory course, BOB did far more than prepare the annual presidential budget. It had a major responsibility for coordinating and safeguarding the integrity of the President's overall program.[56] It had an impact on policy formulation through the preparation of budget requests for departments and agencies, the clearance of all views expressed by federal agencies on pending legislation, review and evaluation of legislative proposals originating in the bureaucracy, and coordination of the process of developing and preparing presidential legislative proposals. In performing its duties, the budget bureau worked closely with the bureaucracy. It developed a professional expertise of its own based on substantive knowledge acquired over time and committed to serving the President. In recent years, BOB played a key role in staffing and organizing the work of presidential advisory groups. Bureau officials served on advisory committees or their staffs, the Bureau analyzed advisory committee reports and recommendations, it participated in high-level consideration of those reports, and it was the mechanism for linking committee proposals and other suggestions for policy change to the annual budgetary process.

Operating with no constituency other than the President BOB provided objective staff assistance over time. Its biases were those of professional careerists in public service. Bureau officials developed a skeptical attitude toward other participants in the policy process—bureaucrats, congressmen and their staffs, and pressure group representatives—and they routinely challenged all suggestions and ideas in the context of their conception of the President's program goals. The Bureau did not, however, serve as a source of information. It was an institutional screen through which all kinds of information and advice was filtered and assayed in terms of its value to the President and his program.

The changes instituted under Reorganization Plan No. 2 will undoubtedly affect the central role of BOB in policy formulation. The emphasis in the new OMB is more on management than on policy development. The Domestic Council and its staff will presumably assume many of the functions formerly performed by BOB. This shift occurred in the realm of national security policy in 1947. It is too soon to determine if OMB's domestic policy role will parallel the rather limited one that it has played with respect to national security matters. Certainly the domestic policy format will be different. Decisions which Budget Bureau officials and White House staff members formerly made apart from department heads will presumably be made in a forum that includes them as principal participants. OMB will be involved

[55] Schick, *The Budget Bureau That Was: Thoughts on the Rise, Decline, and Future of a Presidential Agency*, 35 LAW & CONTEMP. PROB. 519 (1970).
[56] *See* Neustadt, *Presidency and Legislation: Planning the President's Program, supra* note 13; Neustadt, *Presidency and Legislation: The Growth of Central Clearance, supra* note 13; Maas, *In Accord with the Program of the President,* in 4 PUBLIC POLICY 79 (1953).

but as a supportive staff whose major concern is with costs and with implementation. However well these changes work in practice, it is their clear objective to reduce the significance of the budget staff in presidential policy formulation and to utilize it more extensively as a device for coordinating and rationalizing the implementation of policy. Given the great value of BOB to Presidents since Roosevelt it is, in my judgment, questionable whether the revision of its mission and the consequent separation of policy formulation from implementation will "enable the President to have more facts and better options at his disposal when he makes his decisions."[57] It is doubtful if structured enforcement of the politics-administration dichotomy will endure and, if it does survive, whether presidential policy leadership will be enhanced rather than weakened.[58]

E. The Inner Circle and White House Staff Advisers

The absence of formal institutional support for the President in Congress, the fragmented parochialism of the bureaucracy, and the lack of an integrating party structure grounded in an ideology combine to make the task of leadership in policy formulation one of bargaining and manipulation. As Neustadt has so aptly stated, "presidential power is the power to persuade."[59] In approaching the task of policy leadership, modern Presidents have depended heavily on the group of friends, counsellors, secretaries, and other aides who constitute the White House Staff and on an informal inner circle of close associates and confidants. These two sets of advisers are continuously and directly involved with him in the formulation of policy. They have some overlapping members and their composition and operational pattern varies between administrations and over time within a single presidency.

Inner circles, which have also been referred to as "kitchen cabinets," "the invisible presidency," and similar terms, tend to be comprised of a few key White House staff members, one or two Cabinet members who enjoy the special confidence of the President, and occasionally a few personal friends of the President.[60] There is a tendency to attribute great power to these intimate presidential advisers and they no doubt have exercised considerable (but indeterminate) influence over recent Presidents. For example, John Foster Dulles and Sherman Adams apparently predominated over all other advisers to President Eisenhower for the first several years of his presidency. The intimate personal and intellectual relationship between President Kennedy and his brother Robert is well known. And President Johnson placed great reliance on two of his Cabinet members, Secretaries Rusk and McNamara. Although interaction between the President and his informal inner circle is a central feature of policy formulation, it is necessary to guard against overemphasizing this

---

[57] Testimony of Dwight Ink, Assistant Director of the Budget, *Reorganization Plan No. 2, supra* note 1, at 89.

[58] *Cf.* Carey, *Reorganization Plan No. 2: Remarks, supra* note 54.

[59] R. NEUSTADT, *supra* note 7, at 32. *See also* E. HERRING, PRESIDENTIAL LEADERSHIP 24 (1940).

[60] *Cf.* Seligman, *Presidential Leadership: The Inner Circle and Institutionalization, supra* note 2; L. KOENIG, THE INVISIBLE PRESIDENCY (1960); P. ANDERSON, THE PRESIDENTS' MEN (1968).

phenomenon. There exists a collective presidential decision-making process that is not so much the work of a few individuals as the organized effort of many groups including the inner circle, the White House staff, OMB, and a host of presidential advisory committees.[61] Furthermore, national policy-making may center in the presidency, but it involves a considerable number of political elites in different policy areas. These elites, which overlap only occasionally, participate actively with the presidency in shaping national policy.[62]

The inner circle provides the President with broad gauge advice on critical policy choices that is unrestrained by departmental, agency, or pressure group interests. It is held together by a mutual bond: the President's need for advisers who share his values and goals but who can broaden his perspective and the advisers' capacity and desire to meet that need. Membership in the inner circle is prestigious (despite Brownlow's plea for men with "a passion for anonymity") but it may be short-lived. The tasks that its members perform are demanding, and the President's needs and preferences change. According to Seligman, inner circle members function as "buffers," "catalysts," "liaison men," "fixers," "needlers," "communications experts," "policy advisers," and "sometime ideologists."[63] Its members may be selected because of their ability to perform tasks for which the President is unsuited. In this respect, the inner circle complements the President's personality. It compensates for his limitations.[64]

The White House staff, which usually includes some inner circle members, is larger and more formalized. The President enjoys great freedom in setting up his office and selecting his staff, but its functions are fairly well established. Its primary job is to furnish the President with sufficient information and analysis to permit him to make decisions with an awareness of the available alternatives and their probable consequences. The specific tasks of the White House staff include press relations and communications, speechwriting, congressional liaison, pressure group and general public liaison, management of the President's schedule, and policy advice and counsel.

The management of press relations and communications is crucial to building and maintaining a favorable presidential image. The persons who perform these tasks, however, seldom manage to exert influence on major policy decisions. Their advice relates to tactical rather than strategic matters. Speech writers are also involved in presidential communications. Their role affords them the opportunity to exert some influence on substantive policy decisions, but only to the extent that the President has confidence in the judgment of the individual speech writer. For in-

---

[61] Cf. J. BURNS, supra note 2, at 152-53; Seligman, Developments in the Presidency, supra note 2, at 707.

[62] See Thomas, Bureaucratic-Congressional Interaction and the Politics of Education, 2 J. COMP. AD. 52 (1970); Cronin, The Presidency and Education, PHI DELTA KAPPAN, Feb. 1968, at 295.

[63] Seligman, Presidential Leadership: The Inner Circle and Institutionalization, supra note 2, at 412-13.

[64] Seligman, Developments in the Presidency, supra note 2, at 710.

stance, Theodore Sorensen was one of President Kennedy's principal speech writers. His style, tone, and ideas merged with those of his chief so that they were often indistinguishable. On the other hand, the identity of President Nixon's wordsmiths is virtually unknown. They remain anonymous White House artisans who mold presidential addresses to specifications determined by their superiors.

Presidential liaison with Congress and with pressure groups is a White House staff function of twofold importance. It shapes the scope and content of input from Congress and pressure groups to the policy-making process and it affects the level of support for the President's policy goals. Failure to involve congressional leaders adequately at a sufficiently early stage can spell the defeat of the President's legislative program. As a practical political matter, congressional sentiment must be assessed and congressional leaders consulted in determining the administration's policy agenda. The operating responsibilities of the congressional liaison staff include presenting the administration's position on legislation to individual congressmen, coordinating and directing the administration's legislative program on Capitol Hill, gathering information, including congressional sentiment, analyzing legislative issues, assessing the potential impact of presidential statements and actions, and performing auxiliary services for members of Congress.[65] Under Presidents Eisenhower and Nixon congressional liaison has been a line operation somewhat removed from direct access to the Chief Executive. Their liaison staff directors, Wilton Persons and William Timmons, did not enjoy direct access to them.[66] The policy impact of the liaison staff under these circumstances has come from its assessments of probable congressional opinion and actions. Under Presidents Kennedy and Johnson, congressional liaison occupied a more central position in the White House staff. With Lawrence O'Brien, a skilled political tactician, directing the lobbying staff, congressional relations were significantly upgraded, although it took O'Brien and his team some time to master their work. Both Democratic Presidents worked directly with O'Brien in shaping the content of their legislative programs as well as in developing legislative strategy. While all Presidents are dependent on their liaison staffs to shepherd legislation through Congress, the role of that staff in policy-making varies substantially.[67] All presidential lobbyists are agents, salesmen, and contact men. They can become advisers and counsellors if the President wishes.

Until the Nixon Administration, liaison with politically important interests was handled by the congressional relations staff and through the practice of assigning primary responsibility for liaison with groups in specific policy areas to presidential assistants. Access to the White House was generally channeled through these individual contact men who acted as brokers between the presidency and the pressure groups.

---

[65] For an excellent description of President Nixon's congressional liaison operation see Bonafede & Glass, *White House Report/Nixon Deals Cautiously with Hostile Congress*, NAT'L J., June 27, 1970, at 1353.

[66] In November, 1970 President Nixon appointed former Congressman Clark McGregor as a counsellor with responsibility for congressional relations. McGregor's role and relationship to the President is yet to be established.

[67] Cf. A. HOLTZMAN, LEGISLATIVE LIAISON: EXECUTIVE LEADERSHIP IN CONGRESS (1970).

Outside groups knew whom to see if they wished to make a presentation of their views. The assistants who acted as contacts performed these tasks in addition to their other duties. They did not formally coordinate information gathering or the rendition of advice, but were available to groups seeking access. In varying degrees and ways, they filtered the input to the President from external sources. President Nixon, in keeping with his preference for formalizing staffing arrangements, assigned responsibility for contact with organized constituencies to a separate staff.[68] The outside liaison staff acts as a broker between pressure groups and administration policymakers. The lodging of this responsibility in a special staff is an attempt to improve the scope and content of informational input and to more effectively convert the resources of private interests into support for the President. It has the advantage, from the presidential perspective, of systematizing what previously was a random process. Its disadvantages are not yet clear, but one possible difficulty may stem from the inability of a small liaison staff to develop sufficient familiarity with all policy sectors to be able to deal selectively and effectively with them. The liaison staff may simply become a crew of messenger-errand boys with no function other than to receive and direct communications and to perform special chores such as organizing meetings and checking out presidential appointments. An outside liaison staff with no recognized policy impact could become a liability if pressure groups perceived them as buffers between themselves and the real policy-makers. As with congressional liaison, the President must rely on the White House staff to manage relations with organized constituencies. They have great potential value to him as sources of political leverage but they can also be sources of frustration. Dealing effectively with pressure groups requires a skill and tact that gives them a sense of efficacious involvement in policy formulation. The most appropriate approach to this staff function is not yet apparent.

The management of the President's time is another vital task of the White House staff. There are two dimensions to this function: the screening, condensation, and digesting of information that reaches the President and the control of his schedule. Obviously, time is a most precious presidential resource. No President can read all the memoranda, reports, newspapers, and other printed matter that he should to be ideally well-informed. Therefore, he must attempt to minimize the costs of his ignorance.[69] The White House staff performs this task in accordance with presidential reading habits and tastes, but regardless of its directives it necessarily exercises substantial discretion over what the President reads. There is an inescapable policy impact in this staff function that should be recognized even though it cannot be controlled.

The staff members who manage the President's schedule perform an ancient

---

[68] *See* Bonafede, *Men Behind Nixon/Charles W. Colson: President's Liaison with the Outside World,* NAT'L J., Aug. 8, 1970, at 1689.

[69] *Cf.* Downs, *Why the Governmental Budget is Too Small in a Democracy,* 12 WORLD POL. 541 (1960); A. DOWNS, AN ECONOMIC THEORY OF DEMOCRACY (1957).

political task, that of doorkeeper. Since the beginnings of organized government those who guarded the ruler's door have exercised substantial influence and power. Henry Fairlie describes the White House as "pre-eminently a staff of competing doorkeepers," and he argues that the medieval office of chamberlain still exists.[70] The President depends on his schedule makers to reserve his time for those persons and activities which are politically beneficial and to protect him from unnecessary wasting of time. The policy preferences of the President's doorkeepers can determine who sees him and thus, to a degree, exerts an influence on his decisions. To minimize the power potential that inheres in their "chamberlains" Presidents have tended to select men whose personal loyalty is unquestioned and whose policy interests are either so limited as to pose no problem or closely identical to those of the President, such as President Nixon's assistant, H. R. Haldeman.

The members of the White House staff also provide the President with policy advice and counsel. (Those who particularly "have his ear" become, by definition, members of the inner circle.) White House staff advisers fall into two general categories. First, there are the experts and intellectuals whose skills, knowledge, and experience make them valuable as idea generators and as evaluators of policy alternatives. Their professional or academic perspectives complement the political outlook of the President. In the early years of the Nixon Administration, Henry Kissinger in national security policy, Daniel Patrick Moynihan in domestic affairs, and Arthur Burns in economic policy furnished this type of advice. The second basic category of White House advisers includes close political associates and personal friends of the President. These are truly the President's men whose main value lies in their ability to perceive an issue or situation in terms of its effect on the President and his political objectives. Their advice and counsel is political and personal. In the Nixon administration, John Erlichman, and Robert Finch, after his departure from HEW, exemplify the close political-personal adviser. Such advice is necessary and essential to a President, but hardly sufficient. It must be combined with expert and professional advice within the White House and with a wide array of external advice and information.

White House staff advisers are a mobile and transient group. Their ranks seldom hold firm as most Presidents move through several sets of advisers in the course of their administrations. In part this is due to the expendability of presidential staffers who not infrequently drop out when policies they have espoused fail or lose favor. It also stems from changing policy goals and situational factors which alter presidential staffing requirements.

F. Presidential Advisory Committees

The formulation of policy in the presidency and the executive branch also involves extensive utilization of advisory committees. A General Accounting Office

[70] Fairlie, *Thoughts on the Presidency*, THE PUBLIC INTEREST, Fall 1967, at 37.

survey, conducted in late 1969, revealed the existence of 1,573 boards, committees, commissions, panels, councils, conferences, task forces, and other advisory groups.[71] The survey identified 198 "presidential committees," that were so designated when one or more of their members was appointed by the President. These presidential groups are created by statute, executive order, or less formal directive. Their manifest task is to advise and make recommendations, but they perform other functions as well. An analysis of the full range and activity of presidential advisory committees is beyond the scope of this paper. I will limit my discussion to the most salient aspects of those groups which have played a prominent role in presidential policy formulation: public commissions, White House task forces, and White House conferences, all of which operate for a limited time period, and permanent advisory bodies, such as the CEA and the President's Science Advisory Committee (PSAC), that are lodged in the Executive Office of the President.

Modern Presidents have used short-term advisory bodies for the study of specific problems or issues. The end product of these groups is usually a report and a set of recommendations for action. Public commissions are the most well-known temporary advisory committees.[72] Presidents employ commissions for various purposes. The establishment of a commission is a safe response to a serious situation or problem. It dramatizes the President's concern and his desire to obtain expert information and advice. The unstated presumption is that presidential action will follow the report and recommendations of the commission. Although the commission may prove to be an important source of advice, its immediate function is to reassure the public, ease tensions, and alleviate pressures on the President. The Warren Commission, the Kerner Commission, and the Scranton Commission performed this function for Presidents Johnson and Nixon. Their proposals, however, did not serve as major sources of policy initiatives. Commissions have also been used to study less salient but persistent problems such as housing (the Kaiser Committee of 1967-68) and executive organization (the Ash Commission of 1969-71). These groups, although less publicized, tend to be more able to perform fact-finding and analytical activities that will generate viable policy suggestions for the President.

Most commissions, being public bodies, are necessarily broadly representative. This means that all relevant functional constituencies are included in the membership, a condition that has effects on the work of the commission. On the one hand, it may lead to a thorough airing in a highly visible forum of the central policy issues involved. On the other hand, it may result in a blurring of critical differences of opinion because of pressures to produce a consensual document. In most cases the representative character of presidential commissions contributes to their failure to serve as important sources of new ideas. (The 1970 report of the Commission on

---

[71] *Presidential Advisory Committees, supra* note 1, at 5.

[72] *See* F. POPPER, THE PRESIDENT'S COMMISSIONS (1970); Drew, *On Giving Oneself a Hotfoot: Government by Commission,* ATLANTIC, May, 1968, at 45; Bell, *Government by Commission,* THE PUBLIC INTEREST, Spring, 1966, at 3.

Obscenity and Pornography is a notable exception, although its proposals were publicly rejected by the President.) As one critic of the Kerner Commission observed, its purpose was "not so much to develop innovative solutions as to legitimize existing untried solutions."[73]

Sometimes a presidential commission can prove quite embarrassing to the Chief Executive. President Johnson chose largely to ignore the Kerner report's sweeping proposals for new and expanded domestic programs. They were strikingly incompatible with a tight federal budget and with the proud claims of accomplishment for the Great Society. Two years later, in 1970, President Nixon's alleged lack of leadership was a major finding of the Scranton Commission's report on campus disorders. Although Nixon's response to the report was moderate in tone, other members of his Administration rushed to attack the report and castigate its authors. The report of the commission on obscenity and pornography—a group appointed by President Johnson—received open criticism from Nixon, who used it to inject an anti-smut dimension into the 1970 congressional election campaign.

Because the use of public study commissions entails substantial costs that may outweigh their potential benefits, Presidents since John F. Kennedy have also sought information through the employment of other devices such as task forces.[74] These flexible, informal groups have been used to collate a wide range of thinking and generate new proposals in specific policy areas. Presidents Nixon and Kennedy used them as vehicles for easing the transition to their administrations. President Johnson relied upon them as primary sources of ideas for his legislative program. The Johnson task forces were more systematically operated than Kennedy's or Nixon's have been to date. In all three administrations, however, task force personnel and procedures have contrasted sharply with public commissions and with permanent advisory councils. A primary rationale for task forces is that they are not confined by the narrow institutional perspectives of the bureaucracy and Congress or by the parochial concerns of clientele groups. Rather, they permit the President to call upon people outside the government with a proper balance between imagination and practical political considerations for advice in the form of brief appraisals and tentative suggestions. Task force members tend to be university and foundation based experts who have some knowledge of and experience with the government. They are not necessarily representative of all relevant constituencies.

Task forces work with limited staff assistance. Unlike commissions, they do not produce long, documented analyses. Their reports usually are not published and they have no official status. The President may keep the task reports confidential or make all or parts of them public. The ideas contained in them can be accepted or rejected with limited risk of political embarrassment.

---

[73] G. Marx, Report of the National Commission: The Analysis of Disorder or Disorderly Analysis? (paper presented at the annual meeting of the American Political Science Association, Washington, D.C., 1968).

[74] See Thomas & Wolman, supra note 9; Glazer, On Task Forcing, The Public Interest, Spring, 1969, at 40.

The limitations of task forces arise from the very informality and flexibility that constitute their greatest value to the President. They cannot carry as much weight as more formalized and publicized bodies. Their reports tend to be quite tentative and speculative and are unlikely to stand alone as the basis for new policies. They require supportive recommendations and additional studies by other groups in the bureaucracy and the Executive Office of the President. To the extent that task force reports are kept secret, as they were in the Johnson Administration, they engender resentment in the agencies, on Capitol Hill, and in clientele groups. But if the reports are made public, pressure tends to build for the President to react to the proposals regardless of how tentative they may be. Task forces also risk becoming routinized if they are used too extensively. Their success may lead to the destruction of their informal, flexible character. Task forces are a useful but limited means of obtaining the experience, information, and ideas from outside the government.

White House conferences have been held on occasion to draw attention to a specific problem by bringing together a group of distinguished citizens for a public discussion under presidential auspices. In the past decade conferences have been held on such subjects as education, civil rights, and international cooperation. The principal function of such gatherings is support-building through publicity. White House conferences have been criticized as explorations of "the lowest common denominators of their subjects."[75] They have been lauded as manifestations of "meaningful dialogue between citizen and government official."[66] In any case, it would seem that being organized into numerous committees and operating with temporary staff assistance, the conferences are not likely to be of great value as sources of new ideas and information. Their principal utility lies, by virtue of their nature, in the base that they potentially provide among professionals, political leaders, and relevant constituencies for presidential leadership in meeting the problems at issue. There are always risks in staging White House conferences. At least some of the notables who attend are likely to have ideas that are quite at variance with the values and goals of the President and his administration. These participants may be able to make the conference move in unintended and embarrassing directions. Another difficulty that the conferences pose is the generation of expectations that cannot be met. While a good many participants are not so naive as to regard a conference as the solution to the problem, the affected sectors of the public and even some participants tend to assume that there is a presidential commitment to action. In any case, although White House conferences can attract and build support and impart legitimacy to new policy initiatives, they have substantial limitations.

While modern Presidents have had varying success in utilizing temporary advisory groups, they have generally found two permanent advisory councils with supportive staffs, CEA and PSAC, to be of substantial value in the formulation of national

---

[75] Fairlie, Book Review, N.Y. Times, Nov. 27, 1966, § VII (Review of Books), at 32, 34.

[76] Clemens, Letter to the Editor, N.Y. Times, Dec. 18, 1966, § VII (Review of Books), at 15.

economic and science policies.[77] These two bodies are an integral part of the Executive Office of the President and thus represent the most extensive formalization of presidential advisory committees. Both possess independent staffs, but their structure and operating methods are quite dissimilar. The CEA consists of three distinguished economists who devote full time to their task and are supported by a professional staff. The CEA studies economic trends, analyzes macroeconomic policy alternatives, and examines the economic impact of substantive policy proposals in areas such as housing, welfare, and defense. It furnishes the President with sophisticated analysis that provides a rationale for presidential decisions and is a major conduit for funneling new economic ideas to the President. In the Kennedy and Johnson Administrations the CEA often competed with the Treasury and the Federal Reserve Board in shaping economic policy. Under President Johnson the Council became involved as a major participant in certain policy sectors such as housing. It moved beyond a purely advisory to a policy-making role. Presidents Eisenhower and Nixon tended to rely somewhat less on the CEA for basic policy suggestions and used it more as an analytical resource. The CEA's value to presidential staffing lies in its professional character and in the absence of any formal ties to a clientele group (other than the academically based American Economic Association).

The science advisory structure is also highly professionalized, but is somewhat more complex than the CEA operation. PSAC consists of seventeen persons, most of them distinguished academicians, and is chaired by the Special Assistant to the President for Science and Technology. The special assistant, who is the only full-time member of PSAC, also functions as director of the Office of Science and Technology (OST) and chairman of the Federal Council for Science and Technology, an interagency coordinating committee. PSAC conducts much of its business through panels consisting of one or two of its members plus additional personnel. These panels examine specific subjects and problems and file reports and recommendations. OST furnishes staff assistance to the PSAC panels, evaluates scientific research programs, and assists OMB in the development of science agency budgets. Since the establishment of OST in 1962, it along with PSAC and the special assistant have advised Presidents on such topics as the nuclear test ban treaty, the space program, domestic uses of science, and the development and support of scientific research and education. The science advisory system is geared to enable a non-scientist President to make decisions involving the support and use of science that are compatible with his political, social, and economic goals. In an increasingly complex technological environment this is an advisory mechanism of great importance. Presidents since Eisenhower have relied heavily on it to help them shape science policy. According

---

[77] For an analysis of the CEA see E. FLASH, ECONOMIC ADVICE AND PRESIDENTIAL LEADERSHIP: THE COUNCIL OF ECONOMIC ADVISERS (1965). The science advisory system is carefully described and analyzed in M. REAGAN, SCIENCE AND THE FEDERAL PATRON (1969).

to Michael Reagan, the science advisory system has worked to the advantage of both the scientific and political estates.[78]

Thus far I have not mentioned the myriad of committees and other groups that advise the President, Cabinet members, and lesser officials. These include two basic types, interagency committees and public advisory committees. The interagency committee is primarily a coordinating device and is used mainly to monitor policy and program implementation. Occasionally in the Kennedy and Johnson Administrations, interagency task forces were assigned responsibility to develop presidential legislative proposals. Interagency groups are apparently necessary to overcome the structural dispersion of the federal bureaucracy. They have had varying degrees of success depending, at least in part, on the rank and prestige of the chairman. In testimony before the Monagahan subcommittee, William Carey, a long-time budget bureau official, cited the Federal Interagency Council on Education (FICE) as an example of an ineffectual group. FICE, which an Assistant Secretary of HEW chaired, "never did get around to giving advice to the President."[79] On the other hand, Carey observed that the Federal Council on Marine Resources and Engineering Development, which the Vice President chaired, was highly successful.

Public advisory committees are a pervasive phenomenon in national politics. They can provide a steady flow of new ideas to the President and members of the administration and in so doing improve the quality and widen the range of policy options that are open. They can also serve to broaden the participation of individuals and groups in the processes of policy formulation thus improving communication between the government and the public and increasing popular support for various programs. But advisory committees are subject to limitations if not abuse. Agencies tend to use them as crutches or shields. Advisory committee members may be coopted to support narrow bureaucratic rather than broader presidential and public values. It is also possible that committees may attempt to exercise control over the agencies. To the extent that they succeed democratic responsibility to the public is blunted.[80]

The most troublesome problem that advisory committees present the President is not the lack of information and advice, nor the absence of effective means to obtain it. Rather, it is the difficulty of organizing and using the advisory system effectively. What the President does not and cannot know is immeasurable. Most of the proposals, recommendations, and reports of the numerous committees that are advisory to him never reach the President. As William Carey told the congressional subcommittee investigating the matter:

[78] M. REAGAN, *supra* note 77. Reagan believes that the government-science relationship is tenuous because of the continuing threat that use of the government's financial leverage to direct science to the achievement of utilitarian goals will destroy the autonomy of basic science. *Id.* at 317-19.

[79] *Presidential Advisory Committees, supra* note 1, at 161.

[80] For a discussion of policy advisers in the area of education, see Cronin & Thomas, *Educational Policy Advisers and the Great Society,* 18 PUBLIC POLICY 659 (1970); Cronin & Thomas, *Participant Perspectives on Federal Advisory Processes,* forthcoming in SCIENCE.

. . . Government is getting a great deal of advice, and some information, from the legions of advisory bodies which it creates. I am much less clear on what happens to the advice, or who is listening. I do know that very little of the advice emanating from most advisory bodies ever seeps through to the President himself. Most of it is lost through evaporation, some of it leaks out on staff advisers to the President, and no one can say with certainty how much of it feeds into policy decisions. There is no catch basin to filter and synthesize committee advice and recycle it through the executive branch system.[81]

The need for evaluation and analysis of information on a systematic basis has been long recognized and is at the heart of the rationale for Reorganization Plan No. 2 of 1970. There have been some successful ventures in this direction, such as the CEA and the science advisory system, but they were not comprehensive. The policy analysis performed by the former Bureau of the Budget, as important and vital to presidential leadership and planning as it was, did not provide integrative and synthesizing functions at a level of analysis that would solve the problems Carey describes. Perhaps the new Domestic Council will do so.

Advisory committees of all types are indispensible instruments of presidential policy leadership. However, they have been used indiscriminately in recent years with the result that their credibility has been damaged and their potential value reduced. Furthermore, their findings and recommendations have not always been systematically analyzed or regularly used as the basis for further policy development. No doubt Presidents will continue to employ them, but a more realistic appraisal of their capabilities is in order.

III

THE ADVISORY FUNCTION: A SUMMARY

It has been asserted on more than one occasion, both by former participants in the work of the presidency and by students of it, that much of what happens escapes the attention of the President. This is not at all surprising given the complexity of governmental operations, yet there remains the need for effective presidential leadership in the making of basic policy decisions. That leadership is heavily dependent on the advice and information that the President receives. To a considerable extent the President's office and powers are defined in the Constitution and by statute, he must function as head of one of three equal branches of government, Congress and established customs have imposed numerous duties upon him, and as the nation's major political leader he is expected to respond to the demands of partisans and established constituencies. In meeting the many expectations that surround their various roles, modern Presidents have found it convenient and necessary to utilize some basic sources of advice and information that inhere in the institution and the situation in which they must operate.

---

[81] *Presidential Advisory Committees, supra* note 1, at 161.

In this paper I have examined some of the principal advisory mechanisms that Presidents have employed in the process of policy formulation. The Cabinet and its committees, the top echelon councils for national security and domestic policy, the Office of Management and Budget, the White House staff and its inner circle, and the permanent and temporary presidential advisory committees all carry accompanying benefits and costs. For example, the Cabinet as the symbolic embodiment of the representative character of the administration appears ideal for building support and developing consensus when used as a policy-making body. But it is so severely hampered by the fragmentation inherent in the pluralistic basis of departmentalization that frustration often results when Presidents try to use it. Or, when various types of advisory committees are employed to tap vitally needed external sources of information, they may prove unmanageable or even embarrassing to the President. Or, devices designed to provide systematic identification, analysis, and management of issues and problems, such as the NSC system, may be instituted at the expense of policy rigidity that limits the capacity for flexible response in emergencies.

The use of many advisory mechanisms—the White House staff and its inner circle, the OMB, and some type of NSC system—is inescapable and each President must adapt them to his personal administrative and leadership styles and to his policy objectives. The use of other mechanisms—the Cabinet and its committees and presidential advisory committees—is much more discretionary. How Presidents employ them is likely to vary between administrations according to a rough cost-benefit calculus that also incorporates elements of style and political goals.

Generally, it appears that Democratic Presidents have tended to prefer a less formalized, more open advisory system characterized by relatively easy access of individuals and groups to the President, a heavy flow to the President of reports, memoranda, and other written material that has only been partially refined or screened, an absence of strict functional specialization within the system, and a pragmatic flexibility that is adaptable to emergencies but poorly suited to any kind of long-range planning. Conversely, Republican Presidents have tended to organize their advisory systems more formally and elaborately. Their arrangements have featured greater reliance on the Cabinet as an advisory and decisional body, more finely prescribed procedures and routines for obtaining and processing information, more careful management of the President's time through controlled access to him and highly selective filtration of the flow of paper, an insistence on functional separation of intelligence tasks, and strong emphasis on long-range planning seemingly at the expense of adaptability to emergency situations. The greater propensity of most Democratic Presidents to innovate in domestic policy also appears to be associated with their preference for more open staffing arrangements. The Republican Presidents' preference for structural formalism and prescribed routines is, however, at its strongest in the realm of national security policy where there is much less partisan difference of opinion over policy alternatives. This suggests that the partisan factor is an independent determinant of staffing arrangements for presidential policy formulation.

Regardless of party affiliation, the inclination to develop new policies, and personal operating style, the President needs substantial assistance in obtaining and utilizing advice and information. Successful presidential policy leadership requires that the President's goals be sufficiently well defined that governmental performance can be directed and measured according to the standards that the goals provide. The refinement of presidential policy preferences is not an easy task, for the presidency is the strategic focal point of pressures and demands that emanate from independently powerful elites that function in the numerous policy areas.[82] The President acts as a broker and mediator between these competing and usually non-overlapping elites. He can provide leadership and direction in those policy areas that he regards as important, but only if he has secured the needed intelligence.

Unfortunately, there is no specific formula for an effective advisory and information system. As President Nixon has so appropriately observed:

> There is no textbook prescription for organizing the machinery of policy making, and no procedural formula for making wise decisions. The policies of this Administration will be judged on their results, not on how methodically they were made.[83]

Perhaps the most that can be stipulated is that presidential advice and information should be as wide ranging as possible and that it should encompass diverse social, economic, and political perspectives. The advisory system should be structured so that the President is not isolated, yet he must be protected from fatuous incursions on his time and energy. At key points close to the President there should be situated two sets of advisers, one with unquestioning personal loyalty to him and the other with broader professional and political loyalties. Within these limits, the President may use whatever combination of advisers and advisory mechanisms he wishes. The system that he develops will always be characterized by nagging uncertainties as well as promising potential. Consequently there needs to be continuous analysis and evelution of the presidency and its intelligence system. Yet the basic pattern is set and, even with structural shifts such as Reorganization Plan No. 2, is likely to undergo only marginal adjustments. Ultimately it may well be that muddling through is the most that we can hope for. If so, the challenge that remains is still demanding: to manage the muddling so as to produce satisfactory, if not optimal presidential policy leadership.

---

[82] *Cf.* T. Cronin, The Textbook Presidency and Political Science 34-36 (paper delivered at the annual meeting of the American Political Science Association, Los Angeles, Calif., Sept. 1970).

[83] Report by President Nixon, *supra* note 37, at H929.

"EVERYBODY BELIEVES IN DEMOCRACY UNTIL HE GETS TO THE WHITE HOUSE . . . ": AN EXAMINATION OF WHITE HOUSE-DEPARTMENTAL RELATIONS

Thomas E. Cronin*

I

On Directing the Federal Establishment from the White House

A President is expected to perform three overriding functions: to recast the nation's policy agenda in line with contemporary needs, to provide symbolic affirmation of the nation's basic values, and to galvanize the vast machinery of government to carry out his programs and those he has inherited. The slippage and gap between the first and third functions is the primary concern of this discussion. The annual unveiling of a President's legislative program now has much in common with Madison Avenue's broadsides advertising each year's "spectacular new line" of Detroit-made combustion engine automobiles: the perceptive citizenry is increasingly sensitive to performance standards of both.

And so it is that the recently arrived President, aspiring to "unite the nation" and "get the country moving again," expecting that he and his lieutenants will succeed where previous administrations faltered, customarily feels he must order first his own executive branch "household." Recent Presidents often have gone out of their way to solicit the loyalty and support of senior civil servants. President Nixon, for example, immediately after his inauguration, personally traveled to each executive department and met with and addressed thousands of these senior officials. Presidents and their inner circle of aides continuously strive to secure greater internal managerial control over the executive departments. They even learn (after awhile) that one way to do this is to forge a unity on policy priorities among the general American public *outside* of the executive branch.

But, as Bailey has pointed out, the executive branch of the federal government is a many-splintered thing.[1] The President is soon acquainted with the considerable difficulty of promoting unity in the face of the basic pluralism of the American political system.[2] Presidents Kennedy, Johnson, and Nixon have each complained bitterly about the recalcitrance of the federal bureaucracy, and seemingly turned

---

* Research Associate, Governmental Studies Program, Brookings Institution, since 1970. Coauthor and editor, The Presidential Advisory System (1969).

The views expressed in this article are the author's and not those of the Brookings Institution or any of its staff, officers, or trustees. This article is derived from a larger investigation currently in progress on the presidency and the executive establishment during the 1960's.

[1] Bailey, *The President and His Political Executives*, Annals, Sept. 1956, at 24.

[2] *See* R. Fenno, The President's Cabinet 271 (1959).

more and more to their personal White House staffs for help in gaining control of their own executive establishment. And the collective record of Kennedy, Johnson, and Nixon as chief executive, especially with respect to the achievement of their domestic policy goals, has raised considerable questioning and criticism. As Rexford Tugwell concluded:

> The truth is that Kennedy did not function as an executive. He had only the most meager contacts with the secretaries of the domestic departments, largely because he had no interest in their operations.[3] This inability of a president—who must be political leader and chief legislator and who is sole custodian of the national security—to direct the domestic establishment has become almost total.[4]

Kennedy, after being in office two years, publicly complained that the nation's problems "are more difficult than I had imagined" and "there are greater limitations upon our ability to bring about a favorable result than I had imagined."[5]

One Kennedy White House aide put the frustration more bluntly: "Everybody believes in democracy until he gets to the White House and then you begin to believe in dictatorship, because it's so hard to get things done. Everytime you turn around, people just resist you, and even resist their own job." Again, the same John Kennedy who in many ways inspired the country, was moved to quip about a relatively low priority project, the architectural remodeling of Lafayette Square across from the White House, "let's stay with it. Hell, this may be the only thing I'll ever really get done."[6] President Johnson also expressed disappointment over seemingly slow and uncooperative departmental responses. He attempted to "ride herd" on a multitude of programs by insisting on getting up-to-date figures on varied federal and international grant programs and routinely required departmental written reports. But he eventually resorted to vesting more and more authority for departmental coordination in the White House domestic policy aides and his Budget Bureau director. It was a no doubt disillusioned President Johnson, tired with continually battling the bureaucracy, who solemnly warned the incoming Nixon Administration that they should spare no effort in selecting thoroughly loyal people to man key departmental positions. It is as though Johnson believed that a significant portion of the Great Society programs, for which he had fought so hard, had been sabotaged by indifferent federal officials. And, in the wake of the Great Society legislative victories, both Presidents Johnson and Nixon held that the scaffolding of the federal government and the federal system needed extensive revamping, if not major surgery. Said Nixon: ". . . I have concluded that a sweeping reorganization of the Executive Branch is needed if the government is to keep up with the times and with the needs of the people."[7]

---

[3] Tugwell, *The President and His Helpers: A Review Article*, 82 POL. SCI. Q. 253, 262 (1967).

[4] *Id.* at 265.

[5] Interview with President John F. Kennedy televised December 16, 1962.

[6] Quoted in Rovere, *Letter from Washington*, THE NEW YORKER, Nov. 30, 1963.

[7] Nixon, State of the Union address, Jan. 22, 1971, in 117 CONG. REC. H92, H94 (daily ed. Jan. 22, 1971).

The thesis running implicity if not explicitly through this paper is that White House staffs and executive department officials, upon whom contemporary Presidents are exceptionally dependent, are more specialized, professionalized, and differentiated than has been generally acknowledged. Presidents find themselves continuously surrounded—some would say afflicted—by problems of complexity, diversity, and a seemingly endless series of jurisdictional and territorial disputes. Presidential staffs, cabinet members, and advisors are invariably associated with, if not captured by, professionally, politically, or personally skewed sets of policy preferences. No cabinet officer or White House advisor consistently and singularly acts for "Everyman" or "the public interest." Priority setting, budget cutting, and preferred procedural strategies necessarily promote selective interests at the expense of others. Hence, Presidents are constantly, and rightfully, faced with conflicting claims; calibration and management of conflict is the core of presidential leadership. Those who would somehow reorganize the federal government so as to remove or elevate the American presidency away from bureaucratic or societal conflicts should be fully aware that they may at the same time be stripping the presidency of the strategic occasions for exercising essential leadership skills.

To the extent that White House staff and senior department officials maintain close communications and negotiations—or exchanges—we can speak of the existence of an executive branch exchange system.[8] Both sides are needed to perform the functions of the executive branch; each wants certain types of help from the other, and each seeks to avoid overt antagonism toward the other. White House staff members can be viewed as performing important linkage roles in this exchange system, connecting a President with a vast network of administrative officials. Presidents and most of their staff grow well aware that cooperation from the permanent federal departments is earned rather than taken for granted. Loyalty and support as well as crucially needed expertise are eagerly sought, for a basic premise in the exchange system is that departmental officials, especially civil servants, play, or can play, a strategic role in administering federal government activities.

Some of the relationships within this exchange system can be briefly suggested here. Richard Neustadt has commented:

> Agencies need decisions, delegations, and support, along with bargaining arenas and a court of last resort, so organized as to assure that their advice is always heard and often taken. A President needs timely information, early warning, close surveillance, organized to yield him the controlling judgment, with his options open, his intent enforced. In practice these two sets of needs have proved quite incompatible; presidential organizations rarely serve one well without disservice to the other.[9]

---

[8] For more theoretical treatments of the exchange system notion, see G. HOMANS, SOCIAL BEHAVIOUR (1961); P. BLAU, EXCHANGE AND POWER IN SOCIAL LIFE (1964). Cf. Heath, Review Article: Exchange Theory, 1 B. J. POL. SCI. 91 (1971).

[9] Neustadt, Politicians and Bureaucrats, in THE CONGRESS AND AMERICA'S FUTURE 102, 113 (D. Truman ed. 1965).

And Bill Moyers adds:

> The job of the White House assistant is to help the President impress his priorities
> on the Administration. This may throw him into a sharp adversary role between
> two Cabinet members who are also competing with the President for their views
> of what the priorities should be. . . . Their [White House assistants] job is to make
> sure that decisions get implemented; it is not to manage the implementations.
> The follow-through aspect of it is very, very important. In recent years, the
> White House staff may have tended to become far too much of a managerial
> operation and less an overseer.[10]

The general White House view reflects a concern for teamwork, cohesiveness,
interdepartmental coordination, follow-through on the President's program, and
protection of the President's reputation. White House aides generally spend a
sizeable portion of their time engaged in intra-executive branch alliance building.
How best to communicate what the President wants done? How to give the departmental leaders a sense of involvement in presidential decisions? How politely but
firmly to tell "them" of the President's dissatisfaction with department performance?
How to motivate them to give added energy to get "our" programs moving? Should
we promote an inside man into that new vacancy or bring in someone from the
outside? How can we extricate this program operation from that nearly impossible
group of people over there? A standard joke during the 1960's had White House
staff members trying to figure out how to contract out to private enterprise or
foundations the work that the State Department was assigned to perform. A standard
exercise during the late 1960's, especially within the Nixon Administration, was the
design of programs that might shortcircuit the federal bureaucracy with the hope
of getting federal monies and programs more swiftly into the hands of state and
local officials. In short, the problem becomes how to employ the resources and sanc-
tions of the presidency to make the machinery of government act in accord with the
administration's overriding goals?

Senior departmental officials are no less involved in exchanges with the presidential
staff. Some of them are temporary political appointees, most are career civil servants
with a long legacy of dealing with the presidency, especially with the budget officials
attached to the Executive Office of the President. Their concern is often a blend of
wishing to satisfy and cooperate with the objectives of the current presidential team,
but at the same time attending to departmental priorities and the always present
need for maintaining departmental integrity. White House requests for the most
part are honored; pressure and arrogant communications are resented. But the day-
to-day concerns are reflected in the following types of questions: How can we get
White House endorsement and increased budget approvals for this new department initiative? How can we get the White House to side with us in this jurisdictional matter? How can we make an end run around that unsympathetic and

---

[10] Quoted in an interview by Sidey, *The White House Staff vs. the Cabinet*, THE WASHINGTON
MONTHLY, Feb. 1969, at 4.

amateur White House aide and make sure the President hears about this new idea? When should we supply a potentially great news announcement to the White House and risk not being able to use it here to gain publicity for "our" cabinet officer and departmental programs? In short, how do we deal with the White House when necessary, or when it can help us, but otherwise preserve our autonomy?

There are a variety of "rules of the game" governing White House departmental exchanges. Some are easy to define, most are elusive and variable.

The focus of analysis in the following discussions is on the exchange relationships between White House staff and departmental executives, especially on the "middle-man" role of the White House staff. These alliances, often uneasy and almost always fragile, are difficult to comprehend without examining the observations and perceptions of centrally involved participants. With this in mind, I interviewed forty-three members of the Kennedy, Johnson, and Nixon presidential staffs. Of these, twenty-four served under Kennedy, thirty-four under Johnson, and six under Nixon (many staff members served under more than one administration).[11] Additionally, more than twenty-five cabinet and sub-cabinet members from these administrations were interviewed or consulted.

The 1960's and the presidential administrations of John Kennedy and Lyndon Johnson present a fascinating laboratory for examining White House-departmental relations. It seems fair to assume that cooperative and responsive relationships are particularly tested during and immediately after periods of sustained presidential activism, that is, when major new programs are being launched and old ones being discarded or revitalized. That the sixties were a major period for such change is well-documented and need not be retold here.[12]

Simple but previously neglected questions such as the following need to be asked: How much tension and strain exist between White House staff and departmental executives? Why do some White House staffers see considerable conflict whereas others view departmental relations as essentially harmonious? What variance exists over time or among the departments? What are the major sources of perceived conflicts? To what extent should and can conflict be resolved?

II

WHITE HOUSE-DEPARTMENTAL CONFLICT: PRESIDENTIAL AND DEPARTMENTAL PERSPECTIVES

The focus on conflict here deserves a note of explanation. In the strictest sense, conflict occurs when different people "seek to possess the same object, occupy the

---

[11] Since the period under study here is 1961 through 1970, the bulk of these interviews were with Kennedy and Johnson staff aides. These interview/informants serve as substitutes for direct participant observation by the author. From the various "informants," through a careful process of filling in parts of the complex mosaic, we can construct a richer descriptive-analytical account of the exchange relationships.

[12] See, e.g., A. SCHLESINGER, A THOUSAND DAYS (1965); J. SUNDQUIST, POLITICS AND POLICY: THE EISENHOWER, KENNEDY, AND JOHNSON YEARS (1968).

same space or the same exclusive position, play incompatible roles, maintain incompatible goals, or undertake mutually incompatible means for achieving their purposes."[13] Conflict, as well as its closely interrelated opposite, integration or harmony, is always more or less present in any large organization, and indeed in all human relations. If one looks for it, one will surely find it. One of the ironies of our government is that, although it exists to resolve conflict, *i.e.*, to pull together diverse class, regional and ethnic interests and accentuate the common goals of prosperity, liberty, etc., it strives at the same time to make this nation safe for and supportive of certain types of conflict, *e.g.*, business competition in the marketplace, diversity in religion, and the clash of contending ideas and values. Within the federal executive branch there is more contention about the priorities and tempo of federal activity than there is about the basic ends or legitimacy of the government. In this sense, the executive branch exchange system operates much like a trading arena in which different participants hope that their preferences might prevail. Some recent examples of conflict in the executive branch revolved around the following types of concerns—would vocational education programs be better managed and coordinated by the Office of Education or the Labor Department, what types of guidelines should exist for "Model Cities" applications, should we raise or lower tariffs on shoes and textiles, should United States surplus food programs principally serve the interests of agricultural price stability or short term foreign policy aims, to what extent and in what manner should federal agencies enforce the Civil Rights Act of 1964[14] and the Supreme Court ruling in the *Brown v. Board of Education*[15] decision, and how rapidly and to what extent should domestic departments decentralize administrative and evaluation authority to the ten federal regional offices around the country.

Conflict is not always an indicator of weakness or ill health of an organization. Critical adversary relationships may provide a much needed jolt toward system adaptation and renewal, and hence be a notable asset. Coser's suggestions are relevant:

> Conflict prevents the ossification of social systems by exerting pressures for innovation and creativity; it prevents habitual accommodations from freezing into rigid molds and hence progressively impoverishing the ability to react creatively to novel circumstances.[16]

Several former members of the executive branch have made a case that certain federal policies and practices have suffered not from too much conflict, but from too little.[17]

---

[13] North, *Conflict—Political Aspects*, in 3 INTERNATIONAL ENCYCLOPEDIA OF THE SOCIAL SCIENCES 226 (D. Sills ed. 1968).

[14] Pub. L. No. 88-352, 78 Stat. 241.

[15] 347 U.S. 483 (1954).

[16] Coser, *Conflict—Social Aspects*, in 3 INTERNATIONAL ENCYCLOPEDIA OF THE SOCIAL SCIENCES, *supra* note 13, at 232, 235.

[17] *See, e.g.*, C. FRANKEL, HIGH ON FOGGY BOTTOM (1969); R. HILSMAN, TO MOVE A NATION (1967); T. HOOPES, THE LIMITS OF INTERVENTION (1969); D. MOYNIHAN, MAXIMUM FEASIBLE MISUNDERSTANDING (1969); G. REEDY, THE TWILIGHT OF THE PRESIDENCY (1970). *See also* A. ENTHOVEN & K. SMITH, HOW MUCH IS ENOUGH? (1971).

But assessing the utility or disutility of conflict requires an extremely sensitive appraisal of a large number of variables. The analysis here is limited to an exploration of participant perspectives on the existence and presumed sources of conflict in the White House-departmental exchange system.

It is hoped that studying the existence and nature of conflicts in the executive branch exchange system may add to our understanding about what makes the presidency work—or not work. Though contemporary Presidents have been able to provide some semblance of integrating unity via their legislative messages and budgetary controls, Presidents seem otherwise increasingly buried beneath their own institutional machinery. Conservatives and liberals alike join in faulting the executive branch as a bulwark against change, and as largely unresponsive to contemporary needs. The phenomenal growth and differentiation of the executive establishment and the attributed independence of the permanent government (civil servants, foreign service and military officials, and so forth) from the presidential government (the President, his inner circle of White House counselors, and those politically appointed cabinet officials who can be thoroughly relied upon) make assessing the strength of the presidency quite complicated.

Let us examine the major competing schools of thought about functions and responsibilties belonging at the White House and those belonging within the departments. Just as there are those who want to strengthen Congress in all executive-legislative relations and thereby make Congress the "first branch of government," so also there are heated arguments about whether the cabinet and the departments need to be strengthened vis-à-vis the White House staff and the Executive Office of the President. While not doing justice to the richness of varied arguments, it is helpful to sum up the contending polar perspectives characterizing much of recent practice and prescription: the presidential perspective and the departmental. These are presented here as ideal type constructs and as such are not necessarily held by any one person or group. It is likely that admixtures of these perspectives will be found in instances of conflict and in proposals for reducing conflict. Indeed, much of the ambiguity and inconsistency of contemporary reforms stems from an alternation back and forth between these two perspectives. Reform documents are surfeited with a seemingly contradictory, but intentionally conciliatory exercise of saying "on the one hand," we need stronger departments, or a stronger cabinet, but "on the other hand," we must have a strengthened presidency. Illustrative are the Nixon reorganizations of 1970 which call for closer domestic cabinet ties with the presidency under the umbrella of a "Domestic Council," but insist on locating the fairly sizeable Council staff in the President's office (staffed at least initially with highly trusted White House aides recruited from the national and regional presidential campaign entourage).[18]

---

[18] See Reorganization Plan No. 2 of 1970, Mar. 12, 1970, in 1970 U.S. CODE CONG. & AD. NEWS 449.

A. The Presidential Perspective

This perspective, popular among most presidential advisors, university liberals (at least during the 1950's and 1960's), and probably a majority of the Washington press corps, holds that the presidency should be a strong and visible force in making sure that presidential policy objectives get effectively translated into desired policy performance. "This is the great office, the only truly national office in the whole system." The basic premise corresponds with Alexander Hamilton's point of view—that the requisite unity and drive for our political system would only come from a strong executive.[19] Only the presidency should retain discretion over budget choices and over the way federal policies are administered. And only the presidency can provide the needed direction and orchestration of complex, functionally interdependent federal programs. Presidents and their staffs, if properly organized, can assure that the laws of the land not only will be administered faithfully, but also imaginatively. There is an explicit assumption that a strong presidency can make a major difference in the way government works and that this difference will be in the direction of a more constructive (desirable) set of policy outcomes.

Presidentialists invariably also argue that the presidency is not properly organized, staffed, or funded. The presidency needs not just "more help" but a major infusion of skills, talent, tools, and loyalty if it is to gain control over the permanent federal departments. Implicitly, if not explicitly, "More Power To The White House!" is the slogan. Partly because so many previous Presidents have bypassed existing departments and set up their own new independent agencies, and partly because of the sheer size and diversity of the executive establishment, the White House too often serves at the pleasure of the bureaucracy, rather than vice versa. McGeorge Bundy speaks for many believers of the presidential persuasion when he observes that the executive branch in many areas "more nearly resembles a collection of badly separated principalities than a single instrument of executive action."[20]

The presidential camp never completely trusts civil servants, and frequently mistrusts political appointees as well. Whatever of importance needs doing either ought to be done directly from the White House, or should be done with the expectation that the departmental people will temper or undermine the desired policy intentions. As former Kennedy staffer, Arthur Schlesinger, explains:

> At the start we all felt free to "meddle" when we thought we had a good idea or someone else a poor one. But, as the ice began to form again over the government, freewheeling became increasingly difficult and dangerous . . . [and] our real trouble was that we had capitulated too much to the existing bureaucracy. Wherever we have gone wrong . . . has been because we have not had sufficient confidence in the New Frontier approach to impose it on the government. Every important mistake has been the consequence of excessive deference to the permanent government. . . . The problem of moving forward seemed in great part the problem

---

[19] See THE FEDERALIST No. 70 (Hamilton).
[20] M. BUNDY, THE STRENGTH OF GOVERNMENT 37 (1968). See also id. ch. 2.

of making the permanent government responsive to the policies of the presidential government.[21]

The goal of the presidentialists in its crudest form is "to presidentialize" the executive branch. Toward that end there are catalogues of reform proposals, a few of which can be mentioned as examples:

> The strong Presidency will depend upon the Chief Executive's capacity to control and direct the vast bureaucracy of national administration. Ideally, the President should possess administrative powers comparable to those of business executives . . . . What the President needs most can be simply formulated: a power over personnel policy, planning, accounting, and the administration of the executive branch that approaches his power over the executive budget.[22]

Other variations on this theme call for better policy evaluation and program management staffs within the Executive Office. Presidentialists with narrow policy interests are always asking that the formulation and administration of their particular policy concerns be brought closer within the presidential orbit "much along the lines of the Council of Economic Advisers." Another suggestion would give the presidency some field agents or "expediters" (federal domestic program "czars") located in federal regional offices or large metropolitan areas to insure that presidential priorities are being properly effected at the grass roots level.

B. Departmental Perspective

This perspective holds that the success or failure of the federal government's efforts to manage federal programs rests almost entirely on the quality and competence of the executive departments. An assumption here is that all programs at the federal level possess considerable discretionary aspects. Those holding a departmental perspective say that for programs to be effectively administered, discretion and authority must (at least to a large extent) be vested in departmental and bureau leaders. The sentiment here is that the role of the White House, particularly in regard to the administration of domestic programs, should be a highly selective one, and one that is tremendously and rightfully dependent on career civil servants and professional departmental expertise. Certain department officials, for example, deplored the amount of White House involvement in AID grant clearances, HUD model city selections, and HEW desegregation proceedings. To be sure, even the most extreme departmentalist would agree that crisis situations and various types of national security matters necessarily should be subject to substantial presidential discretion.

The departmentalist view has varying support among professional civil servants, among some former cabinet officers, and even among some former White House staff assistants. Moreover, there are increasing numbers of skeptics who are persuaded

---

[21] SCHLESINGER, *supra* note 12, at 683.
[22] L. KOENIG, THE CHIEF EXECUTIVE 417 (rev. ed. 1968).

that a larger and more "resourceful" presidency (or more "institutionalization" of the presidency) is not a realistic answer to the problem of managing a responsive federal government. There are even those who argue that it probably does not make much difference which of the various presidential candidates gets elected. "You can elect your favorite presidential hopeful at the next election but the basic problems of government non-responsiveness will still be with us!"[23]

Some advocates of the departmental perspective come to their position because of a recognition that the political facts of life just do not permit intensive or extensive presidential involvement in most matters of federal policy administration. The limits of the presidency are cited, such as in David Truman's appropriate cautions:

> [the president] cannot take a position on every major controversy over administrative policy, not merely because his time and energies are limited, but equally because of the positive requirements of his position. He cannot take sides in any dispute without giving offense in some quarters. He may intervene where the unity of his supporters will be threatened by inaction; he may even, by full use of the resources of his office, so dramatize his action as to augment the influence he commands. But he cannot "go to the country" too often, lest the tactic become familiar and his public jaded. Rather than force an administrative issue, he may choose to have his resources for a legislative effort . . . [For effectiveness he] must preserve some of the detachment of a constitutional monarch.[24]

And while the President remains detached or "above" the day-to-day operations of the federal government, cabinet members and their staffs want both a relative independence and a vote of confidence with which to carry on their work. As one prerequisite, they insist that White House staff members should not have authority independent from the President to issue directives to cabinet and agency leaders. And when they need it cabinet members and agency heads should have the right to direct access to the President. It follows too that Presidents should get involved only in broad policy questions, not in the nuts and bolts concerns of program execution and application. White House people are viewed as "amateurs and terribly ill-informed nuisances" who are seen as "breathing down our necks."

The more the White House usurps functional responsibilities from their "proper" home in the departments, the more the White House may undermine the goal of competent departmental management of presidentially sponsored programs. A cabinet member who is made to look weak within his department will be treated with less respect by his subordinates as well as by relevant congressional and client support groups. Department officials who must fight strenuously to maintain access and rapport with the White House have correspondingly less energy left over for their internal department management concerns. When the White House staff or other presidential advisors step in and temporarily take over certain departmental functions, the action may further diminish the capacity of the department to streamline

---

[23] This view was expressed by one former cabinet member interviewed for this study.
[24] D. TRUMAN, THE GOVERNMENTAL PROCESS 407-08 (1951).

or revitalize its capability for managing these functions in the future. Too frequent intervention from the White House creates morale problems within the departments. Resentment and hostility are likely to impede subsequent cooperation. Imaginative professional people will not long remain in their departmental posts if they are frequently underused or misused.

Departmentalists, charging that White House aides get rewarded for "meddling" in department affairs, note that on closer inspection it is frequently a disadvantageous strategy for everyone involved, excepting perhaps the White House aide who has to look "busy." George Reedy, a former Johnson aide, notes that "there is, on the part of the White House assistants, a tendency to bring to the White House problems which should not properly be there, frequently to the disadvantage of the president."[25]

If these arguments appear overdrawn and unrealistic, listen to President Johnson's former Housing and Urban Development Secretary, Robert Wood, as he decidedly posits the departmentalist over the presidentialist persuasion:

> The longer one examines the awesome burdens and limited resources of those who help the president from within his immediate circle, the more skeptical one becomes of a strategy for overseeing government by "running" it from 1600 Pennsylvania Avenue. The semiheroic, semihopeless picture has been captured many times in several administrations: dedicated men, of great intelligence and energy, working selflessly through weekends and holidays to master an endlessly increasing array of detail on complex subjects beyond their understanding on which decisions must be made "*here*" because a resolution elsewhere is not to be trusted. They persevere, taking their stand against "the bureaucrats," pushing programs through against sullen, hidden resistance from the departments. Committees are abolished, agencies rejuggled, staff reviews simplified, new reporting forms introduced, all in the effort to assure that more and more decisions are, or can be, presidential. Yet, in the end, after thirty years, the effort to help the president in making government work has not succeeded.[26]

III

A. Amount of Conflict Perceived by White House Staffers

Conflicts in the executive branch exchange system are widely acknowledged by most recent White House staff members. The forty-three aides interviewed for this study were asked whether they experienced major difficulties in working with the federal executive departments: "can you give your view of this; is this really a problem?" As shown in Table 1, approximately two-thirds answered that there were extensive and considerable troubles in dealing with the departments. Some talked of this as the single greatest problem in contemporary government. One man who had worked for both Presidents Kennedy and Johnson said that "it was an absolutely

---

[25] REEDY, *supra* note 17, at 94.
[26] Wood, *When Government Works*, THE PUBLIC INTEREST, Winter, 1970, at 39, 45.

terrible problem. . . . There are major problems with cabinet members and civil servants alike. Even the great cabinet members like McNamara and Freeman were terrible in evading their share of many of our efforts." A senior Johnson Administration counselor observed that the "separation of governments is not so great between Congress and the president as between a president and those people like sub-cabinet and bureau officials, who become locked into their own special subsystems of self-interested policy concerns." Others talked about the increasing defiance of department people toward the White House:

> It's a terrible problem and it's getting worse, particularly with the State Department. The major problem is the lack of any identification [on their part] with the president's program priorities. At State they try to humor the president but hope he will not interfere in their complex matters and responsibilites. It is equally a problem with civil servants and cabinet types. It is amazing how soon the cabinet people get captured by the permanent staffs. Secretary [David] Kennedy [of Treasury] under Nixon, for example, was captured within days . . . and Nixon's staff didn't even try to improve things. They just assumed there was a great problem. Personally, I think you can't expect too much from the bureaucracy. It is too much to expect that they will see things the president's way.

TABLE 1

White House Staff Perception of Conflict with Departments

Problem of tensions and conflict in these exchanges was:	Percentages N = 43
Considerable	65%
Moderate	25
Insignificant	10
Total	100

Source: Personal interviews with forty-three White House staff members serving between 1961 and 1970.

Some aides were more inclined to note that conflicts varied with different departments and with different cabinet members. For example: "yes there are certainly many problems, but it differs from area to area and from president to president. I think the amount of friction is related to the role of the White House staff and what they undertake and what presidents let them do." Another example of a more tempered assessment of the existence of conflict comes from a Congressional relations aide to the Kennedy-Johnson White House:

> Oh, yes—there are problems to an extent. There is deep suspicion around the whole government toward the new president when he comes into power. . . . But the fights you get in are different all around town. . . . We had some excellent men around town, and some bombs. The important thing for a president to do is to get good men and then decentralize the responsibility. Let the department people do their job and don't let your [White House] staff interfere too much . . . .

Some White House staff who had less involvement with departments were the most likely to acknowledge little if any serious conflict.

On balance, a substantial majority of recent presidential staffers complain of considerable difficulty and conflict in their work with the federal executive departments. To a man, all of these aides were proud of having worked for recent Presidents and quite obviously enjoyed the ambiance of White House political life (said one: "It is the ice cream parlor of American politics!"). Most of them, however, left frustrated with the task of making the permanent government responsive to the White House. The modal if not the consensus view was "the greatest difficulty we had was getting things out of the executive agencies. The magnitude of change and effort that is needed to get things back into shape . . . and how futile it all seems to be . . . [as] requests get lost among the bureaucracy and it is so tough to penetrate all their crap."

B. What White House Staffers See as Sources of Conflict

Conflicts in the executive branch exchange system can be attributed to both subjective and objective factors. The difference in allegiance to the presidential or departmental perspectives illustrate a major subjective factor. Some other subjective factors include differing definitions of priorities and roles, personality clashes, and personal ambitions. Objective factors would include such things as sheer size of the federal effort (and the time and communications restrictions that stem from that size), restrictive budget limitations (Presidents and cabinet heads find they have little control over ninety per cent or more of "their" budgets[27]), centrifugal pulls inherent in federalism and in the functionally independent departments, and various knowledge gaps (for example, "we don't have all the answers!"). Presidential staff members seem to be well aware of most of these sources, but seem to stress the subjective differences and the ill effects of the divorce between presidential and departmental perspectives.

Extended interviews with White House staff yield the persuasive impression that no one set of difficulties lies at the root of executive branch conflict. Their discussions often moved back and forth from noting causes to complaining about symptoms. But their multiple citations here (see Table 2) are instructive both for their diversity and for unexpectedly candid criticism of the way the White House itself contributed to these difficulties.[28]

---

[27] See C. SCHULTZE, ET AL., SETTING NATIONAL PRIORITIES (1970); Weidenbaum, Budget "Uncontrollability" as an Obstacle to Improving the Allocation of Government Resources, in 1 THE ANALYSIS AND EVALUATION OF PUBLIC EXPENDITURES: THE PPB SYSTEM 353-68 (Compendium of papers presented to the Joint Economic Committee of the United States Congress, 1969).

[28] The staff perceptions of the sources of conflict shown in Table 2 do not adequately reflect the intensity of the respondents' views. Although they blamed White House staff operations approximately as often as they faulted the departments, the author feels their criticisms of department officials and civil servants were more intense than their criticisms of their White House colleagues.

1. *On White House "Sources" of Conflict*

White House staffers suggest that their own definition of their roles, and the pressures they had to work under frequently exacerbate relations with cabinet and department officials. Presidents and their staffs arrive at the White House charged up to get things done, to produce results, to make good on the pledges of their campaign. The frenzy and simplification of problems and issues generated in the campaign, coupled with the post election victory euphoria result in strategies of over-extension and insensitivity:

> Well, a Kennedy staff hallmark was to seize power from around town. In retrospect I think they often were insensitive to the channels of the existing government. They came in after the campaign with a pretentious "know it all" attitude and they hurt their case by this stance. For example, I think the White House staffers often called people low in the departments and deliberately undercut cabinet people too much in the early years. . . . In retrospect I don't think you can coordinate much from the White House. You just don't have the people and the numbers . . . [and] you can't evaluate all that much [not to mention managing it] . . . .

No Emily Post manual is available for White House aides to learn about the numerous nuances and diverse expectations that come with their staff roles. At best, it is a learning by doing, and a learning from your mistakes type of experience. The goldfish bowl and pressure cooker atmosphere is an invitation to problems, and the opportunities for mishaps and mistakes abound. Hatchet men for the opposition party and aggressive columnists in search of scandal and conflicts of interest are ever-present with their predatory instincts. These frequently arise situations in which White House aides try desperately to get faster results for "their President" from securely tenured officials in the various governmental departments. But White House aides are damned if they become overly arrogant with department people on the one hand, and on the other hand become superfluous or irrelevant men if they grow afraid to use the available resources of their positions. Eager for fast results, there were many staffers who, according to a former White House aide, "if they had the option between (1) giving an order to the bureaucracy, or (2) trying to win their cooperation, would always settle quickly for issuing orders."

Staff insensitivity to cabinet and department executives occurs for a variety of reasons. Presidents often want to "put the heat on" some cabinet member or bureau chief, but prefer not to take the blame for being tough. Presidents understandably eschew the "bad guy" role, hence the bearing of unpleasant news befalls various staff assistants.

Discussions about the problem of staff insensitivity were often ambiguous. On the one hand, aides somewhat contemptuously talked of the need for more "care and feeding" of cabinet members (as though some of the cabinet were kept symbols for window dressing alone). But they would also insist that one just has to be aggressive and "hard-nosed" in order to get anything accomplished. For example:

TABLE 2

PRESIDENCY STAFF PERSPECTIVES ON THE SOURCES OF CONFLICT AND STRAIN IN
WHITE HOUSE-EXECUTIVE DEPARTMENT RELATIONSHIPS

Types and Sources of Conflict	Percentages N = 41
White House "Sources":	
WH staff insensitivity toward department officials	51%
WH staff and President communications failures	44
WH staff usurpation of department roles and/or excessive interference in department affairs	37
WH "tried to do too much too quickly"	29
Departmental "Sources":	
Civil servant and bureaucratic parochialism	49
Cabinet "leadership" too weak or unimaginative	46
Departmental leaders captured by narrow special interests	46
Red tape, and inept staff work	37
Departments unable to work together	24
Complexity/Diversity Factors:	
Sheer size and complexity of federal efforts	37
Lack of time for the needed follow-through/ coordination/implementation	27
Substantive and ideological differences about policy choices within the federal system	27

Source: Personal interviews conducted by the author with forty-one presidential staff members who served at the White House during 1961-70. Respondents could give more than one reply. *See* n.28 *supra.*

I think most of the problem lies in the disregard of some White House aides of the rank, and age, and positional dignity or status of cabinet members and agency heads. Three little words can give a White House aide a lot of power, "the President wants . . . ." You need to combine a proper sense of firmness with deference . . . but you have to know the danger traps and the mine fields and always have to keep in mind the question: "How can I serve the president?" I'll tell you exactly how to deal with this problem: you use two plans. Plan A: get in touch with the cabinet or department head and say "the President is anxious to have your judgement on X matter." If they squirm or delay or fail to comply then you use Plan B: "Damn it Mr. Secretary, the President wants it by 3:00 this afternoon!" You have to be tough in this business.

Some aides stressed that the always delicate distinction between *staff* or advisory roles at the White House, and operational administrative *line* responsibilities in the cabinet departments became overly blurred during the Kennedy and Johnson years. Too many of the staff tried to do more than they were supposed to be doing and gradually came "to give orders" rather than transmit requests. But as mentioned earlier, Presidents frequently encouraged this development and some cabinet members respect decisive and competent White House aides, brusk though they may be. Impatient or disillusioned with some of their cabinet, Kennedy, Johnson and Nixon turned more and more to their White House staff for advice, coordination, and particularly for help in resolving jurisdictional disputes between executive agencies. One result, in the words of one top Johnson aide, was that "after awhile he [Johnson] never even bothered to sit down with most of the cabinet members (domestic cabinet) even to discuss their major problems and program possibilities." Partly because of the war, and partly because he had grown used to leaning on his own staff so heavily, "Johnson became lazy and wound up using some of the staff as both line managers as well as staff and, I think in retrospect, *it frequently* didn't work out!"

Some of the most instructive commentary was devoted to the problem of intra-executive branch communications. Numerous aides mentioned that a "basic reason for conflict is the lack of communications." Fault in this regard is generally placed upon White House staff and sometimes on the President. Often it is not that cabinet and departmental officials fail to respond to White House policy directives, but rather that those directives are too hazy or inadequately communicated. Sometimes it is because Presidents and their aides just have not made up their minds.[29] Occasionally, different White House aides send out contradictory messages to the departments. For example, the domestic program and legislative development staff might be pressing a department for new program ideas while the budget director and his staff are warning department officials of the need to reduce their activities, especially their more costly programs. Often the President has not made his view known forcefully enough to overcome uncertainty and confusion. Presidents are handicapped in this sense because they often have multiple audiences in mind when preparing their remarks. The capacity of the departments to understand what the President means and to believe that he really means it should never be taken for granted. In his farewell pep talk to the Nixon cabinet, Daniel Moynihan posed the problem as follows:

> [I]t is necessary for members of the administration . . . to be far more attentive to what it is the President has said, and proposed. Time and again, the President has said things of startling insight, taken positions of great political courage and intellectual daring, only to be greeted with silence or incomprehension.
>
> . . . But his [Nixon's] initial thrusts were rarely followed up with a sustained, reasoned, reliable second and third order of advocacy.
>
> Deliberately or no, the impression was allowed to arise with respect to the widest range of Presidential initiatives that the President wasn't really behind them.[30]

---

[29] For a discussion of indecisiveness and ambiguity during the Eisenhower years, see N. Polsby, Congress and the Presidency 19-22 (1964).

[30] Farewell comments to the Nixon cabinet and subcabinet delivered by Daniel P. Moynihan in the East Room of the White House, Washington, D.C., Dec. 21, 1970, reprinted in 6 Weekly Comp. Pres. Doc. 1729, 1731 (1970).

Another aspect of the communications problem is rooted in the sheer size of the federal enterprise. One story was mentioned by a former Johnson aide as a lesson relevant to understanding the communications responsibilities of the presidency. He suggested that the dinosaur probably became extinct not because it was too big or too clumsy, but rather because it suffered a failure of communication. Signals were not transmitted from brain to foot, or from foot to brain rapidly or accurately enough to create a picture of reality on which the dinosaur could act. A few weeks after hearing this story, I was intrigued by the seemingly quite analogous but more specific account of another former Johnson aide, who trenchantly summed up many of Lyndon Johnson's troubles in directing the war in Vietnam as follows:

> Even if the Vietnam problem could have been managed by the President of the United States acting as the Vietnam Desk Officer, the system would soon have broken down from sheer lack of communication. It is one thing for Great Men to make policy, it is another to implement it, monitor it, coordinate it with existing policies and programs, and undertake the advance planning to meet foreseeable problems and possible contingencies.[31]

One other problem discussed by close to a third of the White House aides (again, see Table 2) was that their Administration tried to do too much too fast. Even President Johnson was quoted to this effect in the last days of his presidential term.[32] It was not that Great Society programs were ill-intentioned or mis-placed, but rather that not enough planning had preceded implementation. One veteran budget counselor to Presidents explained his view of the conflict this way:

> Too much was attempted under LBJ. We didn't ask ourselves enough questions about whether we could do these things. Expectations outran the capability to work things out. There were too many other demands or problems in the mid and late 60's. Vietnam, inadequately trained manpower at all levels of government, and the structure of intergovernmental relations was inadequate. The space and missile programs had the backing of the people, but public support was terribly splintered over the War on Poverty, etc. . . . It was like a Tower of Babel with no one interested in the other people's programs.

If the departments are, in fact, occasionally "parochial" in their behavior, Presidents and presidential staff can often be overly "political" in their behavior. For example, Nixon's vetoes of various health and education bills—for balancing his political budget—incurred the hostility of several HEW officials. Likewise President Kennedy's highly political decision to support federal subsidies for the construction of the Cross-Florida Barge Canal angered many budget and conservation counselors within his own administration. Likewise the typical Executive office attitude toward the Agricultural Department—"keep prices down and the farmers off our back!"—annoyed many department officials who held expansionary hopes for turn-

---

[31] C. COOPER, THE LOST CRUSADE 414 (1970).
[32] See H. GRAFF, THE TUESDAY CABINET 172 (1970).

ing their department into a rural development and a major conservation agency. The point to be appreciated in several of these illustrations is that the political perspectives and substantive preferences of Presidents and their staffs produce their share of executive branch conflicts.

2. On Departmental "Sources" of Conflict

There is an increasingly popular view that much of the conflict in the federal executive branch can be explained by the fact that the departments are "specialized, parochial, self-interested," while the President and his advisors have "a government-wide point of view."[33] The extent to which this is the overriding explanation is easily overestimated. While House staff members (whom we would expect to be prime enthusiasts for this interpretation) fault the White House and its operations about as often as they fault the cabinet and the departments. The battlefield depiction of the departments as rapacious challengers of the presidential prerogative, as illustrated by the Schlesinger quote below, is, at least in the context of my series of interviews, an overdrawn or embellished position:

> Kennedy . . . was determined to restore the personal character of the office and recover presidential control over the sprawling feudalism of government. This became the central theme of his administration and, in some respects, a central frustration. The presidential government, coming to Washington aglow with new ideas and a euphoric sense that it could do no wrong, promptly collided with the feudal barons of the permanent government, entrenched in their domains and fortified by their sense of proprietorship; and the permanent government, confronted by this invasion, began almost to function (with, of course, many notable individual exceptions) as a resistance movement . . . .[34]

Approximately half of the White House aides mentioned a seeming inability of many government workers to adopt "the presidential perspective." This latter commodity, always ill-defined, seems capaciously to include "the public interest," responsiveness to the electorate, maturity of judgment, virtue, and wisdom.[35] Whatever all this is, quite a number of the White House policy staff assistants are convinced that department people either do not understand it or just stubbornly resist it. "Mostly the bureaucrats are unresponsive, they view themselves as the professionals and see your [White House] impact as purely political. They don't fight you openly, but they don't cooperate if they can help it!"

Another way for White House aides to explain departmental sources of conflict is to question the competence or loyalty of the cabinet member. Cabinet members get faulted for being "too much of an individualist," "too aloof," "too stubborn" and sometimes for not being "a take charge type." In any event, the traditional complaint

---

[33] See, e.g., J. DAVIS, THE NATIONAL EXECUTIVE BRANCH 146 (1970).

[34] SCHLESINGER, supra note 12, at 681.

[35] An attempt to explicate the "presidential perspective" is made in T. SORENSEN, DECISION-MAKING IN THE WHITE HOUSE 78-86 (1963).

that cabinet members get captured by narrow special interests was a frequent response; to some it was the number one problem:

—Often times we appointed weak cabinet people to start with. Luther Hodges at Commerce was very weak. And Ribicoff [HEW] chickened out after he came aboard and saw the mess which he was supposed to administer—so he merely presided over it temporarily while he began making plans to leave and run for a Connecticut U.S. Senate seat.

—It all comes down to people, some people do a great job like McNamara. They really run their show and get great people to help them and don't need White House interference. Rusk and McNamara were talented and loyal, but Weaver [HUD] was very weak and had loyalties mainly to his department's interests. Even John Gardner [HEW] became seduced [by special interests] much faster than anyone predicted. And Willard Wirtz [Labor] was terrible . . . He saw himself as Labor's representative to the president rather than as part of the president's cabinet. He even out-Meanyed George Meany a few times!

One of the most significant factors promoting conflict between the departments and the White House staffs is their different time perspectives. This same variable is also at play in White House-congressional relations.[36] A president and his staff think in terms of two and four year time frames—at the most. They strive to fulfill campaign pledges, convention platforms, and earlier announced priorities as soon as possible, seeking always to build a respectable record for forthcoming election campaigns. The haste with which the White House rushed the announcements of the Model Cities and the Teacher Corps programs may well have damaged the chances for effective design and launching of these programs.[37] Career civil servants, on the other hand, will be around after the elections regardless of outcomes, and more importantly, they are held accountable to the General Accounting Office, the Office of Management and Budget, or to congressional investigation committees for the way federal programs are administered (and for any mistakes that might be made). The work incentives for most careerists are stacked in the direction of doing a thorough, consistent, and even cautious job, rather than any hurried dancing to the current tunes of the White House staff.

C. Conflict as a Result of Complexity

Nearly all of the White House aide commentary on executive branch conflict can be traced back to problems of government size and problem complexity. White House aides become arrogant and insensitive because they are often asked to do too much in too short a time. White House aides "breathe down the necks" of cabinet and department leaders because Presidents become impatient and restless for results.

---

[36] See POLSBY, supra note 29, at 102-03, for a discussion of this same variable in executive-legislative relations.

[37] See H. SEIDMAN, POLITICS, POSITION, AND POWER 76 (1970); Kempton, *Proclaim and Abandon: The Life and Hard Times of the Teacher Corps*, THE WASHINGTON MONTHLY, Feb. 1969, 10-19.

Departments appear inert or unresponsive because they are having difficulty in pulling together diverse specialists to work on complex questions. Cabinet members give the impression of being "weak" (and sometimes are) because they must preside over huge holding companies of diverse, functionally specialized enterprises. White House aides are continuously disillusioned and disappointed by the lack of coordination both within and among departments; but the White House vision of coordination unrealistically presupposes that department people share an understanding of complex problems, and a sophisticated appreciation of the relatedness of one problem to another, of one agency to another. Communications problems exist because large numbers of people are involved in administering programs all over the country and are confronted by constantly changing and shifting circumstances. Legislative or executive intent, or the GAO and Civil Service Commission "rulebooks and regulations," even if they could be memorized, do not have all the answers for all seasons. Uncertainties, changing environment, and shifting priorities all make policy implementation harder (and pleasing the White House near impossible). One White House counselor to President Eisenhower summed up what he refers to as the pervasive fact of political life that continually affected the Eisenhower Administration:

> the sheer size and intricacy of government conspire to taunt and to thwart all brisk pretensions to set sensationally new directions. The vast machinery of national leadership—the tens of thousands of levers and switches and gears—simply do not respond to the impatient jab of a finger or the angry pounding of a fist.[38]

There is, finally, the constantly faced dilemma of choosing between competing values. Ideological preferences enter here. That not many White House aides mention ideological factors as a source of conflict may imply that a relatively common political culture unites executive department officialdom with recent members of the presidential government. But there are differences of view, sometimes reflecting political party points of view, but more often reflecting differences about the role of the federal government in solving local or international problems. There is always the problem of making the critical distinction between what the federal government can do and what it cannot do. The occasional quest to push the governmental system to great levels of commitment and compassion gets generated in presidential elections and later by major presidential policy addresses (*e.g.*, the quest *to end* poverty, *to achieve* equality of opportunity, *to renew* our cities, *to help develop* Latin America, *to return power* to the people, and so forth). However, even the "best laid plans" of Presidents or Congress often get rescinded because of the "bottlenecks" of problem complexity and jurisdictional interdependency. As White House aides well know, however, "you have to start somewhere"—despite manifest

---

[38] E. HUGHES, THE ORDEAL OF POWER 59 (1963).

opposition and complexity. One aide explained the fate of many Great Society programs as follows:

> . . . complexity of problems and complexity of the executive establishment [those were the chief problems]. . . . A program today often needs three or four departments and an equal number of Congressional committees and sub-committees to even get things started. It is the interdependency of policy and responsibilities that slows things down. There are just more and more people and more institutional drags involved. It takes a lot of time and testing to get things to work. For example, in the fields of job training and civil rights—LBJ knew he had to start things even though he couldn't be sure everything would work out well. He was terribly aware that there were so many bottlenecks. . . .

Listening to White House aides' views of these conflicts heightens one's appreciation for the responsibilities of the chief executive. The President has to act, even in the face of uncertainties, complexity, and opposition; eventually the consequences of inaction may outweigh the results of an ill-fated action. The President can ask the right questions, can act as educator, can preside over appropriate compromises, and can do much to shape and sharpen new policy directions, but the constraints on directing an effective application of those policies to problems are enormous. As the general public expects more and more of the presidency, and as its responsibilties for performance become greater and greater, the President is often thrust in the middle of a disillusioning squeeze play.

IV

A DIFFERENTIATED WHITE HOUSE STAFF

Much has been written about the continuous growth and increasing importance of the White House staff. The popular verdict is that the White House staff is the "center of the action" within the executive branch, and that it, more than any other body of counselors, is now the prime mechanism for helping Presidents shape and execute decisions. We are told that recent White House staffs have included favored assistants who have overshadowed the cabinet executives and challenged the importance of the "Distinguished Outsiders" to whom previous Presidents may have turned.[39] Senior presidential assistants often deny any superordinate status over the cabinet and claim they are there merely to help the President communicate with the departments.[40]

To be sure, White House staff have been quite strategically important in policy formulation stages of federal policy. But their apparent "effectiveness" in this one sphere too often obscures an unimpressive record in policy direction or "follow-through." While White House staff may contribute to the distillation of a vast amount

---

[39] See, e.g., S. ALSOP, THE CENTER (1968); P. ANDERSON, THE PRESIDENTS' MEN (1968); C. ROBERTS, L.B.J.'s INNER CIRCLE (1965).

[40] See Murphy, Eisenhower's White House, FORTUNE, July 1953, at 75, 76 (quoting Sherman Adams).

of incubating legislative proposals, congressional subcommittees along with departmental officials are often able to go about the work of steering and administering federal domestic programs with seeming immunity from White House influence.

Presidents, of course, use their staff differently from term to term, and from one season to the next. But several generalizations about the White House staff in the 1960's can be suggested. It is my estimate that the patterns of continuity and similarity of the way recent Presidents (1960-1971) have organized and used their White House staffs far outweighed the differences. First, while the role of the White House staff has grown generally, its greatest increase in responsibility has been in information gathering and "policy distillation" activities: the culling of new ideas from task force and advisory group reports, the drafting of legislative messages, and the subsequent design of legislative strategies.[41] As mentioned above, the execution or direction of far-flung federal enterprises have been less easily assumed by the White House (although there have been attempts). Second, the increased importance of the White House staff in policy making comes not so much at the expense of cabinet and departmental influence, as in proportion to the measurably expanding commitments of the federal government. Furthermore, just as current White House staff are significantly more important as a collectivity than most previous presidential staff, contemporary department leaders (excepting perhaps one or two) have vastly increased mandates, more administrative responsibilities, and larger staffs of their own, than did their predecessors of some twenty or forty years ago. Finally, relatively few White House aides enjoy anything near the prominence of the more important members of the cabinet. Under recent Presidents, only a small number of White House aides (ranging from six to a dozen) have had close and frequent access to the President. In practice, the large majority of White House aides deal much more frequently with sub-cabinet and cabinet secretariat staffs than directly with cabinet mmbers. And White House aides have their largest influence on matters of small importance or in matters with which the President is indifferent. Theodore Sorensen's view of the staff role is relevant:

> In those areas where his [President Kennedy's] interest and knowledge were limited, the scope of our discretion was often large. But even in those instances we did not make major decisions for him. Our role was to enable him to have more time, facts and judgements with which to make them himself—to increase *his* influence, not ours; to preserve his options, not his ego; to make certain that questions were not foreclosed or answers required before he had an opportunity to place his imprint upon them.[42]

And White House staff should not be judged as distinctly superior to the cabinet or departmental personnel, for the quality of White House staff contributions is very often only as good as the cooperation and counsel White House staff can elicit from departmental officials.

---

[41] *See* THE PRESIDENTIAL ADVISORY SYSTEM (T. Cronin & S. Greenberg eds. 1969).
[42] T. SORENSEN, KENNEDY 259 (1965).

The day of the "general purpose aide" with an entirely undefined portfolio seems a thing of the past for White House staff. To be sure, many of the White House jurisdictions are not rigidly prescribed, but those claiming to be generalists thrive not "at large," but in particular functional or substantive assignment areas, within, for example, public relations, foreign policy, or domestic program areas. It is easier than one might suspect to divide recent White House staff into five relatively distinct functional operations. (More could be defined, but a typology of five is sufficient for our purposes.) Overlapping assignments do exist and not a few White House aides claim they serve (or served) as bridges between factions within the staff. But with rare exceptions, presidential aides can be identified as members of one of the following staff units: (1) domestic policy and legislative program, (2) budget and economic policy, (3) national security and foreign policy, (4) congressional relations, and (5) administrative and public relations.[43]

As seen in Table 3, perceptions of executive branch conflict vary quite measurably with the type of White House task assignment. The White House aides with more programmatic or policy oriented responsibilities are far more likely to observe "considerable conflict" with the departments than are the more political or public relations staff assistants to Presidents. Is this just because they have more contact with the departments? Or is the nature of the work assignment responsible? Or is the type of man who is likely to be cast in one job at the White House basically different from the type of man he must deal with in the departments? A closer examination of this differentiated White House staff (at least as it existed from 1961-1970) may

TABLE 3

VARYING STAFF PERCEPTIONS OF CONFLICT IN PRESIDENCY—EXECUTIVE DEPARTMENT
RELATIONS, WITH STAFF FUNCTIONS HELD CONSTANT

	Presidency Staff Functional Groupings				
Levels Of Conflict	Domestic Policy & Legis. Prog. N = (12)	Budget/ Economic (6)	National Security/ Foreign (8)	Congress Relations (5) (Total N = 43)	Administrative Public Relations Staffs (12)
Considerable	100%	83%	75%	20%	25%
Moderate	0	17	12.5	80	50
Insignificant	0	0	12.5	0	25
	100%	100%	100%	100%	100%

Source: Personal Interviews of White House Staff Members serving between 1961 and 1970.

[43] One of the more distinguishing characteristics of the expanding Nixon White House has been its newly-created Office of Communications for the Executive Branch— a public relations and image-making functional group that will no doubt continue to exist in the same or somewhat similar format under future Presidents. *See* Bonafede, *Men Behind Nixon—Herbert G. Klein: Spokesman for the Administration*, NAT'L J. 258-62 (Dec. 6, 1969).

suggest some of the features about White House work and staff "operational codes" which both make life difficult within the White House and shape varying performances.

A. Domestic Policy and Legislative Program Staff

Recent developments have had the effect of enhancing the need for a larger and more professional domestic policy and legislative program staff: the sheer growth of federal domestic programs, the fact that the initiative for setting the budget and formulating legislation has swung over to the President, and the vast increase in jurisdictional questions which are raised by multi-departmental programs such as Model Cities, mass transit, manpower training, early childhood education, and environmental protection. Another new dimension of White House staff domestic policy work has been the increased use and major reliance on presidential advisory networks outside of existing channels (*i.e.*, besides those within or connected with the executive departments).[44]

Most of the Kennedy and Johnson domestic policy staff members were trained as

TABLE 4

BACKGROUND CHARACTERISTICS OF VARIOUS WHITE HOUSE STAFF GROUPINGS
DURING THE 1960's

	STAFF GROUPINGS				
Background Factors	Domestic Policy & Legis. Prog. N = (12)	Budget/ Economic (6)	Nat. Security, For. Affairs (8)	Congress Relations (5)	Administrative Personal Staff (12)
				(Total N = 43)	
Lawyer	75%*	0%	0%	40%	17%
Economist	0	50	50	0	0
University Professor	8	50	38	0	0
Public Relations Journalist	0	0	0	0	58
Former Congressional Staffer	42	0	12	20	33
Former Executive Branch Employment	75	100	75	40	17
Political Activist	50	0	25	100	67

Source: Personal interviews. * Percentages to be read down the column.

[44] *See generally* THE PRESIDENTIAL ADVISORY SYSTEM, *supra* note 41. *See also* H. WOLMAN, POLITICS OF FEDERAL HOUSING ch. 4 (1971).

lawyers (see Table 4). Most also had previous and sometimes extensive Washington experience; the Kenendy aides came directly from the campaign and from Capitol Hill staff positions, the Johnson aides mainly came from within the executive departments. Many had both legislative and executive branch work experience. Presidents Kennedy and Johnson used their domestic policy staff to summarize and analyze departmental proposals, refine conflicting views (insofar as possible), and generally define issues or proposals that deserved presidential attention. The domestic policy staff have been particularly sensitive to the fact that they should help the President "make his decisions [based] on the full range of *his* considerations and constituencies, which no Cabinet member shared."[45] These staff usually see their work in terms of "getting things started," "getting bills to Capitol Hill," and later, once programs start getting enacted, "making things work."

The domestic aides, more frequently than any other group within the White House, usually fashion a distinctively adversary relationship with their counterparts in the domestic executive departments. Patrick Anderson captures some of the disquietude toward Johnson aide, Califano:

> Serving as the chief expediter for an impatient and demanding President, Califano has made many enemies. Cabinet members seeking to carry an issue to the President are often told to "talk to Joe" and this breeds resentment. Part of Califano's job is to knock heads together, and this wins him no friends among those whose heads are knocked. Some Cabinet members call him "Little Joe" behind his back, and they say it without smiling. Others who have crossed his path have called him a "hatchet man," and worse.[46]

These White House staff tend to be younger than the cabinet and senior civil servants with whom they conduct most of their business. Invariably, the White House lawyers explicitly view themselves as counsels to the President (who, of course, is "their" client). Often these lawyers interrogate or prod "their" departmental adversaries much in the spirit of the prosecuting attorney, and with the same tutored and dispassionate disregard for niceties, they soon earn the disapprobation of many a departmental official. Priding themselves on possessing a superior capacity to think analytically, and the insight and foresight of that mysterious element called the "presidential perspective," White House domestic policy lawyers often view themselves as the necessary and indispensable catalysts who must stimulate and prod the departments into compliance with presidential intentions. Insensitive and arrogant as this appears, these aides are encouraged in this behavior by their perceptions of the constant need for speed, and by an often disillusioned and disbelieving President hardened by his inability to bend departmental bureaucracies in the direction of his policy priorities.

---

[45] SORENSEN, *supra* note 42, at 258.
[46] P. ANDERSON, *supra* note 39, at 367.

B. Budget and Economic Counselors

During the 1960's several members of the Council of Economic Advisers and of the Budget Bureau directorate functioned as full-fledged members of the White House staff. The previous distinctions between "Executive Office of the President" and "White House staff" became increasingly blurred as the White House domestic policy lawyers needed more sophisticated counsel on unemployment, tax policy, inflation control and numerous related questions involved in "managing" the national economy. Concomitantly, budget directors and economists—assigned to the Executive Office—assumed a presidential perspective largely indistinguishable from that of senior White House policy aides.[47]

Budget Bureau leadership in the past decade was recruited from among the economics profession or from respected "old hands" who successfully worked themselves up the career ladder within the Bureau. In theory at least, the President's domestic aides and political counselors serve the short term, immediate policy interests of *a President*, whereas the Budget Bureau serves the longer term perspective of *the presidency*, with particular responsibilities for program evaluation and budgeting analysis. By the mid-1960's both the Bureau of the Budget and the Council of Economic Advisers were involved in White House program formulation tasks as well as in quasi-operational activities such as inflation control or anti-poverty program activities. As these so-called Executive Office "staff" became increasingly involved in White House and cabinet-level operations, the distinctions between White House and "Executive Office of the President" *and* the distinctions between presidential *staff* and executive branch *management* became at best hazy, and often confusing.

The Bureau of the Budget—now the Office of Management and Budget—has long played a central role (although with differing success[48]) as an intermediary between White House and the departments. The Bureau has been expected to raise tough questions about program promise and performance: "What will this program really do?"; "Why has this program taken so long to get off the ground?"; "Why does this cost so much?"; "Why haven't you been in closer collaboration with other departments on this part of that program?"; and so forth. Not surprisingly, and in no small part intentionally, these investigative questions and the budgetary examination processes themselves beget a more or less adversary relationship with the departments.[49] Moreover, Presidents and their senior White House staff assistants expect their budget and economic advisors to identify and bring to their attention department inconsistencies and specific program activities that run counter to the President's intentions. That conflict and heated argument result is not something that necessarily upset Presidents. One recalls John Kennedy's comment to two aides

[47] See Gordon, *Reflections on Spending*, in 15 PUBLIC POLICY 13 (J. Montgomery & A. Smithies eds. 1966).

[48] Schick, *The Budget Bureau That Was: Thoughts on the Rise, Decline, and Future of a Presidential Agency*, in this symposium, p.

[49] See A. WILDAVSKY, THE POLITICS OF THE BUDGETARY PROCESS (1964); Davis & Ripley, *The Bureau of the Budget and Executive Branch Agencies: Notes on Their Interaction*, 29 J. POL. 749 (1967).

in the midst of one such heated debate: "The last thing I want around here is a mutual admiration society. . . . When you people stop arguing, I'll start worrying."[50]

Budget officials, even more than White House staff domestic policy aides, are now well accustomed to their often unfashionable role as the "abominable no-men" of the executive branch. Presidents frequently transmit some of their most unpleasant decisions for cabinet leaders *via* Budget Bureau leadership. One former director points out that conflict between the departments and the Budget Bureau is not only inevitable but, on balance, healthy. How else can you ferret out all the problems and possibilities? Said another Budget Bureau leader: "there is actually an inverse relationship between a cabinet member's effectiveness for the administration and his popularity with the Budget Bureau." That is to say, maleable and agreeable department people probably lack the capability for inventing and incubating needed new policy proposals and/or managerial strategies.

C. National Security and Foreign Policy Staff

It might seem that the President's national security staff would enjoy more harmonious relationships with "their" executive departments than is the case between the domestic policy staff and the domestic departments. Presumably the national security staff deals primarily with only two departments, State and Defense, in contrast to domestic policy aides who must deal with about ten departments plus numerous independent agencies. Moreover, it is generally held that the President is granted much greater leeway in determination of foreign policy than is the case in the various domestic policy spheres. But such a view is somewhat deceptive, for the Defense Department alone is really several departments rolled into one huge umbrella, employing at least three times as many *civilians* (not to mention military personnel) as the entire list of domestic departments (with the Post Office now excluded). In practice, the White House national security staff has responsibilities for at least seven or eight major departments and agencies, including Defense, State, Central Intelligence Agency, The Military (Joint Chiefs of Staff), the United States Information Agency, Agency for International Development, and frequently, when appropriate, for Treasury, Agriculture, and Commerce as well.

The hope that a strong Secretary of State and a well organized State Department could act as the central coordinator for United States foreign policy has grown increasingly unrealistic. Contemporary Presidents have generally held that United States national security policy is and must be presidential policy, and concomitantly, there has been a major shift in policy formulation and direction to the White House and away from the various departments.

All recent Presidents have relied heavily on their national security staffs for keeping in close communication with the executive agencies making up the national security establishment. John Kennedy was warned against having a large layering

---

[50] Quoted in P. SALINGER, WITH KENNEDY 64 (1966).

of staff imposed between himself and his national security departments. He was successful in cutting down the size of the complex formal staff inherited from Eisenhower, but he did not lessen the responsibility of his own team of White House aides in this area. Indeed, after the Bay of Pigs embarrassment, Kennedy enlarged the mandate and the functions of this staff. Kennedy and his aides generally viewed the Systems Analysis and International Security Agency groups as well as the Office of the Secretary in the Defense Department as unusually close allies and sometimes even as adjunct staff.

Kennedy's staff had several economists and foreign affairs specialists recruited from university communities. Gradually, both the McGeorge Bundy and Walter Rostow NSC staffs during the 1960's added experienced "regional area" specialists from State Department or the CIA. But relatively few specialists in military or defense policy served on their staffs, though the Nixon-Kissinger staff has been more inclined to add staff in this sphere. Most of the national security aides interviewed for this study saw considerable conflict in departmental White House relations; the exceptions to this generalization were former department aides who felt that their colleagues exaggerated their estimates of conflict. It is possible that men who have spent most of their career working within government find it easier to work with the departments and are generally more patient than those White House aides new to government. That the National Security Council's framework for coordination has existed for twenty years longer than the newly created Domestic Council offers apparently only slight advantage to NSC aides in trying to get the departments to act in responsive compliance with the President's policy agenda.

Recent national security aides at the White House also paint a picture of their work as decidedly located within an adversary process in which they act as presidential agents trying to bring about a more consistent and responsive national security policy performance by the respective areas of the United States government. One aide suggested that his job was much like "an espionage operation, digging out information from whatever source was available in anticipation of problems, and on the outlook for new ideas and problems." Another NSC aide rather bluntly said that the White House had to know how to "stir up the animals in the bureaucracy, know when to rap 'their' knuckles, fire them, create new agencies to make end runs around them, etc. . . ." A somewhat more reflective view of their role was put as follows:

> One of the distressing truths of Washington is that government needs a sense of leadership, a sense of coherence and a sense of purpose and often needs to be told which way to go. Hence, the president and the White House often can do the job of prodding and probing, asking the right questions at the right time. Often there are great ideas or proposals around lower down in the government, but they never get the proper attention because in their words "nobody asked us." So shaping

the issues, shaping them in such a way as it can be resolved or treated is critically important and a job that presidents and the national security council staff can fulfill.

D. White House Congressional Relations Staff

White House congressional relations aides differ from their fellow staff having substantive policy responsibilities in several ways. Their concern is less with policy formulation than it is with policy promotion. While the program and policy staff are busy trying to win support and cooperation for White House policy interests within the departments, congressional relations aides spend their time seeking political support from within congressional committees and among diverse factions on Capitol Hill. Not surprisingly, program and congressional liaison aides sometimes differ over the relative merits and feasibility of newly suggested program ideas. And at least under the recent Democratic administrations, the congressional relations aides have frequently mirrored the more conservative views of congressional chairmen in internal White House staff deliberations. Congressional relations aides only infrequently pay attention to policy implementation activities and on those occasions, more often than not, they argue the case as viewed on Capitol Hill to their White House colleagues.

Several factors help explain the congressional relations staff's more moderate estimates of contention between White House and departments. First, the White House congressional relations staff by vocation are far more geared to political accommodation and compromise than others on the White House staff. Consensus-building rather than policy incubation and program generation is their life style and preoccupation. They define their task as helping the President get his program passed by Congress. They consciously work for the reelections of the President (or his party) and the President's supporters within the Congress. To these ends they necessarily seek to minimize conflict and maximize cohesion. A reasonably unified executive branch is an added advantage for successful enactment of major legislation. Division and dissension within or among these departments will usually hurt a bill's chances for passage. Because they, more than any other staff at the White House, are conscious of the ingredients (*i.e.*, new proposals) that go into the making of the box scores of wins and losses that (albeit simplistically) characterize presidential-congressional relations, the legislative liaison aides favor "practical" proposals. While domestic and budget White House staff often remain disappointed by the dearth of new ideas or the hesitancy of the President to back a controversial proposal, the congressional relations officers are more easily satisfied by modest accomplishments and are also less inclined to encourage new or complicated legislative initiatives that might be difficult to pass—"we obviously don't want to be put in the position of having to sell programs that don't have a reasonable chance of passing."

Second, at least during the 1960's, the congressional relations officials had explicitly designated lieutenants in all major departments.[51] For the most part these

---

[51] *See* A. HOLTZMAN, LEGISLATIVE LIAISON: EXECUTIVE LEADERSHIP IN CONGRESS 263 & ch. 9 (1970).

department officers were loyal partisans who owe allegiance almost equally to their cabinet members *and* to the White House congressional relations office, for the White House legislative liaison team had authority to remove or fire departmental legislative relations aides. These department contacts frequently had "graduated" to their posts from campaign or Capital Hill staff work. In general, the White House staff enjoyed cordial and close (often with weekly meetings) relations with these "compatible" counterparts in the departments. In marked contrast with the White House domestic and budget aides it was quite rare for the White House congressional relations aides to have much if any contact with non-partisan civil servants or "bureaucrats." To some extent, their departmental lieutenants took the brunt of and absorbed department conflicts, thereby leaving the White House congressional relations aides relatively free to deal with senior congressional officials and preside over White House-congressional relations strategies.

Finally, the primary preoccupation of White House congressional relations aides is dealing with the leadership and committee chairmen in Congress. Since congressional aides are employed first and foremost to help forge viable coalitions of congressional support from bill to bill and from one legislative season to the next, their chief opposition consists of dissident members of their own party or influential opponents on the other side of the congressional aisle. Departmental concerns, especially departmental debates about alternative programs, are less appreciated and probably less well understood by congressional relations White House aides; these latter concerns necessarily take a back seat to their principal attention which is devoted to congressional and partisan strategy and tactics. In sum, then, both the fact that congressional relations aides have less actual contact with cabinet members and civil servants and the fact that they have distinctively different functional responsibilities account for less perceived conflict with departments.

E. Administrative and Public Relations Staff

As can be seen in Table 3, the non-policy administrative and personal staff assistants to the President were the least disposed to see serious conflict between the White House and the departments. Strictly speaking, no one on the White House staff is far removed from policy matters, but in a relative sense, there is measurable variation in staff involvement in detailed substantive policy deliberations. We now have White House organizations with large staffs of communication specialists, campaign counselors, ceremony coordinators, and dozens of others who handle speechwriting, mail, T.V. and radio arrangements, travel arrangements, and so forth. One reason for their "happier" evaluation of departmental relations is that they are measurably less involved with the vast executive establishment. Their contact with the departments is either with the usually responsive Office of the Secretary or with their own carefully planted network of political aides.[52]

---

[52] *See* E. CORNWELL, PRESIDENTIAL LEADERSHIP OF PUBLIC OPINION ch. 9 (1965). *See also* Bonafede,

It is not so much that many of these aides do not have some problems in their relations with department officials, as it is that they have grown accustomed to accentuating the positive. That is, they are hired to secure maximum press and TV coverage for presidential accomplishments and, not surprisingly, to insure that the appealing rather than the appalling stories, the harmonious rather than the contentious character of a presidential administration are communicated to the American general public.[53] Just as congressional relations aides experienced their conflicts more with certain members of Congress rather than departmental officials, so also many, if not most, of the administrative and public relations aides to Presidents have their occupational difficulties with columnists, editors, and TV commentators outside the government rather than with department officials inside the government.

The backgrounds of the non-policy aides are also quite different from those of the substantive policy staffers. (See Table 4.) Non-policy aides have had more extensive political and party involvement, less training in economics or law, and few have had experience working in the executive branch. Their backgrounds are no doubt related to the incentives or reward systems that affect their job performance. Non-policy aides are less concerned with the instrumental tasks of government effectiveness and, naturally, more concerned with maintaining or enlarging the President's coalition of political supporters. These differing perspectives which reflect distinctive staff divisions of labor influence the way these various White House staff work with executive department officials and how they assess White House-department relationships.

V

A DIFFERENTIATED CABINET

In the previous section it is suggested that the differentiated White House staff organization may be one of the contributing factors to the variance in staff perceptions of conflict with the departments. So also it is likely that diversity and dissimilarity of the executive departments may also contribute to a variance in White House staff perceptions of conflict. An essential premise here is that an understanding of White House-departmental relations must take into account the differences in the way cabinet and department roles are viewed from the White House.

Though the cabinet is not mentioned in the United States Constitution, Presidents have appointed and consulted with their department heads ever since George Washington began the practice. President Washington actively solicited advice and counsel from his three department heads—State, Treasury, and War. In time he called these three together with his part-time Attorney General (who continued a private practice on the side). Subsequently, cabinet meetings became tradition

---

supra note 43; Bonafede, *Harry S. Dent Digs in as Key White House Political Legman*, NAT'L J., Sept. 19, 1970.

[53] Bonafede, *supra* note 43, at 258, 262.

and almost all Presidents used their cabinets as a political sounding board and as a convenient communications network. Over time, the cabinet changed greatly, especially affected by its growth from three to a dozen departmental members by 1967. While the notion of a cohesive presidential cabinet of collegial and interchangeable advisors persists with remarkable staying power, the cabinet as a collectivity has rarely been a policy making or program coordinating body.[54] Indeed, the cabinet as a meaningful "collectivity" appears to be passing into oblivion (though not out of existence). And as Rossiter predicted more than twenty years ago, in its place there has grown up "a congeries of functional cabinets with reduced and appropriate membership."[55] The following discussion sketches several variables that undoubtedly affected White House assessments of and working relations with the cabinet departments under recent presidential administrations.

Any discussion of the cabinet, of course, should note that personality and individual levels of competence often affect the degree to which cordiality exists between White House and departments. Each cabinet usually has one or two cabinet members who excel in one way or another and become the dominant personalities in their cabinet. Herbert Hoover's aggressive performance as Secretary of Commerce under Harding and Coolidge was of this type. George Marshall's performance in both the State and Defense Departments under Harry Truman earned similar accolades. Treasury Secretary George Humphrey clearly towered over most of the Eisenhower cabinet.[56] More recently, the case of Robert McNamara is particularly illustrative. McNamara enjoyed especially close ties with both Presidents Kennedy and Johnson.[57] His previous reputation and his subsequent performance as a talented manager of large, complex organizations practically mesmerized both of these Presidents and most of the White House staff (almost none of whom had ever managed any organization other than temporary campaign staffs). Both Kennedy and Johnson repeatedly pointed to McNamara and the Defense Department as models for other departments to imitate, conspicuously congratulating their PPBS, cost reduction, and cost-effectiveness operations. McNamara's quite effective capacity to present his own case before the Presidents made it seemingly unnecessary for White House aides to serve as "go-betweens" or intermediate channels; indeed McNamara put such staff functionaries out of business even before they attempted any efforts along these lines. McNamara, for example, personally carried his annual budgetary requests directly

---

[54] *See* FENNO, *supra* note 2. Fenno's study should have a wider reading audience than it has had in the past, as many new Cabinet members—and Washington journalists who should know better—continue to talk about an idealized "textbook Cabinet" in which all members are treated as equals and in which each serves as a counselor to Presidents on matters beyond those within their departments' jurisdictions.

[55] Rossiter, *The Constitutional Significance of the Executive Office of the President*, 43 AM. POL. SCI. REV. 1206, 1216 (1949).

[56] HUGHES, *supra* note 38, at 61-68; A. LARSON, EISENHOWER: THE PRESIDENT NOBODY KNEW 25-26 (1968).

[57] *Compare* the sympathetic perspective on McNamara in W. KAUFMAN, THE McNAMARA STRATEGY (1964), *with* the more critical account in Halberstam, *The Programming of Robert McNamara*, HARPER'S, Feb. 1971, at 37.

to the President, with the President granting the Budget Director the opportunity for selective appeals or disagreements; this was a substantially different if not an exact opposite procedure of the usual for all other cabinet members (and for Defense Secretaries both before and after the Kennedy-Johnson administrations).

Occasionally, too, there are times when the politics of the period and the functions of a department thrust particular cabinet members into prominence, and simultaneously, into close collaborative relations with the White House. Dean Acheson's unusually close and cordial ties with the Truman White House and Lyndon Johnson's highly respectful appreciation of Dean Rusk illustrate the cases of internationally tense periods in which diplomatic political strategy looms large. Secretary John Gardner (HEW 1965-68) enjoyed great prominence and relatively good relations with the Johnson White House during the middle 1960's around the time in which major educational and health legislation were being ratified and placed into operation. Soon thereafter, however, when the Vietnam war began overshadowing all else and consuming more and more of the President's time and potential budget increases, White House communications with HEW's Gardner began to resemble those of most other domestic cabinet members—less frequent and less supportive.

The rise in prominence or fashion of an issue relevant to a department's activities can occasionally also work to the detriment of White House-department relations. The "law and order" issue in the late 1960's occasioned cutting partisan attacks to be mounted against President Johnson's Attorney General. Ramsey Clark resisted most temptations to act in any retaliatory or repressive manner. But, evidently, Clark's response was viewed as overly dispassionate and tolerant by his President.[58] And the more recent case of former Secretary Walter Hickel and his varied efforts apparently illustrates the case of a cabinet member who decides to champion popular issues (environmental protection and youth) measurably further than the Administration of which he is a part.

There are, of course, numerous other reasons why Presidents and their staff may deliberately choose to have "cool" relations with a cabinet member. Sometimes this may be due to presidential lack of interest in a department's domain. Sometimes there is ill will existing between a strong President and a strong and quite stubborn cabinet member. Part of the problem undoubtedly arises because Presidents just don't have time to spend with cabinet officers, not to mention the leaders of independent agencies and major bureau chiefs. The blunt fact of the contemporary period is that approximately two-thirds of presidential time has been spent on national security and foreign policy considerations.

An apparent pattern characterizes White House-cabinet relations over time. Just as there is a distinctive presidential "honeymoon" with the press and with partisan critics, so also White House-department ties usually are the closest and

---

[58] See GRAFF, supra note 32, at 172.

most cooperative during the first year of an administration. The first six months of the relationship is usually cordial, "healthy," and often bordering on the euphoric. The election victory is still being celebrated. A new team of "leaders" has arrived in Washington. New faces provide for extensive news copy. A new federal policy agenda is being recast. The newly staffed executive branch gives everyone an impression of bubbling over with new ideas, new possibilities, and imminent breakthroughs. In contrast to the much publicized arrival of the cabinet members, White House staff receive less publicity at this time. White House ceremonies feature the announcement, installation, and self-congratulatory rituals of welcoming in the recently annointed cabinet chieftains who, at least in the Nixon version, are men possessed of special "extra dimensions." The Washington political community, the executive branch in particular, is a veritable merry-go-round of good will and cheerful open doors. One Kennedy cabinet member, remembering those early days, noted that Kennedy told his cabinet that there would be frequent cabinet meetings and that individual cabinet officers should telephone him or Vice President Lyndon Johnson on anything of importance; when in doubt they should "err on the side of referring too much" on policy matters.[59] Even the egregiously silly or blandest of proposals coming from cabinet members at this time are tolerated and entertained by a deferential White House staff and a happily-elected President.

But as policy formulation is accentuated in the early years of a presidential term, program management and implementation receive increasing attention in the later period (especially if a President has been successful in passing a fair amount of new legislation by then). Critical domestic developments and international crises begin to monopolize the presidential schedule. Presidents gradually find that they have much less time for personally dealing with cabinet members as they had in the administration's early months. Cabinet members become less inclined to refer "too much" to the President, knowing full well that they may prematurely exhaust their personal political credit with him. Additionally, the President's program becomes somewhat fixed; priorities get set and budget ceilings produce some new rules of the game. Ambitious, expansionist cabinet officers become painfully familiar with various Executive Office staff refrains, usually to the effect that "there just isn't any more money available for programs of that magnitude," "budget projections for the next two or three years just can't absorb that type of increment," and perhaps harshest of all—"yes, I agree that this is an excellent proposal, but excellent though it may be, it will just have to wait until the next term."

When, in the course of an administration, cabinet members grow bitter about the way they are treated and increasingly left out of White House affairs, they seldom make their opinions public. There are, of course, some exceptions and privately a good number of cabinet officers will talk about the problem. The case of Interior Secretary Walter Hickel is perhaps an extreme case; the fact that he had only two

---

[59] J. DAY, MY APPOINTED ROUND: 929 DAYS AS POSTMASTER GENERAL 97 (1965).

or three private meetings with his President during a two year period seems an unusually restrictive arrangement. Most recent cabinet officers have had more frequent relations with their White House superiors, but few of the domestic cabinet members have been wholly pleased by the quantity or quality of these meetings. Said one Johnson cabinetman, "I just don't know what you can do—you just have to realize that his day is the same length as yours and become resigned to the reality that he just can't afford to spend much time with most of us—especially with that war going on."

A cabinet member who served both Presidents Kennedy and Johnson stated that there should unquestionably have been more cabinet meetings:

> there are two important things that should be done through the use of the cabinet meetings. First, meetings should be held to inform the cabinet members about major developments or new priorities. Secondly, the president should occasionally bring some major policy issue before the cabinet and open it up for detailed discussion. He should take advantage of the broad gauged abilities of these very able men. For example, never once was there any discussion of whether we should send more troops to Vietnam. This type of policy matter was always confined to the national security council group—but they could have benefitted from our views and ideas on this type of matter, for we had less personal involvement in the earlier decisions and might have been able to give valuable added perspective or fresh appraisals.

An insightful commentary is provided by John Kennedy's Postmaster General in his witty but somewhat bitter memoir-recollections. J. Edward Day suggests that Kennedy had neither the time nor the inclination to utilize the collective judgment of his cabinet; Day also hints that Kennedy hardly made use of several of the cabinet members even in their individualized departmental leadership roles. It is worth citing three of his observations at length, not so much because he is one of the few cabinet members to express his views openly, as because his views are similar to the private complaints of several other cabinet officers:

> . . . President Kennedy had never had the experience of being an executive among lesser but by no means subservient excutives; he had been served by a fanatically devoted band of men of his own creation. His Cabinet was a different run of shad. Each member was independent and quick to express his views, perhaps too much so for the President's taste. . . .
>
> . . . .
>
> The impression was created . . . that the President preferred smaller meetings with those Cabinet members concerned with a specific problem. *But his absorption with politics, publicity, and foreign policy allowed him little time to be concerned about the domestic departments,* unless they had an immediate political aspect. For the domestic Cabinet, *personal meetings with the President became fewer and farther between,* and more than one member grew increasingly unhappy because it was so difficult to see the President.

The atmosphere at Cabinet meetings should have been right for free-and-easy, frank discussion. At the outset it had been only natural to assume that such discussion would be encouraged. . . .

The setting may have been right, but after the first two or three meetings one had the distinct impression that the President felt that decisions on major matters were not made—or even influenced—at Cabinet sessions, and what discussion there was a waste of time. . . . When members spoke up to suggest or to discuss major Administration policy, the President would listen with thinly disguised impatience and then postpone or otherwise bypass the question. . . .[60]

A senior Kennedy staff member tells of the occasion when one cabinet officer had repeatedly requested him to make an appointment with the President. "He kept calling and calling, and so finally about the forty-third time—after I had told him over and over again that this wasn't the type of problem the President wanted to discuss with cabinet members—I finally relented and scheduled an appointment. Immediately after Secretary X completed his appointment and had left, Kennedy stormed into my office and [in emphatically strong language] chewed me out for letting the cabinet member in!"

Cabinet members who went to President Johnson with requests were often faced with a *quid pro quo* situation, and at least for some cabinet members, presidential requests were an added factor in keeping them at a distance. One cabinet officer noted that most of the domestic department heads tried as much as possible to leave the President alone because of the enormous Vietnam war burdens the President was carrying. "But even at that, it was known that the President would welcome visits by domestic cabinet members on Saturday mornings. In retrospect, several of us regret that we did not make greater and better use of those opportunities. But part of the reason we didn't was because Johnson had an uncanny way of asking favors of you or giving you a number of political chores to do that you knew you didn't want and often couldn't carry out."

By mid-term election time, the White House also expects cabinet members to campaign for the administration and to celebrate the administrative and legislative record of the past two years. Like it or not, cabinet members become judged on their capacity to generate favorable publicity, and to proclaim the virtues of the recent "White House" achievements and, above all, to exclaim the performance of the sitting President.

Conventional rankings of the departments are based on their longevity, annual expenditure outlays, or their personnel totals. Rankings according to these indicators can be seen in the first three columns of Table 5. A preliminary appreciation of department diversity can be gained by even a casual comparison of these columns. For example, while the State Department is more than 175 years older than some of the newest departments, its expenditures rank as the lowest of any department.

---

[60] *Id.* at 96-98.

On the other hand, the Department of Health, Education and Welfare although formally less than twenty years old ranks second only to Defense in having more personnel and higher annual expenditures.

Some other ways of classifying the departments deserve note. One is suggested by Stewart Alsop's journalistic appraisal of real political "power and impact."[61]

TABLE 5

VARIOUS WAYS OF VIEWING THE EXECUTIVE DEPARTMENTS

SENIORITY	EXPENDITURES[a]	PERSONNEL[b]	A JOURNALIST'S ASSESSMENT OF "REAL POLITICAL POWER & IMPACT"[c]
1 State	1 Defense	1 Defense	1 Defense
2 Treasury	2 HEW	2 HEW	2 State
3 War/Defense	3 Treasury	3 Agriculture	3 Treasury
4 Justice	4 Agriculture	4 Treasury	4 Justice
5 Interior	5 Labor	5 Interior	5 Interior
6 Agriculture	6 Transportation	6 Transportation	6 HEW
7 Commerce	7 HUD	7 State	7 Labor
8 Labor	8 Commerce	8 Justice	8 Agriculture
9 HEW	9 Justice	9 Commerce	9 Commerce
10 HUD	10 Interior	10 HUD	10 HUD
11 Transportation	11 State	11 Labor	11 Transportation

INNER & OUTER CLUSTERINGS[d]	SUPER-CABINET PLAN A[e]	SUPER-CABINET PLAN B[f]	PRESIDENT NIXON'S 1971 PROPOSAL[g]
State Defense Treasury Justice	National Security Economic Stability and Growth Domestic Policy	Foreign Affairs Economic Affairs Natural Resources Science and Technology Social Services and Justice	State Defense Treasury Justice
Agriculture Interior Transportation HEW HUD Labor Commerce			Human Resources Natural Resources Economic Development Community Development

[a] Estimated budget outlays of the executive departments in 1971.

[b] *Statistical Abstract*, data for 1970.

[c] *See* S. ALSOP, THE CENTER 254 (1968).

[d] Generic clustering according to counseling/advocacy dimensions—see text discussion.

[e] The way some White House aides view aggregate departmental concerns, and the apparent priority of these concerns as viewed by recent Presidents.

[f] An example of cabinet consolidation that is one of many plausible but politically unlikely reforms.

[g] Richard M. Nixon, State of the Union message to Congress, January 22, 1971.

[61] *See* ALSOP, *supra* note 39, ch. 9.

Alsop's 1967 ranking takes into account not only the conventional data mentioned above, but also the Washington, D.C., status considerations toward contemporary cabinet members and departmental activities. Upon closer inspection the Alsop listing varies only slightly from longevity or seniority rankings with minor adjustments added to acknowledge the higher budget allocations of Defense and HEW as well as the personal Washington "celebrity" status of Robert S. McNamara and John W. Gardner (HEW).

The contemporary cabinet can also be differentiated into "inner" and "outer" departmental clusterings as illustrated in the fifth column of Table 5. The inner cabinet, at least throughout the 1960's, was generally recognized as the primary presidential counseling as well as strategic information gathering departments. (A cabinet counselor is a source of information and advice, someone to whom a President can turn for appraisals and consultation on highly sensitive or critical problems.) The outer cabinet are the explicitly domestic policy departments (Justice excepted). By custom, if not by designation these cabinet officers assume a relatively straight-forward advocate orientation that overshadows their counseling role. (An advocate is someone who argues for a cause, who supports, defends and on occasion pleads in behalf of some special concern.)

State, Defense, Treasury, and Justice, each for different reasons (discussed below), are the cabinet posts most consistently considered as part of the inner cabinet. The pattern in the past few presidential administrations suggests somewhat strongly that these counseling cabinet positions are vested with high priority responsibilities that almost naturally bring Presidents and their top staff into close and continually collaborative relations with the occupants of these inner cabinet leadership posts. Sorensen wrote that it was the "nature of their responsibilties and the competence with which they did their jobs" that brought certain department executives particularly close to President Kennedy in this counseling manner.[62] Speaking of the Eisenhower period, Emmet J. Hughes sees a convergence of raw strength of personality and leadership with the Defense, Treasury, and State cabinet posts.[63] Sorensen cites six cabinet members as enjoying particularly close ties to John Kennedy, and one gathers that the general order of their importance and closeness to Kennedy amounted to this: Defense Secretary Robert McNamara, Attorney General Robert Kennedy, Secretary of State Dean Rusk, Treasury Secretary Douglas Dillon, and in varying ways Labor Secretary Arthur Goldberg and Vice President Lyndon Johnson.[64] And it is abundantly clear that Rusk and McNamara continued to hold superordinate status in the Lyndon Johnson cabinet vis-à-vis their cabinet colleagues. On balance, the period between 1961 and 1971 can be characterized by having had an "inner cabinet" group made up of the Defense, State, and Treasury secretaries along with the Attorney General. Then, too, as will be discussed a little later, certain White

---

[62] SORENSEN, *supra* note 42, at 265.

[63] HUGHES, *supra* note 38, at 61.

[64] *See generally* SORENSEN, *supra* note 42, ch. 10.

House staff counselors were also included in an inner circle if not in the inner cabinet.

The inner cabinet grouping of this inner/outer breakdown suggested here corresponds identically to George Washington's original foursome, to Stewart Alsop's journalistic appraisal, and also to Sorensen's account of the Kennedy Administration. Moreover, the inner cabinet departments were the only ones immune to President Nixon's proposed overhaul of the executive branch; all others were nominated for abolition. My own classification of inner/outer derives from the examination of how White House aides viewed the departments. The status accorded these cabinet roles is, of course, subject to ebb and flow, for the status is rooted in performance and the fashions of the day as well as reputation. But, in general, White House staff during the 1960's acted far more deferentially toward these inner cabinet positions and the men who occupied them than toward outer cabinet officials.

With the exception of the State *Department*, as distinguished from the *Office of the Secretary* of State, the inner cabinet and the inner cabinet departments were almost always viewed as executive branch allies of the White House staff. An implicit operational code to this effect seemingly guided the manner in which most White House staff aides participated in executive branch activities during the 1960's. For this reason, these ties deserve further attention.

The State and Defense Departments have long been considered counseling and inner-cabinet departments. And the special closeness of Secretaries Rusk and Mc-Namara with both Kennedy and Johnson is illustrative. One Johnson aide said it was his belief that President Johnson personally trusted only two of his cabinet—Rusk and McNamara (though it appears that the trust relationship between Johnson and McNamara diminished somewhat in 1967). Contemporary Presidents view national security and foreign policy matters as life and death considerations; President Kennedy, for example, noted that while mistakes in domestic policy "can only defeat us [at the next election, mistakes in] foreign policy can kill us." The seemingly endless series of crises (Berlin, Cuba, Congo, Dominican Republic, Vietnam, and the Middle East to name just a few) during the 1960's make it mandatory for recent Presidents to maintain close relations with these two national security cabinet heads. Just as George Washington had met almost every day with his four "cabinet" members during the national security concern over the French crisis of 1793, so also John Kennedy and Lyndon Johnson were likely to meet at least weekly and be in daily telephone communication with their inner cabinet of national security advisors.[65]

It needs to be added, however, that throughout the past decade there has been more than a little White House discontent with the operational lethargy of the State Department.[66] We see here an anomaly in which the Secretary of State clearly

---

[65] *See* GRAFF, *supra* note 32; G. CHRISTIAN, THE PRESIDENT STEPS DOWN (1970).

[66] *See* SCHLESINGER, *supra* note 12; HILSMAN, *supra* note 17; J. LEACACOS, FIRES IN THE IN-BASKET (1968); Campbell, *"What is to be Done?"—Gigantism in Washington*, 49 FOREIGN AFFAIRS 81 (1970).

was regarded as a member of the President's inner cabinet, but the Department of State was regarded as one of the most deficient and inadequate cabinet departments. More than twenty-five per cent of the White House staff interviewed for this study cited the State Department as an excellent illustration of the problem of White House-department conflicts. White House staff scorned the narrowness and timidity of the encrusted and elitist foreign service officers and complained also of the cutodial conservatism reflected in State Department working papers. Part of this problem may stem from the threats and philosophy of the Joseph McCarthy era which intimidated State Department careerists into holding only the puristic interpretations of the accepted policies of the day, thereby inhibiting their imaginative and inventive policy faculties. No doubt though, part of the problem stems from the way recent Secretaries, especially Secretary Rusk, defined their job. The demands on the Secretary were such that the State Department and its management were not Rusk's personal top priority. John Leacacos has surmised that the priorities appeared to have been:

> . . . first, the President and his immediate desires; second, the top operations of the current crisis; third, public opinion as reflected in the press, radio and TV and in the vast inflow of letters from the public; fourth, Congressional opinion; fifth, Rusk's need to be aware, at least, of every thing that was going on in the world; and only sixth and last, the routine of the State Department itself.[67]

The fact that the Secretary of State so frequently serves as the President's representative abroad or his number one witness on foreign policy matters before the Congress undoubtedly is another reason so few Secretaries of State have had the time or energy available for managing the State Department's widely scattered staff. It needs to be added that more than sixty federal departments, agencies, and committees are involved some way in the administration of our foreign policy. Recent Presidents increasingly have vested authority in their own White House-based NSC staff partly to compensate for State's uneven performance as a coordination arm for foreign policy matters and partly because Presidents need instant analysis during international crisis periods. In this regard, McGeorge Bundy's White House national security staff was dubbed by the press as "Bundy's little State Department." In another step to centralize and coordinate basic foreign policy activities, Richard Nixon has instituted a White House-level Council of International Economic Policy with broad authorities. Nonetheless, the Secretary of State still enjoys a relative closeness to the incumbent President and even with the rise in importance of White House national security counselors the Secretary of State is likely to continue as a full-fledged member of future presidential inner cabinets.

The Justice Department, also a counseling department, is frequently identified with the "inner circle" of cabinet agencies and its chieftains usually associated with the inner cabinet. That both Kennedy and Nixon appointed their most trusted campaign

---

[67] Leacacos, *supra* note 66, at 110.

managers to the Attorney Generalship is an indicator of the importance of this position as a presidential counseling location. The Justice Department traditionally serves as the President's attorney and lawyer.[68] This special obligation results in continually close professional relations between White House domestic policy lawyers and Justice Department lawyers. Few people realize that the White House is constantly dependent on Justice Department lawyers for counsel on civil rights developments, presidential veto procedures, tax prosecutions, anti-trust controversies, presidential pardons recommendations, regulatory agency oversight, and a continual overview of the congressional judiciary committees. That this particular exchange sees lawyer working with lawyer may well account for some of the generally higher levels of satisfaction characterizing White House-Justice Department transactions. (The anomaly of J. Edgar Hoover as chief of the FBI which is, of course, within the Justice Department, defies most generalizations, for Hoover has often remained immune from both White House and Attorney General sanction, much to the concern of many of his "superordinates.")

The Treasury Department continues to play an all important role as an interpreter of the nation's leading financial interests and as key presidential advisor on both domestic and international fiscal and monetary policy considerations. At one time, of course, the Bureau of the Budget existed within Treasury. Now the budget staff and numerous economists, particularly within the Council of Economic Advisers, are attached to the White House itself, thereby somewhat diminishing the monopoly of economic counsel once available only from the Treasury. But, Treasury is a department with major institutional authority, having considerable responsibility for income and corporate tax administration, currency control, public borrowing and counseling the President with respect to questions of balance of gold, the federal debt and international trade, development, and monetary matters. By custom, if not by law, the Secretary of the Treasury sits in on deliberations of important national security controversies. Indeed, Treasury Secretary Douglas Dillon played a significant role in Kennedy's Cuban Missile Crisis policy determinations. There is here, as in the case of the Justice Department lawyers, a common professional linkage among economists and financial specialists at Treasury and their professional counterparts on the White House staff.

The inner circle of cabinet members are noticeably more interchangeable than the outer circle cabinet. Henry Stimson, for example, alternated from Taft's Secretary of War, to Hoover's Secretary of State, and then back once more as FDR's Secretary of the War Department. Dean Acheson was an FDR Under Secretary of the Treasury but later a Truman Secretary of State. C. Douglas Dillon reversed this pattern by being an Eisenhower Under Secretary of State and later a Kennedy Secretary of the Treasury. When Kennedy was trying to lure Robert McNamara to his new cabinet he offered McNamara his choice between Defense and Treasury.

---

[68] *See* L. HUSTON *et al.*, ROLES OF THE ATTORNEY GENERAL OF THE UNITED STATES chs. 1 & 2 (1968).

More recently, former Attorney General Nicholas Katzenbach went from Justice to an Under Secretaryship of State, and former Attorney General William Rogers is now the thirteenth Justice Department head to have served in another inner cabinet position. John Connally, once a Secretary of the Navy, became a Nixon Secretary of the Treasury. There have been occasional shifts between inner and outer cabinet (*e.g.*, Harriman—Commerce to State, and Richardson—State to HEW), but such examples are an exception to the general pattern. What this interchangeability means is hard to discern, but it suggests perhaps that Presidents find it easier as well as more necessary to work with inner cabinet members and that inner cabinet members find it easier for their part to adopt a counseling style that allows them to identify more closely with the presidential "perspective" than is the case for outer cabinet members.

Quite related to the interchangeability of inner cabinet roles is the little-appreciated fact that, at least in recent years, White House staff aides recruited from within the executive branch have come mainly from among the inner-cabinet departments, often directly from service as assistants to cabinet members. And many of the recent White House staff who did not come from the executive branch had served (at one time or another) as departmental consultants to inner cabinet officials.

In recent years several members of the White House staff have performed cabinet-level counselor roles. Eisenhower, for example, explicitly designated Sherman Adams as a protocol member of his cabinet. Kennedy clearly looked upon Theodore Sorensen, McGeorge Bundy, and some of his economic advisors as co-equals if not more vital to his work than most of his cabinet members. Johnson and Nixon have likewise assigned many of their "staff" men to cabinet-type counseling responsibilities. Indeed, President Nixon, quite reasonably, has appropriated this term—cabinet counselor— for several of his personal staff, including Messrs. Burns, Moynihan, Harlow, and Finch. These counselors, whether in department posts or on the White House staff, are expected to rise above the narrowing frame of reference of the conventional advocate and, in Moynihan's view "It is not enough [that they] know one subject, one department. The President's men must know them all, must understand how one thing relates to another, must find in the words the spirit that animates them . . . ."[69] The people to whom Presidents turn for White House overview presentations to congressmen and cabinet gatherings provide another indicator of inner "cabinet" status. When Kennedy wanted to have his cabinet briefed on his major priorities, he would typically ask Secretary of State Dean Rusk to review foreign affairs considerations, Chairman of the Council of Economic Advisers Walter Heller would review major questions about the economy, and Ted Sorensen might sum up and give a status report on the domestic legislative program. In like manner, when Lyndon Johnson would hold special "seminars" for large gatherings of congressmen and their staffs, he would invariably call upon the Secretaries of State and Defense

---

[69] Moynihan comments, *supra* note 30, at 1731.

to explain national security matters, and then ask his Budget Director and his Chairman of The Council of Economic Advisers to comment upon economic, budgetary, and domestic program considerations. More recently, President Nixon would typically call upon his Secretary of State, his director of the Office of Management and Budget, and one of his chief White House domestic policy counselors to inform and instruct members of his assembled cabinet and sub-cabinet. These illustrations indicate that recent Presidents often believe that members of their own Executive Office are better equipped to talk about and counsel "significant others" regarding the "President's" program rather than let most cabinet members attempt to do the same. Kallenbach's reasoning in this regard seems appropriate:

> [A]s the departments have grown and supervision of their operations has become more burdensome, the heads have less opportunity to concern themselves with questions of general policy outside their own spheres of interest. Another factor is the steady enlargement of the Cabinet group itself. . . . This creates a condition which tends to induce the President to rely more heavily upon one one or more individuals in the group for general advice, rather than upon all equally.[70]

What has generally happened in recent years is that the Secretaries of State and Defense still remain as prominent national security advisors though the National Security Assistant to the President has joined them as an inner-circle counselor. In domestic and economic matters Treasury Secretaries and most Attorney Generals still play a major role in rendering advice and broad-ranging policy counsel, but they have been joined in the inner "cabinet" by the Budget Director, and variously prominent White House and staff economists and domestic policy coordinators. President Nixon's 1971 cabinet reform proposal is an apparent recognition of the problem of the outer cabinet's "distance" from the presidency. His proposals would abolish some of the outer cabinet departments and attempt to bring four newly packaged or consolidated "outer" departments into closer proximity if not full-fledged status with his inner cabinet. It is impossible to tell whether his recommendations will make any significant difference in this regard, although his motives for proposing this change are no doubt related to the seemingly estranged relationships between the outer departments and the White House.

The outer cabinet is the collection of cabinet posts and departments most often nominated as candidates for reform or abolition. These are the cabinet posts that experience the great cross pressures from clientele groups and congressional interests that often run counter to presidential interests or priorities. It is the outer cabinet departments that have the most intensive and competitive exchange with White House and Budget Bureau staff, and many an outer cabinet member has complained bitterly about the political pressures on and unmanageability of their departments. Robert Finch, a recent outer cabinet member who escaped from the outer into a quasi-inner cabinet status as a White House "cabinet-level" political counselor put

---

[70] J. KALLENBACH, THE AMERICAN CHIEF EXECUTIVE 439-40 (1966).

it this way: "It's great, just great, to be a Cabinet member without having to run a big department. I'm in [here a. the White House] on everything."[71] It was as though he was relieved from the advocate role and graduated to a more congenial and satisfying assignment as presidential counselor.

Most of the White House domestic and budget policy aides interviewed for this study cited five departments as the ones with which they had the most difficult or truculent working relations—HEW, HUD, Labor, Commerce, and Interior. Invariably, the White House staff suspects that outer cabinet departmental executives often accentuate the concerns of their department and their department's more obvious clientele over the concerns that might be broadly ascribed to the President or the President's party. One of Franklin Roosevelt's Commerce Secretaries quite frankly acknowledged his representational and advocate obligations when he said, "If the Department of Commerce means anything, it means as I understand it, the representation of business in the councils of the administration, at the Cabinet table, and so forth."[72] President Nixon says he expects his Secretary of Agriculture will be an advocate-spokesman in behalf of the farmers:

> I want to say . . . that when I did appoint him, I wanted a man who would speak for the farmers and for American agriculture to the White House rather than the other way around. He has done that. Beneath that very pleasant and disarming exterior of his is a very strong and persuasive and determined mind. And in these matters that come before us and the high decisions that have to be made at the White House with the legislative leaders, with the Cabinet, on the budget and other matters, I can assure you that agriculture has a very strong advocate.
>
> I have appreciated that fact, because I do not want those who simply are there to parrot the views that we may have developed in advance. I want somebody there that will represent this community and represent it well.[73]

Most of the reform proposals espoused by White House aides (two of which are noted as columns 6 and 7 in Table 5), would reduce the number of cabinet posts in the hope of strengthening the President's ties with the outer cabinet and increasing the stature of the outer cabinet vis-à-vis the inner cabinet. The implicit (but by no means clear) assumption behind most of these reforms is that the fundamental conflict in the executive branch is not between the President and various cabinet members, but it is rather between special and general (or presidential) interests. Some of the outer cabinet departments could and perhaps will eventually be collapsed into a few broader purpose departments. Alternatives depicted in Table 5 indicate that department reduction could conceivably be pushed to five or even three basic core

---

[71] Quoted in THE NEW REPUBLIC, Oct. 3, 1970, at 14.

[72] Fenno, *President-Cabinet Relations: A Pattern and a Case Study*, 52 AM. POL. SCI. REV. 388, 394 (1958) (quoting Jesse Jones' statement before a House Subcomm. on Appropriations in 1941).

[73] Address by President Richard M. Nixon delivered at the Department of Agriculture Conference on Corn Blight, Beltsville, Md., Dec. 17, 1970, reprinted in 6 WEEKLY COMP. PRES. DOC. 1699, 1700 (1970).

departments (even more "revolutionary" than the Nixon proposals). As is usually the case, talk about the need to reform and the move in this direction (however gradual) has been preceded by an implicit or unconscious set of practices that have already recognized a distinctively differentiated cabinet. The way White House aides define their work and how Presidents allocate their time and energy indicate that there currently exist three specialized "cabinet" concentrations—national security, aggregate economics, and domestic policy affairs. And at least during the 1960's it happened that these three areas were attended to in approximately this same order of importance or deference.

In the future it is likely that regardless of how organization charts are drawn, presidential use of the cabinet and White House staff will take into greater consideration the realities of the differentiated roles and activities of the federal departments. It is likely, too, that Presidents will move in the direction of utilizing specialized "cabinets" for concentrated purposes of the federal government. This is to say, the generalized cabinet will more or less pass into oblivion as a national security "cabinet," an economics directorate and a domestic policy "cabinet" continue to emerge, each of which will be presided over by some combination of presidential counselors, some based in redesigned executive departments and others located on the President's personal staff.[74] Cabinet advocates will surely still exist, but it may be possible to have them operate from posts within rather than on top of the executive departments. (It may well turn out, of course, that these concentrated and re-aligned cabinets will find that their internal rivalries become so intense and so often tumultuous that new reform movements will then champion the goal of breaking up the super cabinet framework.) On balance, the White House staff for the forseeable future is not likely to become much smaller or see its importance measurably diminished by these reorganizational developments, but a redesigned and consolidated outer cabinet might enable White House staff to abstain more often from the temptation of pulling administrative responsibilties into itself than has been the case in the last ten years.

VI

STRENGTHENING WHITE HOUSE-DEPARTMENT RELATIONS?

There is little difficulty in establishing the existence of considerable White House frustration with department "unresponsiveness" or parochialism and the existence of cabinet and department distress at the sometimes unnecessary political and abrasive behavior of the White House staff. But it is much less easy to evaluate the varied prescriptions that are put forth as a means toward improving White House-department relations. This last section discusses some proposals suggested by former White

---

[74] This is not to suggest that President Nixon's particular set of reforms will be passed. In fact I doubt they have much chance of being passed as he would want, although there will no doubt be some consolidation and alteration of the current outer-department organizations.

House staff and concludes with some general observations about strengthening White House relations with the cabinet departments.

We have seen in preceding sections that there is no one single cause of White House-department conflicts; moreover there is no one simple solution. Indeed, it would seem reasonable that the appropriate reforms will vary not only with the type of problem but also according to staff functions at the White House and the differentiated departments involved. Most of the White House aides at least implicitly acknowledge that numerous remedial or regenerating efforts are needed within the White House as well as between the White House and departments.

Many former presidential aides began their discussion of reforms by pointing out the obvious: no two Presidents are exactly alike; styles differ as well as policy preferences. Hence, "each president should organize his office more or less as he sees fit." And not a few aides recalled instances of intentions for remedying bad habits at the White House which quickly evaporated:

> Johnson would occasionally try to organize us into some better relationship to the cabinet and agencies. He would get memos on a certain day from two different White House people with two differing views or competing thoughts. He must have told me several times [after such occasions] and I know he told some of the others on the White House staff to "ORGANIZE THIS PLACE!!—organize it along more coherent lines so there won't be so much overlap." But this, [when tried], wouldn't last for more than a few days, because the President himself wouldn't stick to it or honor it. In practice the White House just does not lend itself very easily to that type of straight line or box-like organization.

As seen in Table 6, rather than uniformly calling for the presidential or "more power to the White House" perspective, these aides support what might be called an integration model just as much, and many of them support a department/cabinet approach as well. Almost eighty per cent of the domestic and budget policy aides offered suggestions that would strengthen White House policy planning and management capabilities. Even those who complained about White House staff arrogance often concluded that Presidents must have tough and aggressive staff help. The following responses provide some flavor of the strong presidentialist beliefs of many of these aides. (One could conclude about the first response that it is less a solution than a source of conflict itself.)

> The presidency has to be the activist within the very conservative federal bureaucracy.

> The bureaucracy is the conservative agent or the custodian of old laws and old policies. They fight against anything new suggested by the White House, hence a president has to be the destabilizing factor in the system. The inability of department institutions to be creative or to take on new responsibilities is fantastic! In my view, the most important thing for a president is to know how to *shake* up the bureaucracy! My own law is that for every new major priority you need to create a new agency—never give it to the existing department. You need a new agency

to get the resources and the leadership to pull off anything that is a major departure—like getting a man to the moon.

I think it is impossible to run the White House staff without having tough men to do the work of the president. Sorensen, Feldman and Dungan (Kennedy aides) were of this type. They could be very tough, abrasive, and uncompromising. But they had to be tough because if they were not the people in the agencies and departments just wouldn't respect the communications that came from the White House. I think it is a fundamental dilemma that people working for a president have to be arrogant, and almost be bastards in order to get White House work done with the departments.

TABLE 6

PRESIDENCY STAFF PERSPECTIVES ON THE QUESTION OF IMPROVING COOPERATION AND REDUCING CONFLICT BETWEEN WHITE HOUSE ANE THE EXECUTIVE DEPARTMENTS

STRATEGY PERSPECTIVES[b]	PERCENTAGES[a] N = 43
I. *Presidential Perspective:*	
—Stronger WH Management-Monitoring System	45%
—More Aggressive WH Sanctions and Controls over Executive Departments	41
—Stronger WH Policy Determinating Capability	33
II. *Integrative Perspective:*	
—Make It More of a "Two-Way Street"	45
—More Collaboration and Departmental Involvement in Policy Setting	40
—More WH Staff Sensitivity and Homework Re: Intra-Departmental Concern	36
III. *Departmental—Cabinet Perspective:*	
—Strengthen Cabinet Secretaries and Cabinet-President Linkage	26
—Delegate More to Departments—Less WH Interference and Primacy; More Trust and Better Communications	24

Source: Personal Interviews of White House Staff Members Who Served During 1961-1970 period.

[a] Percentages here reflect multiple responses.

[b] Aggregate responses to the three perspectives were as follows: 69% of the respondents recommended the presidential persepctive, 69% recommended the integrative perspective, and 40% recommended the departmental/cabinet perspective.

Although there is a good deal of overlap between those supporting the presidential and integrative perspectives, the integration approach was relatively more supported among the administrative and public relations assistants and among the national security policy aides than among the domestic and budget policy advisers. Integrative recommendations are seemingly based on the assumption that the White House is not likely to have much of an effect on federal program implementation unless it can win supportive cooperation from among the middle and higher echelons of the executive branch departments. For example:

> I think the basic solution to the problem of dealing with the departments is to get one or two top staff people in the office of a cabinet member or department head and have these people work closely with the White House team. This helps a lot. It has to be a two-way street between the White House and the Cabinet members. It is very important for White House aides to do favors for Cabinet members when they really want to get a promotion for somebody, or get some projects done. If you don't go along with them occasionally, and do this type of thing for them, they in turn are going to be difficult to deal with for yourself. It should be a bargaining, give and take, two-way relationship.

Some forty per cent of the former White House staff aides noted that a strong presidency could only succeed in an executive branch which also was characterized by the existence of strong cabinet and departmental leadership. Many of these aides felt that Kennedy, and Johnson, and their senior staff had neglected the cabinet members and underestimated their importance in making the government work. One aide insisted that it was a major mistake to let the domestic cabinet departments become so divorced from the White House:

> One way to improve things is to have the president and the cabinet members, particularly in domestic areas, meet at least six or seven times a year and talk in great detail, and in highly substantive terms, about the major priorities of the administration. You have to have better communication. Basically you have to make the cabinet less insecure.

Other aides criticized certain of their colleagues for having taken over operational responsibilties of the regular agencies, adding that too often these aides neither expedited program implementation nor accomplished anything else except possibly enlarging their own importance. Other aides aren't so sure of remedies as they are convinced that past behavior by the White House is no longer adequate:

> I think one major problem is the care and feeding of cabinet members. Most of these guys are people too, and the White House staff must be sensitive to that. Luther Hodges spent four most miserable years there [as Secretary of Commerce] and Ed Day [Postmaster General] was also very discontented. They got the feeling that they were left out. As the White House gets more of the action and much larger—the cabinet people will resent it even more. Even if and when you are able to recruit good people to the cabinet, they are likely to let their jobs go and be less excited about the challenges of their work if they are continually kept at a distance from the White House. . . .

Those aides who held sub-cabinet positions in one of the departments or agencies (either before or immediately after they worked on the White House staff) were significantly more sympathetic to the departmental/cabinet perspective than most of their White House colleagues who had not served "in the other fellow's shoes."

VII

CONCLUSION

A democracy must serve as a forum or arena for the practical and just mediation of conflicts. If our elected chief executive and his lieutenants were not constantly surrounded, or "afflicted," by a wide diversity of conflicts, they would probably be avoiding their legitimate public responsibilties. The conflicts discussed in this paper are those that exist within the executive branch, but it seems fair to assume that executive branch conflicts in large part mirror the existing and potential conflicts of society at large and as such they deserve far more detailed scrutiny. In general, however, we can conclude with Lewis Coser that such conflicts as exist are multi-lateral rather than unilateral, multidimensional rather than unidimensional, and occasioned by mixed rather than single motives. This paper suggests, if anything, that the conflicts which abound in the executive branch admit no single source, nor are they generated by any one set of political actors or agents. Size, complexity, specialization, and differing policy preferences are but a few of the factors con-tributing to that richness of contention that often exists within the American executive establishment.

The intent of this paper has been to answer only the most simple and elementary of questions pertaining to conflict and cooperation within the executive branch. It is tempting to pontificate about "solutions" and "remedies" that might ameliorate these conflicts and "strengthen" White House-department relations. But such an exercise would be premature and diversionary from the much needed analysis that must precede sophisticated political engineering. For example, we know little about the impact of conflict on the way public policies are selected and applied, or the conditions under which conflict in the executive branch is useful or necessary or valuable rather than a liability. It might be feasible to devise some indicators or scales on which to measure the amount and intensity of conflict, and the degree to which it helps or hinders certain sets of actors or certain sets of preferences within given decisional arenas. The very definition of conflict deserves more attention: how to distinguish between *routine* and *critical* conflicts; is there a point at which creative or constructive conflict becomes debilitating to the institutions within which they have been fostered? What are the effects of varied types of conflicts on system stability, system renewal, and system innovation?

But having duly displayed the appropriately detached professional caution, let me at least stick a toe into the water, and indulge just a little in a few suggestions that emerge from this analysis. Some readers may find these suggestions to be mere common sense or unnecessarily overbearing. And to some extent so they are. I would only add that these suggestions are offered in the spirit of experimenta-tion and tentativeness and urge that these too be tested.

Ted Sorensen has written that President John Kennedy was always more interested in policy than in the administration of policies.[75] We can extend that observation to President Johnson and the White House staffs of both Presidents as well. The way in which our elections and campaign systems are run makes it easy to accentuate discussions about policy issues rather than policy strategies, and this emphasis seemed overextended during the 1960's.[76] At the beginning of a presidential term White House staffs are initially comprised of policy-generating and policy-distillating activists who attempt to make good on the sweeping proposals that were vaguely articulated in previous campaigns. The emphasis is on policy change and the development of brand new sets of policies rather than the adaptation or improvement of existing policy. It may well be that the initial investment in a staff gathered for the purpose of developing and selling new policies skews the White House counseling resources in such a way that the White House is less effective in managerial and implementation aspects of policy leadership. Since it appears that White House work emphases are somewhat subject to cycles of accentuated policy formulation or accentuated policy implementation, it may be that staffing patterns should similarly be subject to shifting composition. During the Kennedy-Johnson presidencies, however, the internal composition of the staff did not noticeably change. The domestic policy staff, for example, continued to be comprised of youthful Washington lawyers who were geared to putting together new programs for the next State of the Union. But during periods when program implementation and interdepartmental jurisdictional disputes become the overriding concerns of a presidential administration it may not be enough to rely solely upon this type of staff. And to overcome some of the operational deficiencies of major new programs such as those making up the core of the War on Poverty, Alliance for Progress, and Great Society it may not be enough to have White House lawyers and economists occasionally seek the advice of management consultants or appoint managerial project directors to secondary departmental posts.

Even if Presidents reshuffle their executive branch departments, even if Presidents could redesign the congressional committee structure to their own preference and banish lobbyists from the metropolitan Washington community—conflicts would still exist and flourish within the executive establishment. Therefore, no matter what other reforms are attempted, Presidents and their senior-most advisors ought to give far more consideration to the need for skilled management mediators, who will not be afraid occasionally to widen the scope of conflict, who can selectively step in and divide up controversial pieces of the action. By custom if not by preparation, White House aides have increasingly been forced to serve as arbitrators among competing agencies, competing policies, and competing priorities. Indeed, the increasing prominence and importance of domestic, budget, and national

[75] SORENSEN, *supra* note 42, at 281.

[76] T. Cronin, "The Textbook Presidency and Political Science," a paper delivered at the annual meeting of the American Political Science Association, Los Angeles, Sept. 10, 1970, reprinted in 116 CONG. REC. S17,102-15 (daily ed. 1970).

security policy aides at the White House derive from their sitting as judges on the high court of executive branch jurisdictional claims. But ironically many of these people were recruited to the White House not because of their special talents in this area, but because of their help on the campaign trail or as an academic advisor to a presidential candidate or a President-elect in search of a legislative program. It is an understatement to suggest that the White House is in great need of decisive executive branch mediators who can, with the full confidence of the President, preside over the thorniest of complicated claims and counter-claims by competing cabinet members and know when worthy and important elements of a debate are being seriously neglected or misrepresented within these cabinet level negotiations. In the recent past Presidents have used people who were already "on-board" to perform tasks for which they were ill-suited or unprepared. In this regard, one might want to test out a suggestion put forth by Stephen Bailey (although perhaps first at the state or local government level):

> [Presidents] should create a team of two or three or four presidential "administrators" or "expeditors," removed from the day-to-day preoccupations of existing White House aides, who could be assigned on an ad hoc and short-term basis as troubleshooters to straighten out jurisdictional conflicts among agencies, both in Washington and (on an itinerant basis) in the field. "Ad hoc" and "short-term" must be underlined, for permanent and long-term portfolios for such assistants could only produce impossible tensions with cabinet secretaries, agency heads, and key legislators. Furthermore, they might easily create centers of power in the executive branch competitive with, rather than derivative of, presidential authority. Such administrators or expeditors must be men of considerable personal stature. As surrogates for the chief executive in a system inherently unfriendly to surrogates, they must be skilled in mediation, soft of voice, wise in the ways of politics, and utterly devoted to the President—institutionally and personally. The President must be prepared to support their judgements in the overwhelming majority of cases while being willing on occasion to overrule them on appeal.[77]

Presidents and their White House staff should never assume that departmental executives will intuitively divine presidential intentions. White House staff themselves have sometimes not clearly understood their own and their own President's policy positions and often do not adequately communicate their policy positions when they do know their position. While it is true that department officials sometimes do not want to hear or understand what the White House is saying, just as often White House aides have misunderstood the degree to which their job is that of a communications agent. Ironically, those White House staffs who have had most experience in the field of communications are those assigned to deal with external groups and publics, such as the Congress, the press, and the general public, rather than the various components of the executive branch itself.

We have suggested in this paper the distinction between an inner and outer

---

[77] Bailey, *Managing the Federal Government*, in AGENDA FOR THE NATION 315 (K. Gordon ed. 1968). *See also*, Brown, *The President and the Bureaus* . . . , 26 PUB. AD. REV. 174 (1966).

clustering of the cabinet. Inner cabinet members seem to enjoy closer and more collaborative ties with the White House; outer departments are more characterized by centrifugal pulls that dissipate close counseling relationships with the White House. But there are some implications of this dichotomy which are not entirely clear at first glance; the problem for the White House may not be to try to make the outer cabinet precisely like the inner cabinet, but to consider whether the inner cabinet might not benefit from some aspects of the way in which the White House relates to the outer cabinet. That is, the cordial and frequent contact between White House and Defense, Justice, Treasury, and the Secretary of State may actually camouflage substantive problems that should be contended, and issues that should be subject to the clashing of adversary viewpoints. United States policy in Vietnam, the Bay of Pigs episode, inadequate tax reform, and too casual a concern for civil liberties are general illustrations that come most readily to mind as by-products of the inner cabinet in the 1960's. It may be that because White House relationships with the counseling departments seem so close, comfortable, and professional in comparison with White House relationships with the overt advocate departments, that the White House too readily accepts the judgments of these departments, overlooks potentially divisive issues, and neglects the creation of an effective system of multiple and critical advocacy for the substantive and operational aspects of these departments. Too often in the 1960's the debates and adversary proceedings came too late or were procedurally foreclosed with reference to inner cabinet policy choices. If this be so, then many of the more conventional structural reforms (including some of those which President Nixon proposed in his 1971 State of the Union address) misunderstand an important aspect of White House-department relationships. Efforts must be made to increase certain types of conflicts and advocacy proceedings to ferret out differences of views, to generate alternative policy choices (and their rationale), and to estimate the likely consequences of diverse policies.

Many of the White House staff with executive branch experience previously served within inner cabinet departments, and this may explain both their greater difficulties with the outer cabinet and their preference for reforms which would place presidential counselors, as opposed to advocates, in charge of realigned and consolidated outer cabinet departments. But an assumption by which these aides are guided is that the policies or products of the inner cabinet have somehow been more acceptable or wise than those of the outer departments. There may be a tendency here, mistakenly to interpret closeness and loyalty to the presidency as equivalents of intelligent policy and competent administrative performance. In any event, Presidents should be wary of receiving their counsel exclusively from inner cabinet and staff who maintain only a presidential perspective. I am among those who feel that people who protest that a President is drastically isolated are, more often than not, merely signifying that a President has rejected or ignored their pet preferences, but there is nonetheless often a tendency for Presidents to indulge in only those views and opinions that sound like music to the ear, a situation that can of course lead to a state of alarming deficiency.

No one should dispute that our modern presidency is charged with enormous new obligations to act as an overseer of executive branch *responsiveness* and *integrity*. Who else can recruit talented department leadership? Who else can better motivate, educate, and inspire federal officials to higher levels of public commitment? And who else can both authoritatively mediate interdepartmental squabbles and wage vigilant pressure campaigns against those within the federal government who see themselves as the chief constituency of their own federal departments? All this and more is expected of the modern presidency and the expanded super staffs at the White House. But notions of government integrity and responsiveness are always slippery and should necessarily be subject to continuous definitional disputes. Responsiveness to whom? Is the presidentialists' perspective really free of special interests, or does this depend almost entirely on whether one happens to like the sitting President?

We come back, invariably, to a realization that Presidents are limited in the degree to which they can eliminate executive branch conflicts, and alternatively try to strengthen White House-department ties. Presidents have been and will continue to be frustrated by the sluggishness of the federal executive branch's response to new priorities. And increasingly, Presidents are disillusioned by the seeming incapacity to inspire and recharge the batteries of the sprawling federal government. But there are occasions, I think, when Presidents and their staff are justifiably thwarted from any easy resolution of substantive and procedural conflicts. We must be careful to maintain a political climate in which uncomfortable questions can be asked of a President from within—or without—the White House. Sometimes an issue is of sufficient divisiveness that it is not then amenable to any majoritarian point of view, and displacement or avoidance of conflict may be the best approach. Moreover, certain types of conflict-resolution or coordination are essentially forms of coercion that might threaten the rightfully independent bases of influence and opposing viewpoints in Congress or society.[78]

We might measurably contribute to the health of our presidency by examining and ultimately appreciating those conflicts that are avoidable or unavoidable, appropriate or inappropriate, and by trying to understand how these conflicts can limit as well as strengthen the presidency. Properly conceived and carried through, such analyses will undoubtedly help to limit and refine our expectations and assessments of democratic presidential leadership.

---

[78] This point is made in Wildavsky, *Salvation by Staff: Reform of the Presidential Office*, in THE PRESIDENCY 700 (1969).

WEST GERMANY'S "BROWNLOW COMMITTEE": THE FIRST REPORT*

HANS BAADE**

INTRODUCTION

The present Federal Government of West Germany, which took office on October 22, 1969, is committed to a program of internal reforms, including the improvement of policy planning.[1] The new emphasis on government efficiency is already evidenced by three distinct innovations in Chancellor Brandt's cabinet: the reduction in the number of ministries from 19 to 15; the elevation of the Chancellor's Office to Ministry status; and the establishment of positions of Parliamentary Secretary in all ministries.

These innovations were greatly facilitated, and perhaps even made possible on such short notice, by the work of the Project Group for Government and Administrative Reform, which was established less than a year earlier by a Cabinet Committee of seven, headed by Chancellor Kiesinger. The Project Group submitted its first report on August 31, 1969—too late for consideration before the elections of September 28, and, indeed, so close to them that it was treated as confidential until the votes were in.[2] The report was released early in October, 1969. It is likely to be of interest to American readers not only as an indication of current West German thinking on government organization and reform, but also because of the comparative insights it affords.

Students of government reorganization in the United States will recall that the Brownlow Committee appointed by President Roosevelt in 1936 consisted of three eminent Wise Men (Brownlow, Merriam, and Gulick) in academic and civic research organization positions, assisted by a relatively small staff of experts with similar backgrounds. Not so well known, perhaps, is the fact that Louis Brownlow found it "impossible to get any presidential funds for study abroad," and that Lindsay Rogers, whose work on British and French central administrative institutions was considered to be of signal importance for the President's Committee on Administrative Management, could not be appointed to its staff.[3] While this hurdle was to some

---

* The manuscript of this article has been checked for factual accuracy by the Federal Chancellor's Office of the Federal Republic of Germany. However, the author is, of course, exclusively responsible for all evaluations.

** Professor of Law, Duke University.

[1] See especially Chancellor Brandt's policy statement of October 28, 1969, conveniently reproduced in Die Welt, October 29, 1969 (Air Mail Edition); English translation in 17 THE BULLETIN No. 4 (Supp. 1969).

[2] See DER SPIEGEL, Aug. 25, 1969, at 26-27.

[3] L. BROWNLOW, A PASSION FOR ANOMYMITY 353 (1958). For a collective biography of the Brownlow Committee, see B. KARL, EXECUTIVE REORGANIZATION AND REFORM IN THE NEW DEAL. THE GENESIS OF ADMINISTRATIVE MANAGEMENT, 1900-1939 (1963).

extent bypassed by the use of outside funds, the classic Report of the Brownlow Committee does not contain any foreign country materials and shows little *overt* evidence of the influence of comparative studies.[4]

By contrast, the West German Project Group consisted of ten senior civil servants, headed by an official of the Chancellor's Office and composed of representatives of the ministries that made up the Cabinet Committee, plus a delegate of the Federal Accounting Office who, like his chief in the Cabinet Committee, participated in an advisory capacity only.[5] It thus corresponds more nearly to an Inter-Agency Task Force in the United States. The Project Group had its own Secretariat, conducted extensive investigations, and was solely responsible for the report ultimately submitted. Nevertheless, it obtained voluminous information and some advice from a dozen consultants. These consultants were mainly German political scientists and academic lawyers (two of the latter, including the present author, teaching in the United States); and the substantive topics of their reports ranged from the process of political decision making on the Land (state) level to systems analysis. There are no less than seven country studies: one each on Austria, Italy, Switzerland, France, and Great Britain, and two on the United States.[6] These studies were given careful and sometimes detailed attention in the report of the Project Group. It is perhaps worth noting that at least four of the twelve consultants received part of their training in law in the United States, and that a fifth is an English professor of political science.[7]

The following is a brief survey of the first report of the Project Group and of

---

[4] A classic example of the indirect influence of another system of government is the famous recommendation of the Brownlow Committee that the President be given a small number of executive assistants who "should be possessed of high competence, great physical vigor, and a passion for anonymity." THE PRESIDENT'S COMMITTEE ON ADMINISTRATIVE MANAGEMENT, REPORT OF THE COMMITTEE 5 (1937). This language was apparently first used by Tom Jones to describe Sir Maurice Hankey. In a message sent via Mr. Brownlow to President Roosevelt in summer, 1936, Mr. Jones had expressed the opinion that the President would best solve his problem by finding "that one man who would turn out to be another Maurice Hankey." BROWNLOW, *supra* note 3, at 357, 381, 396-97. *See also* KARL, *supra* note 3, at 230, 282 n.20; T. JONES, A DIARY WITH LETTERS, 1931-1950, at 216, 307-08, 312-13 (1954).

[5] The Cabinet Committee consisted of Chancellor Kiesinger and the Ministers of or for Interior, Justice, Economics, Federal Questions, Scientific Research, and Finance, as well as the President of the Federal Accounting Office. For details, see 1 PROJEKTGRUPPE FÜR REGIERUNGS- UND VERWALTUNGS-REFORM, ERSTER BERICHT ZUR REFORM DER STRUKTUR VON BUNDESREGIERUNG UND BUNDESVERWALTUNG 2 (1969) [hereinafter cited as FIRST REPORT]. *See also* Theis, *Reformen im Regierungssystem der Bundes-republik*, 20 AUSSENPOLITIK 677; Theis, *Führungsinstrumentarium und politische Planung*, *id.* at 735 (1969); Theis, *Stand der Überlegungen zur Regierungsreform in Bund*, 3 DIE VERWALTUNG 72 (1970)— the first reports by an insider.

[6] Reports on Austria, Italy, Switzerland, and France by Professor I. Seidl-Hohenveldern, University of Cologne, 2 FIRST REPORT 1, 35, 71, 101; on Great Britain, by Professor Nevil Johnson, University of Warwick, *id.* 133; and on the United States, by Dr. Christian Determann, Yale Law School, and by the present author, *id.* at 180 & 205.

[7] These are Determann, Baade, Scharpf, and Friauf; and Johnson (*see* note 6 *supra*). The then Minister of Justice and the present Minister in the Chancellor's Office, Professor Horst Ehmke, has also studied in the United States and is a noted authority on American constitutional law. *See* H. EHMKE, WIRTSCHAFT UND VERFASSUNG. DIE VERFASSUNGSRECHTSPRECHUNG DES SUPREME COURT ZUR WIRTSCHAFTSREGULIERUNG (1961); Ehmke, *"Delegata Potestas non Potest Delegari,"* A Maxim of American Constitutional Law, 47 CORNELL L.Q. 50 (1961).

official reactions thereto, and a discussion of the importance of comparative and country studies for this project. In conclusion, an attempt is made to relate the present stage of West German government reform more closely to the United States, using as a background the present author's memorandum to the Project Group, entitled "The Constitutional Position and the Government Machinery of the President of the United States."

I

THE FIRST REPORT: GOVERNMENT REORGANIZATION

The First Report of the Project Group for Government and Administrative Reform, dated August 31, 1969, consists of two volumes, 273 and 681 pages in length. The former contains the Report itself, and the latter, called "Appendix," reproduces the consultants' studies.

In agreement with the Cabinet Committee, the Project Group limited its investigations to three topics: (1) the delimitation of the spheres of competence of the federal ministries; (2) parliamentary secretaries, ministers of state, and ministers without portfolio; and (3) the improvement of the governmental machinery of the Federal Chancellor and Government. Its recommendations were made against the background of three policy decisions of the Federal Cabinet and the Cabinet Committee. First, there were to be no amendments to the Basic Law (or West German Constitution) until Fall, 1969. Second, the Project Group was to set out alternative courses of decision. Third, its recommendations were to take account of pre-existing reform measures, and not to prejudice future, more comprehensive reform measures.[8]

A. Reorganizing the Federal Ministries

By way of introduction, it should be pointed out that the reorganization of the federal government in West Germany, including not only the transfer of functions from one agency to another but also the creation, fusion, or abolition of federal ministries, is basically a preserve of the Executive. The latter's competence in this area is limited only by specific legislative acts of an organizational character which—at least in the absence of appropriate delegations of authority—are binding upon the Executive until or unless amended or repealed, and the general necessity of obtaining Parliamentary approval for budget positions.[9] This latter, in effect, prevents the creation of permanent positions without approval by Parliament. In a Parliamentary system of government, which is premised on the support of the government of the day by a working legislative majority, these two limitations are hardly of overriding significance.

Furthermore, a newly elected Parliament votes only on the Chancellor, not his

---

[8] 1 FIRST REPORT, *supra* note 5, at 3-5.
[9] *See generally* E. BÖCKENFÖRDE, DIE ORGANISATIONSGEWALT IM BEREICH DER REGIERUNG (1964).

Cabinet; and the Chancellor-elect is subject only to political, not to legal, restraints in his initial decision as to the composition of the Cabinet and the number as well as the functions of the Ministries to be kept or created.[10] Thus, with a new Federal Government to be constituted in Fall, 1969, and with a reasonably broad mandate for reform, the Project Group had considerable leeway in its recommendations on reorganization.

1. *The Proposals*

The Project Group proceeded from the basic premise that the composition of the Cabinet should be governed by four principles, which were to some extent in conflict: First, there was to be a division of labor by the allocation of discrete spheres of competence. Second, it was desirable to maximize the participation of politically potent powers in the Cabinet. However, third, the effectiveness of the Cabinet as a decision-making body was not be jeopardized by too large a number of Cabinet positions; and, finally, excessive subdivisions of spheres of competence were to be avoided.

There was widespread agreement among the politicians and senior civil servants consulted that the Kiesinger-Brandt Cabinet, composed of 19 Ministers in addition to the Chancellor, failed to meet the third requirement just listed. Although noting the absence of hard evidence, the Project Group tended to agree with this judgment. However, it rejected the optimum size of collective decision-making organisms, put at seven to nine by modern organization theory, as too small for present purposes. Such a group could not represent the entire political Executive of a complex modern industrial state like the Federal Republic of Germany. (It will be noted that the Federal Cabinet is a constitutional organ of prime importance in West Germany; this will be developed in detail further below.[11])

Instead of seeking to establish optimum Cabinet size at the outset, the Project Group proceeded directly to the study of the existing organization chart of the federal ministries, with a view to determining where there was room for the consolidation of functions and the abolition of redundant agencies. Among the advantages to be derived from such consolidations, it noted the reduction of jurisdictional disputes, of duplication, and of the necessity for coordination at the Cabinet level; greater flexibility in assigning priorities within large organisms; more possibilities for the delegation of tasks to subordinate units; and savings in personnel through the elimination of central administrative agencies.

On a somewhat higher level, the rational consolidation of functions was to lead to a reduction of imbalance between the various ministries, the allocation of competences by "task affinity," and the realization of the optimal size of ministries, taking into account existing possibilities for reducing the workload of cabinet

---

[10] For a recent summary, see Rein, *Die verfassungsrechtlichen Kompetenzen des Bundespräsidenten bei der Bildung der Bundesregierung*, 1969 JURISTENZEITUNG 573.

[11] *See* p. 637 *infra*.

ministers. As regards the factor of imbalance, the Project Group rejected the "budget slice" of the various ministries as a dependable criterion. The number of senior civil servants was a more reliable factor, but the ultimate decision would have to rest on the relative political weight of each individual ministry.

In accordance with its mandate to proceed on the basis of existing structures, the Project Group accepted as given the continued existence of a certain number of ministries. These included the five "classical" or "of" ministries based on the Prussian constitutional tradition: the Foreign Office and the Ministries of Interior, Justice, Finance, and Defense. Among the so-called "neo-classical" ministries, *i.e.*, those "*for*" ministries that antedate the establishment of the Federal Republic, nobody among those interviewed had raised doubts as to the continued existence of the Ministries for Economics, Agriculture, Labor, and Transport. Furthermore, in view of the present preeminent importance of science and technology for modern industrial society, the Project Group added the Ministry for Scientific Research to the organizational core.

That left nine ministries as potential candidates for dissolution. Only one of these, the Ministry for Postal Services and Telecommunications, was neo-classical; the remaining eight were what has become known as "prefab" ministries, *i.e.*, creations of political expediency or necessity since 1949. One of these, the Ministry for All-German Affairs, was declared as off limits: due to the special and delicate nature of intra-German relationships, the tasks of this ministry could not be allocated to the Foreign Office or the Ministry of Interior. This decision was candidly acknowledged to rest on political grounds.

The seven "prefab" ministries marked for possible extinction, along with Postal Services and Telecommunications, were Health, Economic Cooperation, Treasury (Federal Property), Housing, Refugees, Federal Relations, and Family. Since the Project Group refused to accept the premise that the public importance of a specific task area was as such sufficient justification for the establishment of a separate cabinet ministry,[12] it did not hesitate to tear down the "prefabs." All three of the alternative models proposed provided for their elimination. Postal Services and Telecommunications was spared on the ground that its abolition might prejudice more general reforms. Furthermore, it was suggested that cabinet-level status might be desirable in view of the international operations of the postal and telecommunication services.

The minute details of the three alternative reorganization schemes suggested are hardly of interest here. The third model, envisaging twelve cabinet ministries, would integrate the various "prefab" ministries into the existing classical and neo-classical ministries; the Ministry for Federal Affairs was to be merged into the Chancellor's Office under all three models. The first and the second models, each calling for thirteen cabinet ministries, contemplated the creation of one new min-

---

[12] First Report 10. *See also* p. 658 *infra.*

istry, termed Ministry for Social Affairs or Ministry for Structural Planning, respectively. The Ministry of Social Affairs (Model I) would encompass the entire former Family Ministry; the Home Construction Division of the Housing Ministry; and the Human and Veterinary Medicine and Food divisions of the Health Ministry. The Structure Ministry (Model II), on the other hand, would consist of the Health Ministry's Water, Air, and Noise Division and all divisions of the Housing Ministry. All three plans envisaged the merger of the Economic Cooperation Ministry into the Foreign Office, and the Refugee Ministry into the Ministry of Interior. The latter was by far the largest beneficiary under all models; its senior staff would grow from the present level of 254 to 340, 380, and 480, respectively, under Models I, II, and III.

Since these plans were elaborated in constant contact with those directly affected, the Report already reflects some reaction to the proposals that were to emerge. The Ministries for Economic Cooperation and of Housing submitted detailed statements of their positions. Far from being resigned to its fate, the former asserted that optimal efficiency in the area of foreign assistance required the abolition of Foreign Office tutelage as well as the transfer of capital assistance functions from the Ministry for Economics. In the judgment of the Economic Cooperation Ministry, a cabinet of "about 15" would still be able to function as an effective policy-making unit.[13]

The Family Ministry, on the other hand, conceded that initial expectations in the special efficiency and drive of small ministries created for particular tasks had not been justified by experience, and that these special tasks would have been pursued with better results by a larger ministry with major subdivisions. It nevertheless opposed the consolidation of all the "prefabs" into one super-ministry, and proposed the creation of a Ministry for Social Affairs that was to be roughly of the same political importance as the Ministry of Labor, and which would encompass all areas of social policy not covered by the classical and neo-classical ministries. This would include family, youth, sports, health, and social and housing assistance.

The Project Group rejected the proposal of the Economic Cooperation Ministry as unsound, and incorporated the Family Ministry's suggestion into its Model II. It also rejected a proposal by an interest group for the creation of a Ministry for Construction on the same grounds that led to the rejection of all strictly technocratic ministry models.[14] Nevertheless, all three concrete proposals for reorganization were to achieve almost total success.[15]

In addition to the major task of reducing the number of ministries through consolidation, the Project Group also discussed several proposals for the transfer of functions between ministries that would continue to exist. It made several recom-

---

[13] Communication from the Ministry for Economic Cooperation, of July 31, 1969, 1 FIRST REPORT 134; and of May 28, 1969, id. at 110, 130.

[14] See id. at 32-33.

[15] See p. 632 infra.

mendations in this connection, with Models I and II calling for more shifts than Model III. These proposed transfers of divisions and subdivisions do not seem to be of major independent significance. The Project Group expressly rejected a suggestion that monetary policy be concentrated in the Ministry of Finance so as to deprive the Ministry of Economics of its key position in macro-economic planning. It also rejected a proposal to transform the Ministry for Scientific Research into a Ministry for Science and Technology, with responsibility not only for research planning and subsidy, but also for the economic exploitation of advances in technology. However, there was a strong collective dissent on this point from within the Project Group itself. An individual dissent, also relating to this area, called for a radical reorientation of educational and training policy in science and technology, with emphasis on all levels rather than extrapolations from the university prototype.[16]

On a different level, the Project Group opposed the establishment of a Coordination Ministry; experience had shown that coordination among equals was beset with too many difficulties.[17] While noting, and approving of, consultation arrangements between individual ministries, the Project Group also recommended against extensive use of standing cabinet committees. This would, in its judgment, not only unduly tax the time schedules of the ministers and thus lead to stand-in representation by senior civil servants without political authority, but would also limit the information level of ministers who were not members of the committees.

2. Implementation by the Brandt Government

Some indications of the effect of the recommendations of the Project Group can be gathered from the cabinet list as approved on October 22, and from the new Government's first policy statement before Parliament on October 28, 1969. The Federal Cabinet now consists of 15 ministries, or perhaps more accurately, 14 ministries and 15 ministers. Besides the five classical "of" ministries, it includes six of the seven previous neo-classical ministries. Postal Services and Telecommunications has lost ministry status after all, and is currently merged with Transport. Among the "prefab" ministries scheduled for liquidation by the Project Group, Home Construction and Economic Cooperation survive. The former was originally scheduled for extinction but was saved by a massive "mayors' revolt."[18] There is a new Ministry for Health, Family, and Youth, indicating the more or less general acceptance— subject to the exceptions noted—of the Project Group's Model I, which also appears to be the one preferred by it. The Chancellor's Office is now headed by a cabinet minister—the former Minister of Justice who was one of the members of the original Cabinet Committee of seven. The Ministry for Scientific Research has been renamed Ministry for Science and Education, which indicates some responsiveness

[16] 1 FIRST REPORT 59-60, 68-71.
[17] Id. at 21. See also pp. 659, 660 infra.
[18] Eschenburg, Bonns kleine Kabinettsreform, DIE ZEIT, December 23, 1969, at 6.

Interior, Finance, Economics, Defense, and Transport. Thus, at the time of the preparation of the Project Group's first report, an appraisal of the functioning of this new political office in the West German federal system had to be based on slightly over two years' experience in substantially less than half the ministries.

A basic premise of the Project Group Report is that its recommendations on ministry reorganization described above, as well as its proposals for the improvement of the instruments of government of the federal Executive to be discussed further below, are inseparably linked to the need for increasing the political efficiency of individual cabinet ministers. Thus, its approach to the subject of parliamentary state secretaries is generally characterized by a desire to strengthen a budding political institution, taking into account all relevant experience to date.

The Project Group gathered quantitative data as to the politically significant activities of the parliamentary secretaries of state, and gathered additional information through detailed questionnaires. Its most significant finding was that the parliamentary state secretaries had virtually replaced the civil servant-state secretaries as their ministers' representatives in Parliament, especially in question period activities. In addition, the Parliamentary State Secretaries of the Finance and Interior Ministries had made statements of Government policy in Parliament; and the latter had, a few times, delivered the opening statements in support of Government bills.[25]

As regards cabinet affairs, the record was somewhat uneven. In accordance with § 23 of the then current Rules of Procedure of the Federal Cabinet, only the Parliamentary State Secretary of the Chancellor's Office was regularly entitled to attend all cabinet meetings. Cabinet ministers not in personal attendance could authorize either the Parliamentary State Secretary or the (civil-service) State Secretary to attend; in the absence of specific ministerial direction, the latter attended. A minister attending a cabinet meeting may, at his choice, be accompanied by either his parliamentary or his civil-service state secretary, but not by both at the same time. Attendance at cabinet meetings by persons other than the Chancellor and cabinet ministers is for purposes of information only. In view of the constitutional nature of cabinet membership, only a minister may hold another minister's proxy for purposes of cabinet decision.

The figures compiled by the Project Group indicate that only the Parliamentary State Secretaries of the Chancellor's Office and the Foreign Office were more or less regularly in attendance at cabinet meetings, although by no means at all of them. The record of the other Parliamentary State Secretaries in this respect is quite uneven. In one case (Interior) there was a striking reduction in attendance, seemingly coincidental with a change in personnel.[26]

A more important issue, expressly left open in the 1967 law despite initial government wishes to the contrary, is the position of the Parliamentary State Secretary

[25] 1 FIRST REPORT 148-53 and tables I-III thereat.
[26] Id. at 153 and table III.

within each individual ministry, and especially his relationship to the (civil-service) State Secretary. Here, responses to the pertinent six-question segment of the Project Group questionnaire reveals identical practices in only three respects. All Parliamentary State Secretaries were entitled to information and access to the files pertinent to their assigned tasks; all regularly received information on all matters of political or basic significance; and—most significantly—all Parliamentary State Secretaries conducted their relations with their respective ministries exclusively through the conduit of the (civil-service) State Secretary. The Project Group further determined that none of the Parliamentary State Secretaries had been assigned a position that made his office an additional level in the ministry's hierarchy. However, in three ministries, they had been given operative tasks, and were entitled to issue directives (through channels) within the scope of these tasks. Other divergencies relate to the channelling of official papers to the minister from below. In one ministry, these had to go through the Parliamentary State Secretary; in three others, he routinely received copies.[27]

The Project Group recommended that Parliamentary State Secretaries be appointed for all federal ministries; that they be placed in the minister's office so as not to constitute a new level in the ministry hierarchy, and that they be qualified, as before, to assume direct operational tasks at the specific direction of their respective ministers, but only through regular channels, i.e., through the (civil-service) State Secretary. None of these changes required additional legislation. In addition, however, the Project Group also recommended that the Parliamentary State Secretaries be redesignated Ministers of State, and that their selection not be confined to members of Parliament. The former would underline the political nature of the office and possibly add weight to its representational qualities, especially on the international level; the latter would enlarge the scope of political recruitment and at the same time mitigate against the danger of talent depletion in the parliamentary party of the government of the day.

The two recommendations last mentioned would require legislation, which has not as yet been sought. The other recommendations of the Project Group have gained ready acceptance by the Brandt Government. Parliamentary State Secretaries have been appointed for all cabinet positions; their rank initially included Professor Ralf Dahrendorf, the noted sociologist and political "idea man" of the minor coalition partner. This evidences a basic decision in favor of further strengthening the political Executive at the cabinet ministers' level through the expansion of the role of the Parliamentary State Secretaries. Furthermore, the Rules of Procedure of the Federal Government have been amended so as to make the Parliamentary State Secretary the regular representative (to the extent constitutionally possible) of his Minister before both Houses of Parliament and in the Cabinet, and to render him independent of the civil service State Secretary with respect to within-Ministry

---

[27] Id. at 148-50 and table I.

administrative tasks (including the operative supervision of Divisions) specifically delegated to him by the Minister.[28]

II

POLITICAL PLANNING FOR THE SEVENTIES

A. The Frame of Reference

The Project Group had initially been assigned two tasks in addition to government reorganization and the strengthening of the political Executive. These were improvements in the governmental machinery of the Chancellor and in the functioning of the Cabinet. However, in due time, these latter two topics came to be regarded as so intimately interconnected that the Report treats both of them under the collective heading "Improvement of the Governmental Machinery of the Federal Chancellor and Government."

1. Constitutional Considerations

To some extent, this fusion of assigned topics was influenced by constitutional considerations. The mandate of the Project Group, it will be recalled, specifically excluded recommendations requiring amendments of the West German Basic Law, or Constitution, for their implementation. Thus, the balance struck between the various components of the political Executive by article 65 of the Basic Law had to be accepted as given for present purposes. Article 65 is to a large extent the legacy of Bismarck's unique combination of Prussian and Federal elements in the 1871 Constitution, with some accretions in later years.[29] It contains three basic principles governing competence within the political Executive which appear to import separation-of-powers thinking into the realm of one of the classic component powers. The first is the Chancellor Principle: the Chancellor determines the directives of government policy. The second is the Department (*Ressort*) Principle: within the framework of these directives, each cabinet minister has individual authority and responsibility in the administration of his department. The third is the Cabinet Principle: differences of opinion between cabinet members (but not between the Chancellor and one or more cabinet members) are resolved by the cabinet, which consists of the Chancellor and the ministers.

The Chancellor's power to determine general governmental policy is augmented by what has been termed the substantive cabinet formation power of the Chancellor-elect. The latter includes decisions as to the number of ministries and the delimita-

---

[28] Zundel, *Kuddelmuddel um Minister-Stellvertreter*, DIE ZEIT, December 23, 1969, at 6; § 23 of the Rules of Procedure of the Federal Government, as amended on February 19, 1970, conveniently reproduced in U. ECHTER & H. LAUFER, REGIEREN IM VERFASSUNGSSTAAT 252, 258-59 (1970). For a recent account, see DER SPIEGEL, March 1, 1971, at 41-43.

[29] E. JUNKER, DIE RICHTLINIENKOMPETENZ DES BUNDESKANZLERS 4-44, 70-75 (1965). *Cf.* Menzel, *Die heutige Auslegung der Richtlinienkompetenz des Bundeskanzlers als Ausdruck der Personalisierung der Macht?* 2 DIE MODERNE DEMOKRATIE UND IHR RECHT 877 (1966).

tion of their functions, as well as the selection of incumbents. A necessary corollary of these powers, not spelled out in the Basic Law itself but generally recognized by accepted authorities, is the power to secure the dismissal of individual ministers after the process of cabinet formation has been completed.

Still, the department and cabinet principles are more than mere ornamental trappings of what has been referred to as a "Chancellor's Democracy." The cabinet principle is of special vitality, since virtually every important political action by the Executive is termed a Government action by the Basic Law, and hence requires a cabinet decision. There might be more doubt as to the value of the department principle; attempts by constitutional lawyers to endow it with justiciable constitutional protection have met with some levity by seasoned political observers. Nevertheless, it is quite clear that all three principles enunciated by article 65 of the Basic Law are constitutional principles; and that at least in theory, they can be enforced by constitutional adjudication which in West Germany extends to jurisdictional disputes between organs of government. Much more importantly, it is also generally recognized that while the working interrelationship of these three principles shifts from time to time and in response to political and personality factors, there is a general obligation of constitutional magnitude not to create additional imbalances through organizational devices.[30]

To sum up: the Project Group had no mandate to recommend changes of the Constitution, and thus necessarily had to shun all schemes that would permanently dislocate the precarious but nevertheless constitutionally ordained balance between the Chancellor, the individual cabinet ministers, and the Federal Cabinet as an aggregate political organ. This meant, as a practical matter, that the task of improving the efficiency of the Chancellors' Office could not be pursued independently of the objective of making the machinery of the cabinet more effective. (The Department Principle had already received special attention in the portions of the Report dealing with reorganization and, more particularly, parliamentary state secretaries and ministers of state.)

2. Intermediate-term Budget Planning

In addition to the above-discussed constitutional constraints, the Project Group was subject to the cabinet's directive that preexisting reform measures be taken into account. Chief among these was intermediate-term budget planning—a secular contribution of the Kiesinger-Brandt Government to the West German political system.

Students of public administration will recall that in August, 1965, President Johnson had directed the extension of the Planning-Programming-Budgeting System to all federal departments and agencies. Almost exactly one year later, an astute man-

---

[30] See the consultations of Professors Klaus Stern and Heinrich Friauf, both of the University of Cologne, in 2 FIRST REPORT 563, 607.

agement analyst could still confidently observe, with respect to West Germany: "Politically, any overt extension of programming or planning schemes is less feasible now than it has even been."[31] West Germany was regarded as fully committed to the "Politics of Non-Planning," and even a leading expert study of budgetary processes, while recommending intermediate-term budget planning at the federal level, had carefully added that this would be for informative forecasting purposes only. It solemnly warned against any attempt to make forecasting the basis of control "by any means," and against any far-reaching subdivision of the data, "or else the market economy would be in danger."[32]

Endangered, indeed, it was. Late in 1966, the holy cow developed lactation problems; and almost overnight, everything changed. West Germany's economic recession was reflected in the governmental sector by a budget crisis. Public disclosure of a monumental overestimate of revenues not only brought down the government of the day, but also gravely impaired confidence in the budgetary tools and methods then available and practised. The Kiesinger-Brandt Grand Coalition Government that took office on December 1, 1966, was indeed not so much a product of coalition arithmetic as the political expression of a general realization that radical governmental reforms were called for. In a federal state saddled with the legacy of a paleo-liberal ideology with pretensions of constitutional anointment, such reforms could only be achieved by a government that commanded the requisite support for amending the Basic Law practically at will. While a coalition backed by over 90 per cent of Parliament was clearly recognized to be a serious deviation from the norm of responsible parliamentary government, this deviation was expressly accepted, on a temporary basis, as the only device suited to bring about the basic reforms now demanded by all concerned.

The Kiesinger-Brandt Government promptly secured a constitutional amendment designating macro-economic equilibrium as a goal of federal and state budget making, and authorizing Parliament to enact guidelines for anti-cyclical budget management as well as "budget planning for periods of several years." This express constitutional recognition of planning as a governmental task was accompanied by the Act of June 8, 1967, for the Support of Economic Stability and Growth. The latter lists four specific budget planning goals: price stability, high-level employment, foreign trade equilibrium, and economic growth. The Government is directed to elaborate and to lay before Parliament intermediate-term budget plans. These plans cover periods of five years, and are regularly adjusted in the light of subsequent insights and developments. Federal ministries are directed to maintain investment plans on a current ten-year basis.[33]

---

[31] H. ARNDT, WEST GERMANY: POLITICS OF NON-PLANNING 122 (1966).

[32] Quoted in id. at 99.

[33] See generally Stucken, Die Haushaltspolitik im Gesetz zur Förderung der Stabilität und des Wachstums der Wirtschaft vom 8. Juni 1967, 27 FINANZARCHIV 202 (1968); Weichmann, Finanzplanung als staatliche Aufgabe, id. at 220; Hettlage, Probleme einer mehrjährigen Finanzplanung, id. at 234; and for

Budgetary estimates are still prepared by the various ministries and revised, as well as coordinated, by the Budget Division of the Ministry of Finance. Intermediate-term budget planning is also initiated by a special subdivision of that Ministry, and then channeled through a Cabinet Committee headed by the Chancellor and composed so as to exclude the "major consumers" of federal funds. Initially, this Committee included the Ministers of and for Finance, Economics, Federal Property, and Federal Questions. While the Cabinet Committee is responsible for the coordination of the intermediate-term budget planning process and for the elaboration of alternative planning proposals, the ultimate power of political decision rests with the whole cabinet as a constitutional organ.

In the past, cabinet decisions in this area have consisted of ceilings for individual ministries worked out primarily on the basis of ministry estimates, but also incorporating decisions as to magnitude and priorities based on more general considerations of economic policy (*e.g.*, high-priority support of transport and research). In time, and as experience accumulates, it is expected that decisions of the latter type will become the central factor in intermediate-term federal budget planning.[34]

The process of intermediate-term budget planning described above has now been extended to the states. A constitutional amendment of May 12, 1969, authorizes federal legislation establishing common guidelines for the federal and state governments for budgetary law, anticyclical budget management, and multiple-year budget planning. An Act of August 12, 1969, adopted just before the recess of Parliament precedent to the September elections, makes the adoption of intermediate-term budget planning mandatory on the state level as of January 1, 1972, and establishes a mechanism for joint state-federal budget policy making.[35] These constitutional and legislative extensions of the intermediate-term budget planning system would appear to provide the federal government with an ideal panel of instruments for the economic and monetary policy guidance of a dynamic modern economy.

It is, perhaps, good to recall that on the eve of West Germany's constitutional crisis that triggered the developments here described, a senior official of the Bundesbank had pessimistically compared the federal administrative apparatus to a symphony orchestra which, while proficient in the classics and in the "popular operatic melodies" preferred by the Adenauer Government, was likely to reveal serious weaknesses when asked to perform modern compositions. Even a star conductor might

---

legal discussion, K. STERN & P. MÜNCH, GESETZ ZUR FÖRDERUNG DER STABILITÄT UND DES WACHSTUMS DER WIRTSCHAFT (1967) and the minutes of the annual meeting of German academic constitutional lawyers in Bochum on October 3, 1968, with reports on *Öffentlicher Haushalt und Wirtschaft* by Professors Friauf and Wagner in 27 VERÖFFENTLICHUNGEN DER VEREINIGUNG DER DEUTSCHEN STAATSRECHTSLEHRER 1 & 47 (1969). Friauf, *id.* at 10-39, furnishes exhaustive further references.

[34] 1 FIRST REPORT 192-95; BUNDESMINISTARIUM DER FINANZEN, FINANZBERICHT 1968 at 106-15, 231-39 (1967). *Cf.* G. DENTON, M. FORSYTH & M. MACLENNAN, ECONOMIC PLANNING AND POLICIES IN BRITAIN, FRANCE AND GERMANY 227-29 (1968).

[35] Act of May 12, 1969, [1969] 1 BGBl. 357 (art. 109(3) of the Basic Law); Act of August 19, 1969, [1969] 1 BGBl. 1273.

fail before an orchestra that approached Schönberg, Bartok, or Stravinsky (*scil.* anti-cyclical economic policy, intermediate-term budget planning) with hesitation; "and let us remain politely silent about Stockhausen and Boulez (modern weapons systems; research planning)."[36] Less than three years after this devastating indictment, the Project Group Report notes:

> Intermediate-term budget planning is the most completely developed instrument of planning at the federal government level. In its methodology and technique, it occupies a leading place in the Western world even if compared to the PPB System of the United States federal government.[37]

B. Goals and Critical Inventory

The Project Group regarded its task of recommending improvements in the governmental machinery of the Chancellor and the Cabinet as tantamount to a mandate to develop organizational schemes for effective political planning by the Executive. It started with the assumption that only the service state is adequate to the needs of modern man in modern society, and that "the service state which actively shapes society . . . must increasingly develop a policy based on concepts derived from a comprehensive view of social, economic, and technological change, and thus able to constantly supply innovation impulses, *i.e.*, impulses for new, consciously directed developments."[38] A few years ago, such a basic premise would have been rank heresy; today, it has become common property. The Project Group was even able to cite as authority a policy declaration by Chancellor Kiesinger on March 11, 1968.

But although the ideology of political planning had been received into conventional wisdom, government and administrative institutions had not fully responded to present-day requirements. The Project Group found that while on the whole, the West German system of government and administration was generally deemed to stand up to critical comparison with economic enterprises or with foreign political systems, it was quite widely regarded as unequal to the task of political planning as defined above. Critical voices referred to a basic style of pragmatic case-by-case reaction instead of the consistent pursuit of long-range policy; to the lack of adequate planning tools and methods in the Chancellor's Office, the Cabinet, and the ministries, especially as regards the basis of information; and to ambiguity and short-term orientation of political goal decisions and value judgments of the Chancellor and the Cabinet. On a somewhat more technical level, there were complaints about the dual function of cabinet ministers, with department management encroaching upon political functions. The traditional bureaucratic apparatus of the ministries was felt to be unequal to its new tasks, prone to prefer quick compromise to the elaboration of political alternatives, and inclined to pursue its own goals or tradi-

---

[36] Hüttl, *Koordinierungsprobleme der Bundesregierung*, 6 DER STAAT 1, 15-16 (1967) (manuscript of a lecture given on October 20, 1966).

[37] 1 FIRST REPORT 192. *See also id.* at 244-45; p. 660 *infra*.

[38] *Id.* at 184.

tional tasks. The isolated creation of planning sections in various ministries was criticized as leading to imbalance in the Cabinet, and to patchwork rather than comprehensive planning.

This wide array of criticism was sufficient to induce the Project Group to undertake its own inquiries into the most important phases of the political decision process within the federal government. These inquiries revealed, in its judgment, that the traditional system had some inherent limitations which were bound to increase with further governmental expansion and compartmentalization. The subdivision and compartmentalization of substantive responsibilities within the hierarchical organization scheme of ministries was found to have no less than four dysfunctional effects upon the intake and the evaluation of information. Since information intake was determined by subject-matter competence, the perspectives of lower organizational units were necessarily limited. Routinization of the intake process was conducive to blocking both the intake and the evaluation of decisive information. Information tended to be more complete where there was pressure by social groups or organized interests; hence there was the danger of an information disequilibrium within the organization. This danger was further enhanced, finally, by the dominance of individual information preferences, made possible through the lack of a uniform information system.

On a somewhat different level, an increase in the number of organizational units was likely to limit the interaction between leadership and the line, thus further enhancing the significance of the value preferences of individual line officials in the decisional process. Finally, there was a general lack of organizational units for the elaboration of long-range perspectives. Planning staffs presently in existence were plagued by limitations of substantive competency; lesser units were too hard-pressed by routine duties to make significant contributions to the process of long-range goal definition.

The Project Group found that some of these difficulties inherent in the hierarchical compartmentalization of ministries had been mitigated by the increasing use of inter-ministry committees.[39] Still, in its judgment, this committee device was unlikely to be a satisfactory tool for the collective shaping of a concept-oriented policy. The prevalent technique of assigning the chairmanship ((*Federführung*) to the ministry most directly concerned tended to favor competence-oriented bureaucratic thinking; and chairmen were likely to keep their committees as small as possible, thus minimizing conflicts of interests or potential conflict situations. Standing committees might be more useful, but in addition to the difficulties just mentioned, the limited powers of the participants militated against the development of innovative functions.[40]

---

[39] See, in this connection, H. PRIOR, DIE INTERMINISTERIELLEN AUSSCHÜSSE DER BUNDESMINISTERIEN (1968).

[40] 1 FIRST REPORT 188-89.

Probably the most devastatingly negative finding of the Project Group concerns the control of political decision making. Current mechanisms were mainly limited to controlling the administrative execution of the measures decided upon; this was true even as regards budget control. In the absence of sufficiently clear definitions of the goals to be achieved, there could be little if any control of the efficiency of actions in terms of purposes.

This searching critique of extant instruments for policy planning was to some extent counterbalanced by the conclusions derived from the foreign-country and West German State studies commissioned by the Project Group. These showed, in its judgment, that the problems found to exist in the West German federal government were also to be found, to a lesser or greater extent, in these other systems of government; that certain peculiarities were essentially the products of historical developments; and that all governments included in the survey were facing new tasks that required adaptations of the traditional systems of government. The most important finding in this regard deserves quoting in full:

> The constitutional position of government institutions is only of minor significance in relation to existing inadequacies. Comparable deficiencies are found in the Presidential, Cabinet, and Chancellor systems. Therefore, none of the problems could be solved merely by, for instance, introducing the Presidential system in the Federal Republic.[41]

C. Improving Policy Planning Through Reorganization

1. Policy Planning and Budget Planning

As already mentioned, West Germany has an intermediate-term budget planning system which compares favorably, in the opinion of the Project Group, to the PPB System at its current stage of development in the United States. Since reform proposals were to be integrated, so far as possible, into pre-existing reform programs, an obvious question was whether the intermediate-term budget planning system might serve as the nucleus for a general policy planning system. The Project Group considered this possibility at some length, and arrived at a negative conclusion.

In essence, the view prevailing would appear to have been that policy planning and budget planning are complementary but not coextensive; that both derive advantages from a dialectical relationship based on independence but interdependence; and that both would suffer from the fusion of budgetary and political planning processes. Budget planning took no account of nonmonetary capacities; it was geared to relatively short-term sequences (five years). An expansion of its functions would necessarily lead to the inclusion of the "largest consumer" ministries in the Cabinet Committee for intermediate-term budget planning. This would be highly undesirable. Furthermore, the preeminent position of the Finance and, to a lesser extent, the Economics Ministries in intermediate-term budget planning

---

[41] *Id.* at 190. *See also* p. 659 *infra.*

would not be extended to policy planning as such without strong resistance to the notion of an "inner cabinet" which was in derogation of the cabinet principle (article 65 of the Basic Law).

Another reform proposal called for the transfer of intermediate-term budget planning responsibilities from the Ministry of Finance to the Chancellor's Office. This proposal, and even a more modest variant which called for the transfer of *Federführung* to the Chancellor's Office, did not find the Project Group's approval. In its judgment, the intermediate-term budget planning process was so intimately connected with the general process of estimate revision and consolidation that it could not be carried out effectively by any unit other than the Budget Division of the Ministry of Finance. The specialized knowledge of the latter would be impossible to duplicate elsewhere. On the other hand, the Project Group recommended that the intermediate-term budget planning memoranda of the various ministries be made available, as a matter of course, to the Chancellor's Office. This would increase the flow of information and eliminate duplication of efforts at the individual ministry level.

2. *Expanding the Chancellor's Office*

The Project Group noted that in recent years planning sections had been established in several federal ministries. While these had undoubtedly contributed to the rise of "problem consciousness" in the bureaucracy, their effectiveness had suffered from the organizational polarity between staff and line. The planning sections did not have independent information networks; and the line divisions and subdivisions could not be depended upon to supply the information required. Furthermore, privileged access to the political executive by units without line responsibilities gave rise to frictions.

The planning mechanism of the Chancellor's Office, on the other hand, was regarded as more promising. This is not discussed in detail in the First Report, but some pertinent information has become available recently.[42] Early in 1967, the Kiesinger-Brandt Government created a Planning Staff in the Chancellor's Office. This staff was headed by a civil servant of Division Chief (*Ministerialdirektor*) rank; but its personnel included non-career civil service academic and other experts employed on a contractual basis. Furthermore, the Planning Staff had an advisory council composed of seven professors of various disciplines at German universities; and it had authority to contract for outside policy research and advice. A textbook illustration of the workings of this, in Prussian-German terms, fairly revolutionary planning organism, is the government reorganization project here described.[43]

---

[42] Lompe, *Die Rolle von Sachverständigengremien im Prozess der politischen Willensbildung*, 16 ZEITSCHRIFT FÜR POLITIK 223, 250-59 (1969).

[43] Böckenförde, *supra* note 9, at 187-91, goes so far as to assert the unconstitutionality of the establishment of a political planning staff in the Chancellor's Office. We are reminded of Heinz Wagner's remark that the West German academic constitutional lawyer receives his journeyman's certificate

The Project Group recommended that the policy planning functions of the Chancellor's Office be substantially expanded. It also recommended that these functions be directed by a close associate of the Federal Chancellor of the day who had ready access to the latter, and whose position in the hierarchy of the political Executive was such that he would be accepted as an equal by the cabinet ministers. As for the organization of individual policy planning projects, within-government task forces were deemed most promising. Such task forces were to be composed of members of the ministries concerned and the Chancellor's Office, under the direction of the latter. The federal ministries had the highest level of information in their respective sectors; and "without the intake of this information, but also without knowledge of the sectoral balance of competing social interests achieved by the various ministries, uniform political planning on the Cabinet or Chancellor's level would hardly be possible."[44]

The Brandt Government appears to have accepted these recommendations. For the first time in West Germany, the Chancellor's Office is headed by a cabinet minister. Personnel changes within this office seem to have been particularly rigorous, with apparently full utilization of the power to dismiss political civil servants, and some transfers of career civil servants as well. The current budget authorizes 80 new positions in the Chancellor's Office, bringing its total personnel to over 300. The Planning Staff, which is now headed by a professor of economics in his middle thirties, has been enlarged in size. Its members participate in top-level policy conferences within the various ministries. There is a budget item for the development of systems analysis in the Chancellor's Office.[45]

On the other hand, this massive increase of the powers of the Chancellor's Office (and, hence, of the Chancellor and his "personal" cabinet minister) has given rise to some resistance. The new Minister of Defense, in particular, is reported to have demanded a binding delimitation, in writing, of the functions of the Minister in charge of the Chancellor's Office; and one of his first acts has been the establishment of a Policy Planning Staff in the Ministry of Defense. It is perhaps significant to note that this latter staff was organized by a well-known, American-educated strategy commenator on temporary six-month leave from the leading West German weekly paper.[46]

---

upon proving that something is unconstitutional, and becomes a master craftsman upon showing that it cannot even be done by constitutional amendment. Wagner, *Um ein neues Verfassungsverständnis*, 1968 DIE ÖFFENTLICHE VERWALTUNG 604, 605.

[44] I FIRST REPORT 201.

[45] *See* DIE WELT, May 2, 1970, at 6; June 22, 1970, at 2 (air mail edition). For a recent detailed account, see DER SPIEGEL, Feb. 1, 1971, at 28-38.

[46] Dr. Theo Sommer of Die Zeit. *See* DIE WELT, November 3, 1969, at 1 (air mail edition). The Minister in the Chancellor's Office has also had difficulties in replacing a number of career civil servants in the Chancellor's Office with persons more receptive to the policies of the present Government. For one view of this matter, see Reuter, ". . . *ausserhalb der Legalität*"? 20 DER DEUTSCHE BEAMTE 43 (1970).

D. Towards New Departures in Planning Organization

The Project Group did not regard its recommendations for the expansion of the planning facilities in the Chancellor's Office as a substitute for a more basic re-structuring of the political planning process. The expansion recommended would be useful primarily for testing, experimentation, and personnel training purposes; it would not obviate the need for a comprehensive political goal-planning machinery.

In view of its limited mandate, the Project Group did not consider mechanisms such as an Inner Cabinet, which required constitutional amendments for their implementation. Instead, it developed three alternative organizational prototypes against the background of article 65 of the Basic Law, which, as discussed above, bars the creation of a functional disequilibrium between the Chancellor, Cabinet, and Department principles therein laid down.[47]

All three models call for a permanent central Task Force or Working Group for Political Planning. This agency is to be headed by an official of the Chancellor's Office whose position is such as to assure close contact with the Chancellor and the cabinet ministers. The other members of the Task Force are to be the planning officials of the various ministries. Their designation is to depend, from case to case, upon the task at hand.

Political goal decisions are, of course, reserved to the Chancellor and the Cabinet. Program planning decisions, on the other hand, are to be made in the ministries. Each ministry is to have a Planning Board directly subject to the Minister and the State Secretary, but the planning process is to be largely the work of *ad hoc* task forces at the Division level. These task forces are to include at least one member without line responsibilities, who will serve as his division's representative on the ministry's Planning Board.

As regards personnel, the Project Group deemed political confidence and innovative potential to be of prime importance. It therefore recommended that especially in the higher positions, public servants be assigned planning positions on a non-permanent basis; and that care be taken, on the Chancellor and Cabinet level, to include officials from all ministries. Significantly, it also recommended that efforts be made to attract experienced personnel from private industry and the universities— presumably on a short-term basis.

The three alternative prototypes for the central Task Force for Political Planning are, in the main, reflections of different concepts of the optimal balance between the Chancellor, Cabinet, and Department principles governing the organization of the political Executive pursuant to article 65 of the Basic Law. Model I emphasizes the Cabinet principle. The Task Force receives its impulses from its members as instructed by their respective superiors, *i.e.*, the Chancellor and the various Ministers. Draft political programs are submitted to the Cabinet for discussion and general approval, and then routed to the various ministries with instruction to develop

---

[47] See p. 637 *supra*.

implementation plans. These are checked by the Task Force for compliance with basic policy decisions and for optimal coordination, and submitted by it to the Cabinet for final approval. This latter also serves as the basis for intermediate-term budget planning.

Model II is based on the predominance of the Chancellor principle. It contemplates the establishment of a well-staffed Planning Division in the Chancellor's Office. Planning impulses are transmitted to it by the Chancellor, acting either on his own initiative or in response to suggestions by the Cabinet or individual ministers. Draft political programs received by the Cabinet for initial discussion are thus the product of the Chancellor's Office as instructed by the Chancellor. The Task Force becomes operative only at the penultimate stage of checking and coordinating individual Ministry implementation plans for final approval by the Cabinet. Again, this latter serves as the basis for intermediate-term budget planning.

Model III is a combination of the Chancellor and Cabinet principles. It generally corresponds to Model I, with the difference that both the Chancellor and the Cabinet can give instructions for the initial planning phase to the Task Force, and that the latter has a policy planning staff that corresponds in size to that contemplated by Model II but is organizationally independent of the Chancellor's Office.

At the present writing, the Brandt Government does not appear to have decided in favor of one or the other of these three prototypes. However, the enhanced position of the Chancellor's Office suggests a built-in bias in favor of Model II. There would seem to be some political as well as constitutional objections to this model, which are not entirely dispelled by the First Report of the Project Group and its supporting consultations.[48] A search for a "non-political" alternative, such as a Planning Office headed by the (large ceremonial) federal President,[49] seems somewhat quaint. Still, the current West German Federal Government, which has achieved so much by way of government reform in so little time, is not likely to expose itself needlessly to major constitutional criticism when developing its long-range political planning mechanism. While the three organizational prototypes suggested by the Project Group will undoubtedly have some impact, none of them seems currently destined for formal adoption.

III

THE USES OF COMPARATIVE ANALYSIS

Louis Brownlow, it will be recalled, found it "impossible to get any Presidential funds for study abroad."[50] The West German Project Group, on the other hand, was quite unencumbered by parochial purse strings. It commissioned no less than

---

[48] See note 30 *supra* and, for the constitutional problems arising from the separation of powers doctrine, the consultation of Professor Friauf, 2 FIRST REPORT 607.

[49] This was envisaged by Köble, *Wider die Expertokratie*, DIE WELT, November 8, 1969, Geistige Welt section, at 1 (air mail edition).

[50] See p. 626 *supra* and note 3 thereat.

seven country studies, two of which deal with the United States and were undertaken there. These studies are reproduced in full in the Appendix of the Report, and their findings are summarized in a special section of the Report itself.[51] Repeated references, to be discussed further below, indicate a pervasive awareness of foreign institutions and practices.

In the following, an attempt will be made to gauge the significance of these foreign studies, and of the comparative insights based on them, for the work of the Project Group. By focusing on the present author's report on the United States, it is hoped to obtain some insights which might be of interest to American students of government organization. Furthermore, an analysis of "comparative government at work" might furnish some more general insights as to the practical utility of that discipline.

A. "The Constitutional Position and Government Machinery of the President of the United States": Seven Questions and Answers

The foreign country studies are based on a uniform set of seven questions drafted by the Project Group, in some instances augmented by subsequent inquiries on specific points. The seven questions concern (1) the real position of the Chief of Government in the governmental system, especially as regards establishing and enforcing uniform governmental policy; (2) his major instruments for executive leadership, including machinery for policy planning and supervision; (3) the Chief of Government's information system, including the reporting methods of the ministries (departments) as well as information derived from other sources; (4) the real division of power at the summit of the governmental system, especially problems of coordination and methods for their solution; (5) permanent representatives of the Chief of Government, and their competences; (6) parliamentary state secretaries, ministers of state, or ministers without portfolio, and their relations with the regular departments and the bureaucracy; and finally (7) the deficiencies of the present system and efforts at reform. In addition to these standard inquiries, the Project Group also requested information from the present author on problems of coordination between the President's political staff and the federal bureaucracy, and on the current status of the PPB System.

The standard inquiries are clearly inspired by the West German system of government and by the mandate of the Project Group to recommend improvements not requiring constitutional amendment. They are therefore more pertinent to parliamentary government than to a presidential system. Nevertheless, the Bureau of the Budget was mentioned by way of illustration in question 2; there were two country studies on the United States which together take up almost one-third of the space allotted to foreign materials; and the specific inquiries just mentioned indicate a lively interest in the practical workings of the American system.

---

[51] 2 FIRST REPORT 1-265; I *id.* at 248-68.

There is hardly any need here to set forth in detail those portions of our study that are descriptive of the formal constitutional system of the United States. Starting with Professor Hermens' felicitous description of the President as "combining the functions of the British Queen and Prime Minister, and absorbing, in his second capacity, the constitutional powers of the entire British cabinet,"[52] it is pointed out that the constitutional problems posed by article 65 of the Basic Law[53] simply do not exist in the United States. The real constitutional problem is coordination between the President and Congress, not coordination within the Executive. The limitations imposed upon Executive leadership by the separation of executive and legislative powers is illustrated by fairly detailed references to government reorganization, the appointment power, legislation and budgetary matters, and control over independent regulatory commissions. Not much time is spent on the problems referred to in questions 5 and 6, relating to permanent representatives of the President and executive representation in Congress; the personalized unitary executive principle inhibits the former and the incompatibility rule obstructs the latter. Nevertheless, it is pointed out that in recent years, there has been an amazing extension, both by statute and by executive order, of the functions of the Vice President—a development that has since continued.[54] Furthermore, mention is made that the constitutional prohibition of membership in Congress by persons "holding any office under the United States" has not prevented the occasional use of Senators and Congressmen on diplomatic missions, nor even the formal codification of that practice in the United Nations Participation Act of 1945.[55]

Like so many other things, it is observed, such practices and even institutional mechanisms are entirely dependent upon their political and practical attractiveness for the current incumbent of the White House. This reflects the cardinal conclusion of the study, made in the context of information networks (question 2) but

---

[52] F. HERMENS, THE REPRESENTATIVE REPUBLIC 464 (1958).

[53] See p. 637 supra.

[54] At the time of the preparation of our study for the First Report, the Vice President was a member of the National Security Council; the chairman of the National Aeronautics and Space Council and of the National Council on Marine Resources and Engineering Development; the alternate chairman of the Council for Urban Affairs, the Cabinet Committee on Economic Policy, and the Council on Environmental Quality; the Office of Intergovernmental Relations was under his immediate supervision. 50 U.S.C. § 402 (Supp. 1970); 42 U.S.C. § 247 (Supp. 1970); 33 U.S.C. § 1102 (Supp. 1970); 3 C.F.R. 102, 103, 122, 105 (1969). In the meantime, the former Council on Environmental Quality has been transformed into a Cabinet Committee, of which the Vice President is again the alternate chairman, 35 Fed. Reg. 4247 (1970). He has also been made the alternate chairman of the Council for Rural Affairs, 3 C.F.R. 206 (1969); and, perhaps most importantly, he is a member of the Domestic Council established pursuant to Reorganization Plan No. 2 of 1970. For historical background, see David, *The Vice Presidency: Its Institutional Evolution and Contemporary Status*, 29 J. POLITICS 721 (1967).

[55] 22 U.S.C. § 287 (1964). Literature on this arrangement is quite sparse. See A. BEICHMAN, THE "OTHER STATE DEPARTMENT." THE UNITED STATES MISSION TO THE UNITED NATIONS—ITS ROLE IN THE MAKING OF FOREIGN POLICY 194-96 (1968); and, for the dilemma posed by conflicting loyalties, Sen. Vandenberg's letter of January 9, 1947, to Mrs. Roosevelt, A. VANDENBERG, THE PRIVATE PAPERS OF SENATOR VANDENBERG 330-31 (A. Vandenberg, Jr., ed. 1952).

also applicable to other questions, including coordination (question 4). The authority "to require the opinion, in writing, of the principal officer in each of the executive departments," conferred upon the President by article II, section 2, of the Constitution, it is stated,

> has apparently never been seriously considered, in the United States, as an insti-
> tutionalization of informatory and advisory authority. Quite the contrary, the
> prevailing view appears to be that a statutory channelling of the President's
> sources of information would be unconstitutional. The view expressed in (West
> Germany) that political advice to the government is a public function and hence
> is subject to limitations imposed by constitutional law, appears strange to Amer-
> ican constitutional thought. Thus, every President informs himself from what-
> ever source and by whatever procedures he deems appropriate.[56]

This passage was to find its way into the report of the Project Group.[57]

Just as there is little purpose to be served by repeating here our observations on the formal constitutional position of the American federal executive, there is almost equally small need for a repetition of the rather extensive descriptions of Presidential information networks and coordination mechanisms. To a large extent, these are based on quite familiar publications and on a few interviews conducted within the academic and research communities; contributors to the present symposium are prominently represented under both headings.[58] On the purely descriptive level, there is hardly any claim of originality—except, perhaps, for the discovery that entries under "Management Consultants" in the Washington yellow pages yield a good bit of otherwise quite elusive information about federal policy contract research, including the gem, in at least one advertisement, "Governments Only."

Evaluation of American institutions and practices with a view to their suit-ability to West German conditions is likely to be of more interest here. The Project Group had not, in terms, called for such an evaluation by its consultants in charge of country studies. However, it quite understandably expressed an interest in in-formation as to the defects of foreign systems in actual experience, as indicated especially by question 7 (deficiencies of the present system and efforts at reform). After all, it is greatly preferable, for governments as well, to learn from the failures of others.

This frame of reference necessarily gives our recommendations and conclusions

---

[56] 1 FIRST REPORT 221, citing BÖCKENFÖRDE, supra note 9, at 187 et seq.; 249 et seq. for the view expressed by some authorities in West Germany (see also note 43 supra); and Bundy, How Foreign Policy is Made—Logic and Experience, 30 U. PITT. L. REV. 437, 441 (1969), for the prevailing American position.

[57] 1 FIRST REPORT 254.

[58] Our study acknowledges invaluable assistance from Professors Thomas E. Cronin and Norman Thomas; Allen Schick gave of his time to introduce us into the mysteries of PPBS. 2 FIRST REPORT 212. Professor Harvey C. Mansfield's then unpublished paper on federal executive reorganization, pre-sented originally at the 1968 annual meeting of the American Political Science Association, furnished most of the information for our discussion of government reorganization; see 2 FIRST REPORT, 213-15, 258 n.14. Mansfield, Federal Executive Reorganization: Thirty Years of Experience, 29 PUB. AD. REV. 332 (1969).

a somewhat negative bias. It is hoped, however, that what was said in that connection, and what will be repeated below, will not be taken as implying any personal dissatisfaction with an exceptionally generous and pleasant host country.

The American system of government appears to have two built-in dysfunctional elements of constitutional magnitude. First, the President has only limited, and frequently insufficient, means for the legislative and budgetary implementation of his program. Secondly—and somewhat paradoxically—his responsibilities within the executive department, encompassing the totality of the functions of Queen, prime minister, and cabinet, are dangerously close to requiring superhuman talents and energy.

It is believed that these structural weaknesses are not outweighed by the advantages of a uniform personalized executive with stable tenure for a period of years. In any event, the very history of government reorganization on the federal level is strong evidence that there are serious and persistent problems of government efficiency in a presidential system. It was concluded, therefore, that the adoption of such a system would not, by itself, offer substantial advantages to a country with a functioning system of responsible cabinet government. This conclusion is again echoed in the Project Group report. It seems to receive added weight from the amazingly swift and comprehensive implementation of the recommendations of that report, especially if contrasted with the markedly different experiences of the Brownlow Committee.[59]

On the other hand, the United States has had, for some time, the most vital and productive economic system in the world. Furthermore, its social system, while not quite as open and egalitarian as sometimes claimed, is still in marked contrast to West Germany's "two societies," or *"halbierte Gesellschaft"* so eloquently described and decried by Professor Dahrendorf.[60] It seems reasonable to assume that the exceptionally high degree of receptivity and adaptability of the American federal executive is, in good measure, causally interrelated with the dynamism of the American economy and the openness of American society. If this assumption is accepted, the three phenomena of American federal government singled out as particularly startling to orderly minds trained in the German civil service tradition are highly likely to be prized assets rather than curious liabilities. These are (1) the massive uncertainties and manifest neglect of organizational constitutional law; (2) the heterogeneous origins, short tenures, and hence, seemingly somewhat amateur character of the top ranks of the federal political executive; and (3) the inclination to farm out to non-governmental organisms, on a contract basis, the formulation of federal public policy.

---

[59] *See* p. 632 *supra*; BROWNLOW, *supra* note 3, at 383-402, 413-22; and especially R. POLENBERG, REORGANIZING ROOSEVELT'S GOVERNMENT. THE CONTROVERSY OVER EXECUTIVE REORGANIZATION 1936-1939 (1966).

[60] R. DAHRENDORF, GESELLSCHAFT UND DEMOKRATIE IN DEUTSCHLAND 301 (1968). Professor Dahrendorf's own translation, SOCIETY AND DEMOCRACY IN GERMANY 273 (1967), uses the term, "divided society."

1. *Organizational Constitutional Law*

The neglect of organizational constitutional law in the United States is, *prima facie*, nothing short of scandalous. Again and again in interviews and conversations with knowledgable persons in and out of government, we heard the complaint that "nobody teaches you how the government is run." Standard books of instruction on constitutional law used at American law schools, even if called "Cases and Materials," proved to be literally without the slightest guidance for our study. As Professor William W. Van Alstyne demonstrated by a postcard poll of teachers of constitutional law at American universities, this neglect of the subject is rather firmly rooted in lack of basic knowledge.[61] Monographic legal literature on organizational constitutional law is almost totally lacking.[62]

It might be contended that this neglect is merely the result of a division of labor, traditional at least since the epic Burgess-Dwight confrontation at Columbia University,[63] between litigation-oriented law schools and institution-oriented departments of political science, and that, in any event, the rather remarkable expansion of the concept of justiciability in recent years[64] is likely to kindle the interest of professional lawyers in constitutional questions not previously capable of judicial resolution. However, this would presuppose, at least until the total eclipse of the political-questions doctrine and the disappearance of all obstacles to justiciability grounded on the cases-and-controversies doctrine and on standing, that political scientists are carrying on the traditions of Burgess, Willoughby, and, perhaps, Corwin.[65]

---

[61] Letter to the Editor, N.Y. Times, Apr. 8, 1965, at 38, col. 3 (Late City Edition):

"In a mail poll I submitted [four] questions . . . based on the Twelfth Amendment to the Constitution, to all professors currently teaching constitutional law in American law schools. Each was asked to respond impromptu, without looking up the answers in advance.

"Ninety-six responses to each of the four questions were received. Over-all, 70 per cent of the answers submitted were technically incorrect. Specifically, 62 per cent, 82 per cent, 66 per cent and 69 per cent of the answers submitted to the first through the fourth question, respectively, were incorrect."

[62] By way of contrast, see Professor Dagtoglou's *Comment*, [1969] PUB. L. 101-111, which reviews over 50 West German monographs on constitutional law published in 1968. *Cf.* his *Comment*, [1970] *id.* at 317-29, which lists a somewhat lesser number for 1969.

[63] J. GOEBEL *et al.*, A HISTORY OF THE SCHOOL OF LAW, COLUMBIA UNIVERSITY ch. 4 (1955); J. BURGESS, REMINISCENCES OF AN AMERICAN SCHOLAR, THE BEGINNINGS OF COLUMBIA UNIVERSITY, ch. 6 (1934).

[64] Baker v. Carr, 369 U.S. 186 (1962); Flast v. Cohen, 392 U.S. 83 (1968); Powell v. McCormack, 395 U.S. 486 (1969); and, after our study was completed, Association of Data Service Org., Inc. v. Camp, 396 U.S. 150 (1970); Barlow v. Collins, 396 U.S. 159 (1970).

[65] A. SOMIT & J. TANENHAUS, THE DEVELOPMENT OF AMERICAN POLITICAL SCIENCE: FROM BURGESS TO BEHAVIORALISM 18-19 (1967); J. BURGESS, POLITICAL SCIENCE AND CONSTITUTIONAL LAW (1890); W. WILLOUGHBY, THE CONSTITUTIONAL LAW OF THE UNITED STATES (2d ed., 1929). E. S. Corwin would seem to be more correctly classified as a political and constitutional historian, *see*, *e.g.*, E. CORWIN, THE PRESIDENT, OFFICE AND POWERS 1787-1957 (4th rev. ed. 1957), and as an outstanding "case law"-oriented constitutional lawyer, as witness his perennial, THE CONSTITUTION AND WHAT IT MEANS TODAY (12th ed. 1958) and his monumental THE CONSTITUTION OF THE UNITED STATES ANNOTATED, ANALYSIS AND INTERPRETATION (1953). He does not appear to have been much persuaded by the one attempt to set forth American constitutional conventions in the British understanding of that term, which significantly was undertaken by a British author writing in England. H. HORWILL, THE USAGES OF THE AMERICAN CONSTITUTION (1925); Corwin, Book Review, 20 AM. POL. SCI. REV. 436 (1926).

Manifestly, that has not been the case. We might speculate on the causes, and especially on the relative weight to be attributed to the scramble for a slice in the lucrative market made up by an estimated one million captive buyers *per annum* of assigned textbooks on American Government; the two-step process of professional legal education which stamps much of political science instruction as undergraduate and "pre-legal" (perversely adding incentive to the emulation of law teaching at a "lower" academic level); and the general decline of public law as a prestigious discipline in increasingly behavior-oriented political science departments.[66] On purely intellectual grounds, the reason suggested last seems to be the only one intrinsically worthy of respect. Still, it is acceptable only to the extent that the behavioral approach faithfully reflects the reality of organizational constitutional law in the United States.

This depends, quite simply, on whether American organizational constitutional law is dominated by political behavior or governed by constitutional convention. The answer is not necessarily foreclosed by the predilection of common-law trained minds for judicially enforceable rights; the British constitution and its overseas transplants illustrate that a common law system is indeed eminently capable of generating the *opinio necessitatis iuris* which distinguishes constitutional convention from politically convenient custom.[67] However, it is quite useless to pursue this question further with regard to the United States. Here, political behavior not subject to judicial sanction is manifestly treated as free from legal restraint. The prevalence of the "bad man" theory of the law[68] on the constitutional level even extends to the interpretation of constitutional provisions that are not, or not as yet, subject to judicial scrutiny.

To mention some examples: When testifying before the Jackson Committee, Governor Nelson Rockefeller asserted that the Vice President was a member of the Legislative department by virtue of his constitutional position as president of the Senate, and could therefore not be delegated executive functions in view of the

---

[66] As to the decline of public law as a prestigious discipline, see Somit & Tanenhaus, *Trends in American Political Science: Some Analytical Notes*, 57 AM. POL. SCI. REV. 933, 940-41 with tables IV-VI (1963). Schubert, *Behavioral Research in Public Law*, 57 AM. POL. SCI. REV. 433, 445 (1963), speaks of "the long period during which public law was an exotic bayou, cut off from the mainstream of theoretical and methodological advances in political science." Whether or not behaviorism has come to the rescue as there predicted is immaterial for present purposes, since judicial behaviorism comes rather close to being the exact antidote to any threat of the revival of interest in organizational constitutional law on the part of political scientists. *Cf.* Verney, *The Education of a Political Scientist*, 3 CAN. J. POL. SCI. 345, 352 (1970): "Presidential government . . . has succeeded in the United States but has never been successfully adopted by other countries. (Perhaps this explains why American students of comparative politics have ignored traditional governmental institutions, which indicate the uniqueness of the United States, and have concentrated on the political process where Americans behave, or are thought to behave, like people elsewhere.)"

[67] *See* A. DICEY, INTRODUCTION TO THE STUDY OF THE LAW OF THE CONSTITUTION, ch. 14-15 (10th ed. 1959); I. JENNINGS, THE LAW OF THE CONSTITUTION, ch. 3 (5th ed. 1959); J. MITCHELL, CONSTITUTIONAL LAW 26-39 (2d ed. 1968); British Coal Corporation v. The King, [1935] A.C. 500, 511 (P.C.); Madzimbamuto v. Lardner-Burke, [1968] 3 All E.R. 561, 573 (P.C.) *Cf.* Adegbenro v. Akintola, [1963] A.C. 614, 631-32 (P.C.).

[68] First set forth in Holmes, *The Path of the Law*, 10 HARV. L. REV. 457, 459 (1887).

incompatibility rule.[69] (The real reason for the sparing use of the Vice President in the Executive department is not this quaint construction of the vice presidency as a Legislative estate with an Executive remainder, but rather the fact that the President has no control over the Vice President's term of office.[70]) The constitutional locus of the reorganization power is largely unsettled. The prevalent practice under the Reorganization Acts of executive reorganization by presidential plan subject to congressional veto is open to grave constitutional objections. The "congressional veto" was, in fact, deemed unconstitutional by President Roosevelt.[71]

The current Reorganization Act, in keeping with the somewhat wavering tradition established by the Reorganization Act of 1939, requires an act of Congress for the creation, abolition, or complete merger of government departments. Their principal officers are, collectively, a constitutional organ by virtue of the Twenty-fifth Amendment; and their appointments are subject to approval by the Senate. Yet, nothing seems to prevent the President from conferring personal cabinet rank, without the necessity of Senate approval, on members of the White House staff.[72]

More recent examples would include the assertion of a presidential prerogative in the appointment of Supreme Court justices that is clearly contrary to historical precedent.[73] At the other extreme, we find a veto message described as containing

[69] H. Jackson, Jr., The National Security Council—Jackson Subcommittee Papers on Policy-Making at the Presidential Level 179 (1965) (testimony of July 1, 1960).

[70] This point is generally regarded as settled by former President Hoover's testimony of January 16, 1956. Hearings on the Administrative Vice President Before the Subcomm. on Reorganization of the Senate Comm. on Government Operations, 84th Cong., 2d Sess. 13-14 (1956) (testimony of Mr. Hoover).

[71] Jackson, A Presidential Legal Opinion, 66 Harv. L. Rev. 1353 (1953). See generally Ginnane, The Control of Federal Administration by Congressional Resolutions and Committees, 66 Harv. L. Rev. 569 (1953). For an excellent brief discussion of the reorganization power which had previously escaped our notice, see J. Kallenbach, The American Chief Executive. The Presidency and the Governorship 380-87 (1966).

[72] Dr. Arthur Burns received this rank in January, 1969; that seems to have set a precedent for the top White House Office officials of the Nixon Administration.

[73] In a letter of March 31, 1970 to Senator William B. Saxbe of Ohio concerning his (ultimately unsuccessful) nomination of Judge G. Harrold Carswell to the U.S. Supreme Court, President Nixon stated:

"What is centrally at issue in this nomination is the constitutional responsibility of the President to appoint members of the Court—and whether this responsibility can be frustrated by those who wish to substitute their own philosophy or their own subjective judgment for that of the one person entrusted by the Constitution with the power of appointment. . . .

"[U]nder the Constitution it is the duty of the President to appoint and of the Senate to advise and consent. But if the Senate attempts to substitute its judgment as to who should be appointed, the traditional constitutional balance is in jeopardy and the duty of the President under the Constitution impaired."

116 Cong. Rec. S4937 (daily ed. April 2, 1970).

The assertion that the President is "the one person entrusted by the Constitution with the power of appointment" (emphasis supplied) is contrary to the wording of the Constitution, which provides, in article 2, § 2, ¶ 2, that the President "shall nominate, and by and with the advice and consent of the Senate, shall appoint . . . judges of the supreme court. . . ." (emphasis supplied). The letter quoted above is said to be in large part the work of Charles Colson, the President's legal adviser, who has been quoted as saying, "The legal brief we prepared on this used the word 'nominate' all the way through, but it came out 'appoint' in the letter." Newsweek, April 13, 1970, at 15. Surely, state papers deserve more discriminating attention. Quite apart from this, however, the cardinal contention that the Senate may not substitute its own philosophy or its own subjective judgment for that of the President in

a "political-science lecture on Presidential prerogatives" in point as if there could be the slightest doubt about his legal entitlement to veto federal enactments at will.[74]

2. Personal Mobility of the Political Executive

American observers are likely to be troubled more by the current scholarly neglect of organizational constitutional law than by its actual state. They would tend to regard massive ambiguity and uncertainty in this area as, on balance, a positive factor, since the absence of clear rules prevents the ossification of traditional structures by constitutional mandate. However, they are likely to be somewhat less complacent about the selection and tenure of the political Executive below cabinet level. There are roughly 125 government officials in the ranks of Secretary to Assistant Secretary, and in corresponding positions with different nomenclatures. A Secretary can be expected to have a tenure of about three years; the average tenure of Assistant Secretaries, on the other hand, is likely to be around two years. It is generally estimated that the first year in office is largely spent on what might be called on-the-job training.[75]

Small wonder, then, that in 1960, the Senate at the request of the Jackson Committee on National Policy Machinery adopted a resolution expressing

> the sense of the Senate that individuals appointed to administrative and policy-making posts should be willing to serve for a period long enough to permit them to contribute effectively in their assigned tasks . . . .[76]

As the Brookings studies have shown, the record is not quite so bleak. The average public service record of the political executive at the time of initial sub-cabinet level appointment is five years; and there is a substantial flow of appointments from within political and professional civil service ranks of the various departments. On the other hand, the recruiting process is hardly likely to inspire confidence in the professional soundness of the appointments made. The appointment of a specially qualified Assistant Secretary pursuant to the recommendation of an equally qualified Secretary might not be a mere chance event, but it is plainly rather exceptional.[77]

The disadvantages of this top-level spoils system with payoffs in social prestige or public service satisfaction are substantial. Besides the obvious drawbacks of amateur administration as such, there is above all the lack of confidence of the top levels of

---

judicial appointment matters is contrary to historical precedent and the overwhelming weight of the informed opinion. See, e.g., KALLENBACH, supra note 71, at 393. Cf. Black, A Note on Senatorial Consideration of Supreme Court Appointees, 79 YALE L.J. 657 (1970), which quite unintentionally underscores our remarks above.

[74] Semple, Jr., The Middle American Who Edits Ideas for Nixon, N.Y. Times Magazine, Apr. 12, 1970 at 32, 69.

[75] See generally D. STANLEY, D. MANN & J. DOIG, MEN WHO GOVERN—A BIOGRAPHICAL PROFILE OF FEDERAL POLITICAL EXECUTIVES (1967); D. MANN AND J. DOIG, THE ASSISTANT SECRETARIES (1965); Mann, The Selection of Federal Political Executives, 58 AM. POL. SCI. REV. 81 (1964).

[76] S. Res. 338, 86th Cong., 2d Sess., 106 CONG. REC. 15705 (1960).

[77] See STANLEY, supra note 75, at 41, and generally Mann, supra note 75.

the professional civil service in departmental leadership, and a consequent strengthening of the Bureau-Congress-clients triangle which obstructs the implementation
of presidential policy.[78] On the other hand, it is difficult to envisage a system that
is more conducive to the rapid exchange of ideas and information between government, industry, and the academic community.

3. Government Policy Formulation by Research Contract

The Executive Office of the President owes its existence to the recommendations
of the Brownlow Committee; the PPB System is a creation of the RAND Corporation. These two standard examples serve to demonstrate the significance of contract research for the formulation of public policy in the United States. However,
they may be likened to the tips of otherwise rather unexplored icebergs. "Hard"
information about federal contract research on government policy, as contradistin-
guished from science and technology,[79] is not so readily obtainable.

We know that the sixteen Contract Research Centers of the Defense Department
at one time employed a total of 346 social scientists (enough to staff the departments
of economics, political science, and sociology of at least three universities), and that
the Department spent about $30 million a year on policy research contracts.[80] This
figure is in marked contrast to the $5 million budget of the Bureau of Intelligence
and Research in the State Department.[81]

Critics have called attention to the possibility of conflict between the policy
planning operations of the State and Defense Departments, to the "hawkish" bias
of the latter's principal consultants, and to errors in judgment in the formulation of
projects and the choice of contractors. The classic example of the latter is the
"Pax Americana" project, which charged the Douglas Aircraft Corporation with the
task of projecting the world political situation in 1985.[82] Seemingly, a somewhat
more short-range analysis of the economic future of Douglas Aircraft would have
been more appropriate.

---

[78] See Brown, The President and the Bureaus: Time for a Renewal of Relationships? 26 PUB. AD.
REV. 174 (1966).

[79] C. DANHOF, GOVERNMENT CONTRACTING AND TECHNOLOGICAL CHANGE (1968); M. REAGAN, SCIENCE
AND THE FEDERAL PATRON (1969). G. LYONS, THE UNEASY PARTNERSHIP—SOCIAL SCIENCE AND THE FED-
ERAL GOVERNMENT IN THE TWENTIETH CENTURY (1969), a veritable goldmine of information, appeared
after the conclusion of our study.

[80] For details, see Hearings on Defense Department Sponsored Foreign Affairs Research Before the
Senate Comm. on Foreign Relations, 90th Cong., 2d Sess. (1968).

[81] Platig, Research and Analysis, 380 THE ANNALS 50, 56 (1968). For the origins of this disparity,
see D. ACHESON, PRESENT AT THE CREATION, ch. 18 (1969); and for the reorganization of State Department research activities since our study, 61 DEP'T STATE BULL. 74 (1969).

[82] Green, Science, Government and the Case of Rand, A Singular Pluralism, 20 WORLD POLITICS 301
(1968); Kaufman, As Eisenhower Was Saying . . . "We Must Guard Against Unwarranted Influence
By the Military-Industrial Complex," N.Y. Times Magazine, June 22, 1969, at 10; Rice, The Cold-War
College Think Tanks, WASHINGTON MONTHLY, July, 1969, at 22. Quite another question, and a somewhat neglected one, is the effect of such contract research on the universities. Cf. Jaffe, Professors
and Judges as Advisors to Government: Reflections on the Roosevelt-Frankfurter Relationship, 83 HARV.
L. REV. 366, 368-73 (1969).

It should be recalled, however, that we are dealing with a subject that is discreet but not discrete. Federal contract research on policy questions is pervasive but not centralized; and failures and conflicts, being more newsworthy, have greater surfacing power. The advantages of seeking guidance for decisions involving federal public policy by contract research seem obvious. These offer almost unlimited flexibility in the choice of informants; ready access to the most current levels of insight of the academic and research communities; and savings, both in funds and in maneuverability, by the avoidance of the alternative solution of creating *ad hoc* bureaucracies for policy problems as they arise.

On the other hand, a traditional view of responsible government would require that public policy be formulated by politically and legally accountable officials and public servants. While such ultimate responsibility is not necessarily waived by the contractual procurement of policy ideas and programs, there seems little doubt that this practice does, in fact, shift public decisions to a non- or pre-public sphere. That is especially the case where the progress of the study commissioned has already led to a crystallizing of informed opinion, or where as yet unresearched possibilities are obscured by carefully elaborated alternative recommendations.

4. Summary: State and Society in the United States and West Germany

Our conclusion was that the lack of clarity in organizational constitutional law, the remarkably high mobility of a heterogeneous political executive, and the extensive use of contract research were phenomena of a political system that did not recognize a significant distinction between "state" and "society." As already mentioned, these factors were deemed crucial for a highly receptive and adaptable political leadership system, and at the same time causally interconnected with an open society and a vital economy.

Implicitly accepting Professor Dahrendorf's trenchant critique of West Germany as a *"halbierte Gesellschaft"* managed by a law-trained "service class" quite unreceptive to the needs and aspirations of the "lower" half of the population,[83] we posed the question whether a radical reduction of the influence of the German service class was not in order. This could be achieved, it was suggested, by a substantial increase in the number of political officials and, possibly, the massive use of contract research on policy questions.

Such a course of action would be likely to decrease the significance of the Rule of Law in organizational constitutional law. Indeed, greater flexibility in this area might even be the pre-condition for the creative activity of a broad and dynamic political leadership group co-opted by constant interchange with the universities

---

[83] DAHRENDORF, *supra* note 60, 106 *et seq.* of the German and 94 *et seq.* of the English editions. Note, incidentally, the recently declining prestige of lawyers in West German society, discussed by W. KAUPEN, DIE HÜTER VON RECHT UND ORDNUNG. DIE SOZIALE HERKUNFT, ERZIEHUNG UND AUSBILDUNG DER DEUTSCHEN JURISTEN (1969), and by Rasehorn, *Juristen auf dem soziologischen Prüfstand*, [1970] NEUE JURISTICHE WOCHENSCHRIFT 24.

and the economy. But would West German society still respect a State that had so drastically opened itself to the people?

A somewhat different question was whether the added costs of such drastic reforms were worthwhile. As one of the two super-powers in a still basically bipolar world, the United States necessarily had to aspire to a position of leadership in all fields of significance. States with more modest means simply could not attempt to operate on the same scale.

This was not to say, we concluded, that the American example was, but for some technical details, only of anecdotal or antidotal interest for West German government and administrative reformers. The point was, rather, to draw attention to the possible consequences of the reception of those constitutional and administrative institutions of the United States which were substantially shaped by the American social system and a specific "American way of life." There will be occasion to return to these remarks further below.[84]

B. Foreign Materials in the Report

As already indicated, several references to foreign systems of government found their way into the Project Group Report. In the following, these references will be mentioned as they occur. It is hoped that this will afford some insights into the practical value of comparative government which might outweigh the tedium of recital by rote.

The first part of the Report, dealing with the delimitation of the spheres of competence of the federal ministries, contains about half a dozen such references. At the outset, it is pointed out that here, foreign experiences were found to be helpful only as to some details. These latter would appear to include the following: First, on the issue of special-purpose ministries, the French experience with its tendency toward the "technocratization" of political leadership is invoked to buttress a negative recommendation. Second, the rejection of the "optimal" small group figure of seven or nine as a criterion of cabinet size is reinforced by reference to British and French experience, although "in view of differences in constitutional structure, such comparisons with foreign countries . . . do not afford an even approximately reliable standard." This is followed by a rejection of the Inner Cabinet device as not only

---

[84] *See* p. 664 *infra.* For a striking parallel, see Ridley, *French Technocracy and Comparative Government*, 14 POLITICAL STUDIES 34, 52 (1966):

"Technocratic leadership depends on the French educational system and on the general structure of careers. We could not early copy French administrative or managerial instiutions, even if we should want to, because we live in a different society with a different culture. That is only saying, of course, what is often said by those who argue that we need to reform our own educational and recruitment systems if we are to modernize Britain. Even this, however, would not necessarily give us anything like the French technocracy. British technocrats would not automatically develop the same sense of responsibility that flows from the French notion of the positive state. One cannot so easily acquire a tradition that has been built up over centuries. We are back at the starting point. What practical lesson can one in fact learn from comparative studies?"

For some tentative answers to that question, *see* p. 663 *infra.*

beyond the mandate of the Project Group because it would require constitutional amendment, but also as reportedly unsuitable for German constitutional life.

Third, the creation of a Ministry for Coordination was not recommended because domestic and foreign experience showed the futility of coordination especially of fundamental views on the same level. Fourth, on the positive side, cabinet status for the Post Office was justified, *inter alia*, by similar status in other countries. Finally, in reiteration of previous comments on coordination between equals, British as well as West German experience is invoked in support of the proposition that a minister without portfolio might be more effectively used for primary political tasks than as a coordinator at the cabinet level, as he was hardly likely to be successful in the latter task.[85]

The section on parliamentary state secretaries, ministers of state, and ministers without portfolio apparently does not contain a single mention of foreign materials. On the other hand, some key references thereto are to be found in the third and last part of the report, relating to the improvement of the machinery of the Federal Chancellor and Government. The conclusions drawn from the foreign country and West German state studies are summarized as follows:

> The problems found to exist in the machinery of the [West German] federal government are to be encountered, to a lesser or greater extent, in all foreign countries covered by this inquiry. They are equally present in the government machinery of the [West German] states.
> Certain peculiarities are essentially the products of historical developments.
> The constitutional position of government institutions is only of minor significance in relation to existing inadequacies. Comparable deficiencies are found in the Presidential, Cabinet, and Chancellor systems. Therefore, none of the problems could be solved merely by, for instance, introducing the Presidential system in the Federal Republic.
> All of these systems of government have, in addition to conventional tasks, met with new problems that make it necessary to further develop the traditional system.[86]

There also is a reference to the PPB System which is found to be less effective than the West German system of intermediate-term budget planning; and to British thought on the reduction of cabinet size, the French Planning Office, and the Swedish system of executive government (the latter had not been the subject of a special study[87]).

By far the most detailed and frequent mentions of foreign materials are to be found in the two appendices to Part III of the Report. The first, which is a methodological survey entitled "Basic Remarks on the Process of Political Decision," contains the following observation:

> The organization of professional advice in the governmental system requires detailed studies, which the Project Group has only been able to initiate in the few

---

[85] 1 FIRST REPORT 7, 10, 11, 12, 21, 24.
[86] *Id.* at 190.
[87] *Id.* at 192, 205.

months of its activities. Here, it will be especially necessary to have recourse to the manifold experiences in France, England, and the United States, in order to utilize further sources for the critical evaluation of our own system.[88]

The Project Group then singled out for special mention some methods of political planning developed in recent years in the United States. Here, it was able to rely on a particularly thorough report on "Political Planning," prepared for the Project Group under the direction of Professor Oberndörfer. The planning techniques referred to include the Delphi Method, systems analysis, cost-benefit analysis, relevance procedure, operations research, PPBS, network planning, and electronic data processing. Discussion is mainly descriptive, but in connection with PPBS, it is stated:

> In view of political and constitutional conditions that differ from those of the United States, and the (in some respects) already further developed budgetary process of the Federal Republic, the PPBS cannot simply be adopted by German administration. Nevertheless, the focal points of the system . . . are of significance for German planning processes as well.[89]

The second appendix to Part III of the Report contains summaries, by the Project Group, of the studies on Great Britain, the United States, France, Italy, Austria, Switzerland, and the West German states. Except for these latter, *all* references, of course, are to foreign institutions. Nevertheless, occasional comparisons with West German conditions, and especially selections of subjects for further study, supply some evidence as to the practical value of the comparative approach in the judgment of the Project Group.

There are two such references to Great Britain, both of them of the former variant. First, British opinion as to the ineffectiveness of a twenty-member cabinet as a working group for the development of policy guidelines is related to a similar judgment prevailing in West Germany. Secondly, and more significantly, the process of information circulation within the political system is described as working "much better" in Great Britain than it does in West Germany. This is traced to the central organization of public administration. There are also some remarks, not expressly comparative, as to the lack of a need for legal norms on coordination of government activities. Such rules have not been necessary in the past, in the judgment of the Project Group, in view of the prevalence of a basic political and social attitude characterized by a desire to cooperate and a willingness to compromise. Furthermore, attention is called to the inhibitions of British civil servants against

---

[88] *Id.* at 238-39.

[89] *Id.* at 240-245. The Oberndörfer study, entitled "Political Planning," will be found in 2 *id.* at 313-459. More recently, a higher civil servant has expressed the opinion that while West Germany has an exemplary legal framework for fiscal planning, the United States has furnished the exemplary methods and techniques for modern intermediate-term fiscal planning. Mennel, *Mehrjährige Finanzplanung im Ausland*, 29 FINANZARCHIV 75, 88 (1970). *But see* Brümmerhoff, *Das "Planning-Programming-Budgeting System,"* *id.* at 64, 74.

political activity, which is said to be rooted in English mentality.[90] It seems reasonable to see some traces of implied self-criticism in this passage.

With respect to the United States, there is little attempt at comparison, save for a reference to the obvious difference between the presidential system and the unique combination of the Chancellor, Cabinet, and Department systems in West Germany in article 65 of the Basic Law.[91] However, no less than three areas are singled out for further study. First, the Project Group notes a trend toward the evolution of the Executive Office of the President, and more particularly of the White House staff, into a de facto presidential cabinet with a position superior to that of the federal cabinet. Its interest in additional research of this development is probably traceable to apprehensions about the constitutional implications of the creation of a planning staff in the Chancellor's Office.[92]

Secondly, the Project Group expresses interest in the non-fiscal activities of the Bureau of the Budget, especially as regards planning, coordination, direction, and control of government activity. Finally, it singles out for detailed future attention what is termed the "expansion of planning horizons" through the use of presidential advisory committees and of contract research, especially to the extent that the latter "impinges upon political goal planning and has for this reason met with special scepticism."[93]

The French system of government is described in somewhat greater detail in the Report than is the American, but interest in it seems substantially more limited. The Project Group is understandably interested in the working of the Commissariat Général du Plan, and expresses an intention to seek more information both as to the type of plan elaborated (i.e., whether it is unilinear or alternative), and as to the planning methods and techniques employed by the French General Planning Commission, with a view to determining their suitability for West Germany. Other than that, it merely notes that the extensive employment of special staffs by French cabinet ministers has kept the category of political public servants relatively small as compared to West Germany.[94]

Interest in Italy is minimal:

> In judging the capacity of the system for political planning, the short tenures in office of the governments will have to be considered. This circumstance hardly permits comparisons with the Federal Republic, especially as regards political goal definition.[95]

A similar lack of interest is manifested in Austria, because the unanimity rule for cabinet decisions, as contrasted with the vital position of the Chancellor under

---

[90] I FIRST REPORT, supra note 5, at 250, 251.

[91] Id. at 253. See p. 637 supra.

[92] I FIRST REPORT B53-54; see p. 647 supra.

[93] I FIRST REPORT 254, 255. Cf. Jaffe, supra note 82.

[94] I FIRST REPORT 259, 260.

[95] Id. at 262.

the West German system, has inhibited the development of central planning institutions.[96] As regards Switzerland, the Project Group limits itself to noting what is termed the most advanced level of government reform thinking of all countries studied, and the "almost complete" identity of Swiss and West German criticism of the respective systems of government.[97]

Rather expectedly, such similarities are also observed with respect to the West German state governments studied. Here, the Hamburg "Planning Triangle" is singled out for special attention.[98] It should be noted that the superb report on German state governments made under the direction of Professor Fritz Scharpf also included substantial amounts of confidential information which were omitted from the published version.[99]

In its introduction to the appendix volume, the Project Group mentioned the need for further studies on the United States, France, Great Britain, and—somewhat surprisingly—on Italy, as well as on the West German states. Its estimate of the value of the foreign country and West German studies for the First Report itself is summed up in one sentence:

> With respect to some aspects of the problem studied, the assumption has been confirmed that there are in foreign countries, but also in the West German States, methods, techniques and beginnings of organizational forms for an improvement of the political decision process which deserve special attention in continued work on government and administrative reform.

This will have to be read in conjunction with an earlier characterization of reports on the West German states as "in part, very instructive"[100]—an evaluation that is not repeated in the passage just quoted.

CONCLUSION

The first two sections of the present paper seek to summarize the main features of the First Report of the West German Project Group for Government and Administrative Reform, and to outline the impact of that report on government reorganization in West Germany. Although it is hoped that they will be of interest to students of government organization in other countries merely by virtue of the subject matter chosen, they are, at base, secondhand descriptions by a relative outsider in another language—the dreary standard fare of what used to be so euphemistically called "Comparative Government."[101]

---

[96] *Id.* at 265.

[97] *Id.* at 267.

[98] *Id.* at 271-73. The "Hamburg Triangle" consists of the Planning Staff of the City-State Council Office (Senatskanzlei), the central Organization Authority, and the Finance Department. For details, see 2 *id.* at 287-88.

[99] 2 FIRST REPORT 267-313; *see* the Project Group's introduction to that volume, *id.* at v, vi.

[100] *Id.* at vi.

[101] Von Beyme, *Möglichkeiten und Grenzen der vergleichenden Regierungslehre*, 7 POLITISCHE VIERTELJAHRSSCHRIFT 63, 78 n.36 (1966), notes "drops in information levels at linguistic and political frontiers," and observes, with refreshing candor: "A book is seldom found worth translating into

The third section, on the other hand, pursues somewhat more ambitious aims. It seeks to render a reasonably comprehensive account of those portions of the Report and of the author's country study on the United States which might be of significance in assaying the practical value of foreign country studies in connection with government reorganization or, more generally, the analytical utility of comparative public law.

The conclusion will have to be that assaying itself. It will rest on three criteria, first alone and ultimately in combination: (1) the utility of foreign country studies for West German government reorganization planning; (2) the significance of the West German experience for the United States; and (3) the value of studies such as the ones here discussed for insights into the nature and the workings of political institutions generally.

The utility of the foreign studies for West German government reorganization planning seems directly proportional to the distance of their findings from the distinguishing characteristics of the respective foreign political systems described. There is more interest in methods than in institutions, and more interest in techniques than in methods. This might be another way of saying that while political planning and decision-making may in time become a truly international discipline in the same manner as the rather obvious precursor, business management,[102] the study of political institutions is not likely to achieve the same degree of cosmopolitanism. Political institutions *do* differ from country to country; and apples are better compared with other apples than with oranges.[103] This explains the marked preference of the Project Group for the West German state studies over the foreign country studies.

For the United States, there are, in the nature of things, only some incidental insights. The current academic neglect of organizational constitutional law seems shocking and inexcusable, even though flexibility in this area is likely to be an asset rather than a liability. Flexible rules are quite capable of study. On a more mundane level, it is hoped that the partisans and critics of PPBS will not ignore the gauntlet of the challenger from overseas.[104] PPBS discussion, which has been quite parochial, might well profit from an infusion of foreign ideas, based on experience

---

the language of the country investigated." A notable recent exception would be G. LOEWENBERG, PARLIAMENT IN THE GERMAN POLITICAL SYSTEM (1966), which is generally acknowledged to be by far the best work on the Bundestag, and has indeed appeared in German translation: G. LOEWENBERG, PARLAMENTARISMUS IM POLITISCHEN SYSTEM DER BUNDESREPUBLIK DEUTSCHLAND (1969). *See also* Scharpf, *Judicial Review and the Political Question: A Functional Analysis*, 57 YALE L.J. 517 (1966), which is a condensation of his study, GRENZEN RICHTERLICHER VERANTWORTUNG. DIE POLITISCHE QUESTION-DOKTRIN IN DER RECHTSPRECHUNG DES SUPREME COURT (1965); and Ehmke, *supra* note 7.

[102] The causes for that development become apparent from a reading of Vagts, *The Multinational Enterprise: A New Challenge for Transnational Law*, 83 HARV. L. REV. 739 (1970).

[103] Acknowledgment is due to Hardin, *An American Lawyer Looks at Civil Jury Trial in Scotland*, 111 U. PA. L. REV. 739 (1963).

[104] *See* pp. 641, 660 *supra*. Certainly the charge of parochialism cannot be levelled against German authors on intermediate-term fiscal planning. See especially Mennel, *supra* note 89.

with West German intermediate-term budget planning. A third insight would appear to be that in view of the significance attributed by the Project Group to the West German state studies, there might be some utility in similar within-country comparative studies in the United States. On this score, more of the fault (if any) would seem to lie with the cosmopolitan preoccupations of the comparativists than with the parochialism of students of public administration; and both appear to be already in the process of mending their ways.[105]

Finally, there is the question as to the utility of comparative studies for a better understanding of political institutions generally. Because of its limited mandate which excluded recommendations requiring constitutional amendments for their implementation, the Project Group felt little temptation to engage in speculation on this august level. There might also have been some unexpressed preference for the West German form of government—surely not an entirely misplaced sentiment in the light of the speedy implementation of the major recommendations of the First Report.

It is difficult to approach the subject here treated without being drawn into emotionally charged discussions about the relative merits of the presidential and parliamentary forms of government.[106] Perhaps, however, we can still utilize some insights of this study in order to clarify the ultimate issues.

A chief realization for the present author was that at least as regards the (presently crucial) central executive and legislative institutions, there is less difference between the British constitution and Continental constitutionalism than there is between the British and the United States systems of government. The British model appeared to us as much more rational and appealing; constitutional life in the United States seemed persistently bedeviled by essentially personal power conflicts and an undercurrent of disregard for the public character of public office.

This appraisal coincided to a remarkable extent with the trenchant critiques of a noted British political journalist in Washington.[107] However, somehow two key pieces of the puzzle seemed to be missing. Did the United States really combine

---

[105] Much of creative American research into state and local government and into political behavior at these levels has been at least intuitively comparative in nature; see, e.g., KALLENBACH, supra note 71. Recent studies tend to be more explicit as to the method employed; e.g., Chaffey, The Institutionalization of State Legislatures, A Comparative Study, 23 WESTERN POL. Q. 180 (1970). H. JACOB & K. VINES, POLITICS IN THE AMERICAN STATES, A COMPARATIVE ANALYSIS (1965), although primarily a teaching tool, might have heralded the beginning of a new era.

[106] BROWNLOW, supra note 3, at 356, notes "the curious notion, especially widespread among political scientists, that the American government would be better if the presidential system were abandoned and the parliamentary system adopted or at least if every step short of the utter subversion of the constitutional separation of powers were undertaken that would bring us nearer to the better British model." C. FRIEDRICH, THE IMPACT OF AMERICAN CONSTITUTIONALISM ABROAD 17-39 (1967) would appear to be quite immune against this "curious notion"—although not, perhaps, against some others. See Ryan, Book Review, 47 CAN. B. REV. 330 (1969). For the classic debate on this issue, see Price, The Parliamentary and Presidential Systems, 3 PUB. AD. REV. 317 (1943); Laski, The Parliamentary and Presidential Systems, 4 PUB. AD. REV. 347 (1944); and Price, A Response to Mr. Laski, id. at 360.

[107] Fairlie, Help from the Outside, in THE PRESIDENTIAL ADVISORY SYSTEM 144 (T. Cronin & S. Greenberg eds. 1969); Fairlie, Thoughts on the Presidency, THE PUBLIC INTEREST, Autumn, 1967, at 28 (1967).

"the world's most modern society with one of the world's most antique polities"?[108] If so, is such a society really compatible with a modern polity?

The first piece has fallen into place by a belated reading of Professor Samuel Huntington's seminal study from which the quotation is taken. As he convincingly demonstrates, the United States political system is essentially an English export, but of Tudor vintage. Even "nineteenth-century Europeans had every reason to be fascinated by America: It united a liberal society which they were yet to experience with a conservative politics which they had long since forgotten."[109]

Rather obviously, such a system is not readily exported in turn. However, we are still looking for the second piece missing from the puzzle, which has now assumed more definite but also more forbidding shape. Is the political system of the United States a beneficial, a detrimental, or, perhaps, simply an indifferent factor in the quest for a modern society? At least one perceptive observer would embrace the first of these alternatives;[110] there are, no doubt, others—now possibly including Professor Huntington[111]—who will espouse different views. The student of public administration and of comparative government can leave this ultimate question open once he has realized its existence. By concentrating on the more down-to-earth problems of improvements in political planning methods and techniques, it is hopefully concluded, he can seek to achieve insights that are useful and politically acceptable both to advanced societies and to developed polities.

---

[108] Huntington, *Political Modernization: America v. Europe*, 18 WORLD POLITICS 378, 406 (1966), in S. HUNTINGTON, POLITICAL ORDER IN CHANGING SOCIETIES 129 (1968).

[109] HUNTINGTON, *supra* note 108, at 133. Professor Huntington's thesis is accepted by Long, *Reflections on Presidential Power*, 29 PUB. AD. REV. 442, 443-44 (1969), but rejected by LaPalombara, Book Review (of Huntington), 78 YALE L.J. 1253, 1269-70 (1969).

[110] D. PRICE, THE SCIENTIFIC ESTATE (1965). *See also* HUNTINGTON, *supra* note 108, at 132: "The American experience demonstrates conclusively that some institutions and some aspects of a society may become highly modern while other institutions and other aspects retain much of their traditional form and substance. Indeed, this may be a natural state of affairs. In any system some sort of equilibrium or balance must be maintained between change and continuity. Change in some spheres renders unnecessary or impossible change in others. In America the continuity and stability of governmental institutions has permitted the rapid change of society, and the rapid change in society has encouraged continuity and stability in government. The relation between polity and society may well be dialectical rather than complementary."

[111] Professor Huntington's 1968 monograph qualifies his views as set forth above with the following statement:

"These conservative institutions could well change more rapidly in the future than they did in the past. External security and internal consensus have been the principal factors militating against the modernization of American political institutions. The former disappeared in the early twentieth century; the latter appears at times to be on the verge of disruption. The political institutions suited to a society which did not have to worry about external dangers may be inappropriate for one continually involved in a balance of terror, cold war, and military interventions in distant portions of the globe. So also, the problems of race relations and poverty strengthen demands for action by the national government. The needs of national defense and social reform could undermine the traditional pluralism inherited from the past and hasten the centralization of authority and structural differentiation in American political institutions." HUNTINGTON, *supra* note 108, at 133. So far as can be determined, this is the only variant from the 1966 text that is not generally supportive of the views therein expressed.